THE SIEGE OF
KÜSTRIN, 1945

THE SIEGE OF KÜSTRIN, 1945

Gateway to Berlin

Tony Le Tissier

Pen & Sword
MILITARY

First published in Great Britain in 2009 by
Pen & Sword Military
an imprint of
Pen & Sword Books Ltd
47 Church Street
Barnsley
South Yorkshire
S70 2AS

ISBN 978 1 84884 022 5

A CIP catalogue record for this book is
available from the British Library

Typeset in Sabon by
Phoenix Typesetting, Auldgirth, Dumfriesshire

Printed in the UK by
CPI UK

Pen & Sword Books Ltd incorporates the Imprints of Pen & Sword Aviation,
Pen & Sword Maritime, Pen & Sword Military, Wharncliffe Local History,
Pen & Sword Select, Pen & Sword Military Classics and Leo Cooper.

For a complete list of Pen & Sword titles please contact
PEN & SWORD BOOKS LIMITED
47 Church Street, Barnsley, South Yorkshire, S70 2AS, England
E-mail: enquiries@pen-and-sword.co.uk
Website: www.pen-and-sword.co.uk

Contents

Introduction

This work is largely based on the works of Herr Fritz Kohlase and Herr Hermann Thrams with their most kind permission. In the 1990s Herr Kohlase published his experiences in the latter part of the siege and his work attracted a lot of feedback from other Küstrin survivors, whose accounts are included here. The late Herr Thrams was a Küstrin teenager at the time of the siege and later wrote a diary-based history of the siege that provided much of the background information.

I am also grateful to the management and staff of the Seelow Museum, who proved extremely helpful in my research.

A.H. Le Tissier
Lymington, Hants
May 2008

List of Maps

Chapter One

The Development of a Fortress

Küstrin began as a lucrative customs post at the junction of the Warthe and Oder rivers, which remained important communications routes until the Oder became part of the revised east German boundary at the conclusion of the Second World War in 1945 and all river traffic came to a standstill.

The town was originally known as Cüstrin and was first mentioned in official records in 1232 when it was entrusted until 1262 to the Knights Templar, who reinforced the existing castle there and established a market. In 1397 the town was pawned to the Knights of St John and was then sold in 1402 to the German Order of Knights, who constructed the first bridge across the Oder there, built a castle to protect it and occupied the castle with a garrison of armed knights. In 1455 the German Order sold the town to the Markgraf Albrecht von Hohenzollern, in whose family's hands the town was to remain until the abdication of the Kaiser in 1918.

Markgraf Hans von Hohenzollern built the new Schloss (fortified palace) between 1535 and 1537, and then had the fortress that is still recognisable today constructed by the engineer Giromella, with its four corner bastions (König, Königin, Kronprinzessin and Philipp) and the central northern bastion (Kronprinz, or Hohen Kavalier).

When King Gustav Adolf of Sweden conquered the Mark Brandenburg in 1631, he also acquired Küstrin. The Swedes reinforced the fortress and added the Albrecht and August Wilhelm ravelins, as well as two lunettes to the Oder bridgehead. (The remains of the upriver lunette were still visible on 1945 aerial photographs.) The Swedish king was killed at the battle of Lützen in 1632 and three years later the Mark Brandenburg was back in Prussian hands.

On 5 September 1730 Crown Prince Friedrich (later King Frederick the Great) was brought to the fortress under guard with his companion Second-Lieutenant von Katte, having been caught while

1

The Russian siege of August 1758

The siege lasted from 14 to 22 August 1758, when Frederick the Great attacked the Russian army from the rear and defeated it at the battle of Kutzdorf. The plan is taken from the volume *Neues Kriegstheater oder Sammlung der merkwürdigsten Begebenheiten des gegenwärtigen Krieges in Deutschland* (Leipzig, 1758).

Key:

A. The town and fortress of Küstrin

B. Russian artillery and mortar batteries that set fire to the town on 22 August 1758

C. Advanced Russian corps besieging the town

D. The camp of the imperial Russian troops under Field Marshal Graf von Fermor trying to desert from his father's army. He was incarcerated in the Schloss, from where he was later obliged to watch the beheading of von Katte, and remained imprisoned there until 26 February 1732.

Küstrin was first besieged by the Russians in 1758 during the Seven Years' War, as a result of which the town was burnt to the ground. Frederick ordered the immediate reconstruction of the town and within ten days of the fire defeated the Russians at the battle of Zorndorf nearby. That same year work was begun on the Friedrich-Wilhelm Canal; when it was finished in 1787 it provided a new outlet for the Warthe into the Oder north of the town.

In 1806 the Prussian army was defeated by Napoleon at the battles of Jena and Auerstädt. The fortress at Küstrin was subsequently surrendered to the French, who proceeded to reinforce the defences. The fortress was besieged again by the Russians from March to July 1813, and then by the Prussian Landwehr, to whom the French garrison capitulated in March the following year. The Schloss then became a barracks.

In 1817 the course of the Warthe where it joined the Oder southeast of the fortress was blocked, and work was begun on the Sonnenburger Chaussee six years later. The Oder-Vorflut Canal was constructed in 1832 to take the strain off the town's bridges during the annual floods, being designed with a dam across it so that the water could only flow across it once it reached a certain level, while ensuring the busy navigation of the Oder throughout the summer. In the 1850s the resulting 'Island' was provided with Lunettes A and B to cover the upstream Oder approaches, and Lunettes C and D to guard the road bridge across the canal from the west bank; of these, only Lunettes B and D still survived in 1945. Only the moat of Lunette A remained and C had been completely removed and filled in. However, the military remained conscious of the importance of the annual flooding of the Warthebruch in particular as a defensive measure.

The first railways arrived with the construction of the Küstrin–Landsberg–Kreuz line in 1856–7, after which the town soon became an important railway junction, but the connection to Berlin was not effected until 1867, when the Oder bridgehead fortifications were removed to make way for the Altstadt station. The two-level Neustadt station was built in 1874–6, when new lines linked Küstrin with Stettin on the Baltic and Breslau in Upper Silesia. In 1885 the Küstrin–Stargard railway line was opened, and in 1896 the Küstrin–Sonnenburg line, the same year that the line to Berlin was doubled. A further connection was made in 1884 with a line to Neudamm. Küstrin now formed the nodal point for two important express train lines running east to west and north to south, as well as being the start point for the other lines. The town had four railway stations: the main station in the Neustadt, Küstrin-Altstadt on the Island, Küstrin-Kietz and Kietzerbusch, which was little more than a halt.

This was also a time of military expansion. The Neues Werke fort was built adjacent to the Neustadt railway station in 1863–72, and the Hohen Kavalier was adapted to take heavy guns. Following the Franco-German War of 1870–1, an attempt was made to preserve the 300-year-old fortifications at the mouth of the Warthe, despite the introduction of longer-ranged guns using Alfred Nobel's far more powerful explosives than hitherto, and outer forts were constructed at a distance of 5 to 10 kilometres east of the Oder at Zorndorf, Tschernow and Säpzig, and to the west at Gorgast. However, presumably as a security measure, none of these external works was shown on the official maps of this area.

Then in 1902–3 the new Artillery Barracks were built on the Island opposite the Altstadt railway station, and in 1913 barracks for an engineer battalion were constructed on Warnicker Strasse. The dwindling defensive value of the medieval citadel could only have been welcome to the citizens, hemmed in as they were by the walls and ditches. After years of negotiation the town managed to obtain a considerable amount of the fortress property from the state in order to be able to lower the walls and fill in the ditches. The First World War delayed this process but, none the less, most of the works fell into civilian use, with a casemate becoming the town museum, one lunette a home to a canoe club and another a youth hostel. Eventually, in 1930, part of the Hohen Kavalier was demolished together with the northern ramparts, allowing the improvement of the stretch of main road (Reichsstrasse 1) running through the Altstadt between the Oder and Warthe bridges.[1]

Another wave of military construction began under the Nazi government with the provision of a large supply depot and bakery. New barracks, later named 'von Stülpnagel', were built to accommodate an infantry regiment on Landsberger Strasse, the engineer barracks were extended, and a garrison hospital was constructed on Warnicker Strasse nearby.

From the invasion of Poland in August 1939 onwards the town became an important transit centre for the war in the east, but was spared immediate involvement in the war until January 1945. Only twice were bombs dropped here during the night raids on Berlin, landing on the outskirts without causing any noticeable damage. Right at the beginning of the air war an apparently inadequately blacked-out farmhouse off the Sonnenburger Chaussee had attracted attention and next day the curious could see deep craters scattered over the fields nearby. Then in 1941 raiders spotted the chimneys of the Cellulose Factory sticking up above the fog bank, but only the factory toilets and washrooms were hit.

The apparent lack of interest shown by the staffs of the Anglo-American air forces in the vulnerable communications nodal point of Küstrin – five large and three smaller railway and road bridges spanning the Oder, Warthe and Vorflut Canal in a so-called multi-level railway station, a rare design enabling the important west–east (Berlin–Königsberg/East Prussia) line to cross over the north–south (Stettin–Breslau) line – simplified the requirement for effective anti-aircraft defence.

For a while during the opening stages of the war heavy flak batteries were deployed in the open fields near Manschnow on the road to Seelow as part of the Berlin defences. Later the flak defences were reduced to the garrison's machine-gun troops, who were stationed at night at various points near the bridges. Luckily for the place and its inhabitants, the effectiveness of these old, water-cooled weapons was never put to the test, but the pointless firing of re-conditioned tracer bullets into the night sky occurred whenever the sound of an aircraft engine could be heard, however far off.

There was also a Home-Flak battery manned by schoolboys and elderly men. Its 20mm cannon were stationed at the river crossing points, mainly on hastily assembled metal scaffolding towers, but also on wooden platforms on school and factory roofs near the Oder bridges. There were also some small searchlights. In daytime the gun crews either went to work or to school, taking it in turns to assemble in the evenings at the provisional accommodation at these positions. The same applied to the whole troop whenever there was an air raid alert. However, their weapons never fired a live round in anger. Two or three times they fired at a target pulled by a single-engined Ju W 34 at a reasonable height with practice ammunition. The gun crews' duty time was mainly taken up with theoretical instruction, preparatory exercises and even with drill conducted by a small group of regular Luftwaffe personnel. These guns were unable to reach the Anglo-American bomber fleets that attacked Berlin from 1944 onwards, using the eastward-running railway as a guide to the Oder before turning north for the Baltic, and eventually they were dismantled at the beginning of 1945.[2]

The Nazi influence on the town could be seen in the renaming of streets after Nazi heroes. Brückenstrasse and that part of Zorndorfer Strasse between the Stern and the Warthe river was renamed Adolf-Hitler-Strasse, Drewitzer Oberweg in the Neustadt became Schlageterstrasse, while the section of Reichsstrasse 1 running through Kietz became Horst-Wessel-Strasse. The town mayor, Hermann Körner, also doubled as Kreisleiter or District Party Leader, his immediate superior being the Gauleiter of Brandenburg, Emil Stürtz, whose offices were in Berlin, although Berlin itself had its own Gauleiter, Josef Goebbels. Next in the Party chain of command was Reichsleiter Martin Bormann, Hitler's head of chancellery, to whom Körner would duly report.

Refugees began arriving in the town by train on 20 January. The first ones arrived on scheduled trains and mainly with a destination in mind. Some were evacuees from Berlin, fleeing from the devastating air raids there, and hoping for emergency accommodation with someone they knew. Then there were the families of civil servants and lower ranking Nazi officials from the Warthegau (the senior ones returned by motorcar). Then there were those who had not waited for orders to evacuate or to join the Volkssturm. These people were tired and irritable from constantly delayed journeys in cold and overfilled trains, but in this they did not differ much from other railway passengers in Germany in those days. Their preparations for the journey had clearly not been made in haste, for they wore suitable clothing and the belongings they brought with them were manageable and solidly packed, ready for frequent alighting from the trains. The assistance they needed from the improvised services at the railway stations, apart from the free distribution of refreshments for the journey, was very little. Those who had not managed to get aboard a passing train nearly always stayed in the station waiting rooms. The danger of missing the next connection to the west was far less there than in the emergency accommodation provided outside the station.

But this picture soon changed. At first there were a few individuals, then small family groups, then the numbers began to grow until the carriages arrived filled to the last inch. Now they were having to sacrifice some of their luggage in the fight to obtain a place on a train. Adherence to train schedules was no longer the norm. Fast and express trains were being slowed down throughout the whole country, and passenger trains could only be used without special permits for journeys of up to 75 kilometres. Shuttle services arrived irregularly, having been hurriedly assembled somewhere. Almost all the trains finished their journeys at Küstrin and were emptied there, a fact which was accepted without protest by the exhausted travellers. There were stories of deeply snowed-under roads with wearying waits at train stops on branch lines and, often enough, of having to walk on to the next big station. At Küstrin, there was at least the chance of spending a night in a heated room, resting on bundles of straw for a few hours. The classrooms to which they were taken could not be illuminated as there was no blackout, but bread and coffee were handed out in the corridors. Those who had lost family members could have the names noted down to be called out at the other locations offering shelter.

As late as Sunday, 28 January 1945 it seemed that life in the town was going on as normal. The local children were enjoying themselves with toboggans and skates, paying little attention to their parents' warnings to remain within call. No one could say whether the factories and businesses would reopen after the weekend break. But then the first treks began arriving in the town, having left distant villages several days ago. The people and their animals were exhausted. The horses were tended to in the streets wherever shelter from the wind could be found, and the refugees asked at the houses for warm drinks for their children. The columns then moved on. Others wanted to stay at least one night under a proper roof. Some had given up completely, their horses having been overwhelmed by the snowdrifts during the last stage; often their wagons could only move on when everyone got off, removing the heaviest loads until the wheels could get a firm grip on the ground. After three or four such incidents, boxes and baskets were often left behind, for it was not worth saving them if one was going on by train.

Until this point individual cases had been distinguishable in the great passing stream, and some compassion had been shown according to the degree of need, but now all those arriving in open railway wagons were in the same lowest state of misery. It took a long time for the trains to be loaded, but things calmed down a little when the trains moved off with shapelessly bundled figures huddled together, packed on the bare floors of the wagons. Here and there a piece of sailcloth or even a carpet provided some basic shelter from the cutting cold. The overcoats of those who had found places inside protected them from the shower of sparks coming from the engine.

Two wagons in which typhus had broken out were detached and medical orderlies carried off a corpse on a stretcher. Several women and children were admitted to hospital with frostbite. The others remained incapable of doing anything, sitting on the platform until they were led away, several forgetting their baggage.

All the accommodation near the station was filled to capacity and more. Even the seats in the cinemas had been removed to provide space. Two schools in the Altstadt had also been made available, but that involved a 1.5 kilometre walk as there was no transport available. No one had thought of providing an adequate aid service or making proper arrangements when this evacuation began. Because of the propaganda put out by the government, the lower level civil servants were unaware of the extent of the approaching avalanche. Consequently only the relatively limited resources deployed for the reception of the evacuee trains from Berlin in the late summer of 1943, providing a brief stop for refreshments, had been implemented. Now considerable improvisation, mainly using helpful members of such organisations as the German Red Cross, the Frauenschaft (Mothers' Union) and Jungvolk (junior branch of the Hitler Youth), had become necessary for the preparation of sandwiches and hot drinks, laying down straw in classrooms for overnight accommodation and providing medical care for the worst cases.

The boys served as guides to the emergency accommodation scattered all over the town, carrying baggage on their toboggans, while the girls assisted with handing out food and looking after the youngest refugees. After the numbing stress of the journey, aggravated by the sudden cold, exhaustion and other ailments, many refugees had fallen ill but there was now a shortage of simple medicaments for the unskilled helpers in the mass accommodation to hand out. Adolescents were determining requirements on their own initiative, obtaining them from an understanding chemist, who gave them a wide selection of medical items free of charge. Such good will, sympathy and ingenuity lessened the distress of the refugees and made survival possible.[3]

Werner Melzheimer wrote about this period:

1945 began in Küstrin with crackling cold and worrying events. The first refugee transports arrived in the town, showing the state of collapse of the German eastern front. The first groups came by train in about the middle of January. But no one could believe that the east front had completely collapsed. But when the transports continued and the refugees started arriving in open goods wagons in temperatures of minus 15 Celsius and more, it became obvious that catastrophe was impending.

The care of the refugees required the commitment of all available resources. Almost without exception, the Küstrin women volunteered to help. They stood on the railway platforms and in the goods station handing out food prepared in the Reichsbahn kitchens. The four big steam cauldrons heated nourishing soup in regular sequence, while the Küstrin women prepared sausage sandwiches for the refugees at long tables. The number of arrivals streaming in increased. At first they came by railway, but then the streets of the town became filled with vehicles of all kinds. They were blocked with the horses and carts of refugee treks arriving packed with the freezing refugees and their bare necessities. All halls and schools were filled. New kitchens had to be set up, such as in the old gun club and the Lyceum. The bakeries were no longer able to cope and the garrison bakery had to assist.

Ever more threatening was the news brought by the people fleeing from the east, from East Prussia, West Prussia, then from Schneidemühl and finally Landsberg on the Warthe, all flowing through the town. Then on the 31st January it suddenly stopped.[4]

The Küstrin battalion of the Volkssturm was mobilised on 24 January under Commander Hinz, head of the Küstrin Technical School. Volkssturm weapons were supposed to come from Party resources, but none could be found, so the battalion was sent off unarmed by rail to Trebisch, north-west of Schwerin on the Warthe. Their allotted positions were already occupied and Hinz, unable to obtain further instructions, decided of his own accord to bring his battalion back to Küstrin. Meanwhile the men's wives had been pestering the local authorities for news and eventually a vehicle was sent to find them. Some 35 kilometres beyond Sonnenburg the car was stopped by sentries, who warned the men in it not to go any further, as the Russians were thought to be in the next village. On the way back, about 20 kilometres from Landsberg, they took a break in a village pub that was full of soldiers drinking while Hitler's speech on the anniversary of the Nazi assumption of power in 1933 went unheeded on the radio.[5]

At this time there was a group of about forty German officers imprisoned in the Schloss, mainly members of families believed to have been involved in the attempt against Hitler's life on 20 July 1944. They included Generals Hans Speidel (Field Marshal Erwin Rommel's former chief of staff), Ferdinand Schaal, Hans-Karl Freiherr von Esebeck, Groppe, Adolf Sinzinger, Leopold Rieger, and von Hollwede, as well as the former commander in chief of the Royal Netherlands Army, Lieutenant-General Jonkher van Roëll. The prison commandant was Major Fritz Leussing, an unusually tolerant character for such a role, who allowed his prisoners to listen to foreign broadcasts behind closed doors. An inspection by an SS general at the beginning of the year had found the commandant's Party credentials wanting and the general had departed leaving the fate of both the commandant and his charges in doubt. General Speidel then persuaded Major Leussing to prepare a travel order for them all that was deliberately smudged. Speidel then signed it as 'Chief of the General Staff' and they set off on 30 January for Württemburg, where Jonathan Schmid, the former head of the civilian administrative staff at military headquarters in Paris, was now regional Minister of the Interior. A Waffen-SS unit then moved into the Schloss.[6]

Stalag IIIc, the big prisoner-of-war camp on the outskirts of Drewitz, had already been emptied, the prisoners being driven off to the west towing their possessions on home-made toboggans. Some of them had passed through Küstrin, but the majority had crossed straight over the frozen Oder. Many of the village inhabitants followed them, but an equal number remained behind while the village Nazi Party chief awaited instructions.[7]

Chapter Two

The Vistula–Oder Operation

In mid-January 1945 a red tidal wave broke over the German front lines in Poland and began sweeping before it westwards all that survived the initial onslaught. The senior German commanders were sacked and hasty attempts were made to reorganise what resources remained.

The Red Army had been astride the Vistula upstream from Warsaw since August 1944 when Marshal Georgi Zhukov had brought Operation Bagration to a successful conclusion, clearing the Germans from Soviet soil. To do this he had been given overall command of three Red Army Fronts, or Army Groups, the 1st and 2nd Byelorussian and the 1st Ukrainian. As Stalin's Deputy Supreme Commander he had already brought victorious conclusions to such campaigns as the defence of Moscow, Leningrad and Stalingrad, and the battle of Kursk. However, his successes had aroused Stalin's jealousy, and as early as 1942 the Russian leader had commissioned Viktor Abakumov, head of the Special Department in the Ministry of the Interior that was later to be renamed SMERSH, to try to discover something with which to discredit Zhukov. Abakumov had begun by interrogating Zhukov's former Chief of Operations in an unsuccessful attempt to produce such evidence. Then Stalin had tasked the Commissar for Defence with finding some error or omission with which Zhukov could be charged, and eventually two artillery manuals were found that Zhukov had personally approved without clearing them with the Stavka, the supreme high command, and an order was then distributed among the upper echelons of the command structure openly warning Zhukov not to take hasty decisions. This activity gave Zhukov serious cause for concern, to the extent that he was prepared to be arrested at any moment on some trumped-up charge.

In early October 1944 Stalin informed Zhukov that he proposed

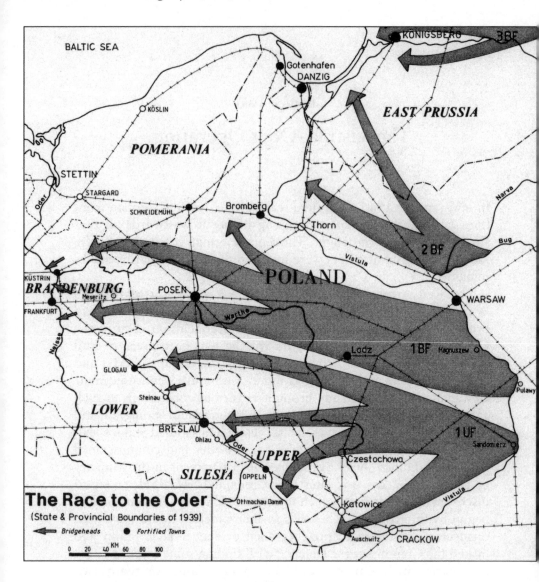

The Race to the Oder
(State & Provincial Boundaries of 1939)
Bridgeheads   Fortified Towns
0   20   40   KM   60   80   100

taking over the supervision of the three Fronts facing Berlin himself, but that Zhukov would have command of the 1st Byelorussian Front tasked with taking the city. Presumably Stalin believed that he now had sufficient experience to do this, being confident of ultimate victory in an atmosphere in which post-war political considerations were beginning to come to the fore. This decision amounted to a humiliating demotion for Zhukov but, as a loyal soldier, there was nothing he could do but accept it, and he assumed the appointment on 16 November 1944 after a spell at work on the operational plans at the Stavka.

The initial campaign was called the Warsaw–Lodz Operation after its somewhat limited aims. For Zhukov's 1st Byelorussian Front this meant breaking out of the Maguszev bridgehead, eliminating the German forces in the area between Warsaw and Radom, and then pushing forwards via Lodz to Posen to form a line extending north to Bromberg and south towards Breslau, which Marshal Ivan Koniev's 1st Ukrainian Front should by then have reached in its clearance of Upper Silesia. Nothing was planned in detail beyond that stage, for the outcome of the type of breakthrough battle envisaged could not be gauged with any accuracy.

Koniev began the offensive with his 1st Ukrainian Front on 12 January, followed by Marshal Konstantin Rokossovsky with the 2nd Byelorussian Front on the 13th sweeping northwards on Danzig and Gotenhafen, and lastly Zhukov joined in with the 1st Byelorussian Front on the 14th. By the time Zhukov attacked, the 9th Army opposing him was fully alert, but to little avail. By the end of the following day the 9th Army's defensive system had been destroyed and Zhukov's 1st and 2nd Guards Tank Armies were through and advancing up to 100 kilometres beyond their start lines. To the south Koniev's forces were enjoying similar success with a rapid advance.

The Soviet progress was aided by the weather. There was little snow to hinder them, and as the frozen ground and iced-up waterways could take the weight of the infantry and light artillery pieces, they did not have to stick to the roads and thus built-up areas could easily be bypassed. The movement was so swift that the Soviets were constantly catching the Germans unprepared, their defences unmanned. Consequently, on 17 January, the day the two 'Berlin' Fronts drew abreast and Warsaw fell, Stalin ordered Zhukov to reach the Bromberg–Posen line by 3 or 4 February.

The Soviet advance continued with increasing speed. Posen was reached on the 22nd and Bromberg fell the next day, a full week ahead of schedule. However, Posen was an important communications centre, where seven railway lines and six major roads met, and it would not be taken that easily. It was a genuine nineteenth-century fortress city with an inner citadel and a ring of massive forts manned by a garrison of some 60,000 troops of various kinds. But a single city could not be allowed to hold up the Soviet advance, so the leading troops pressed on while Colonel-General Vassili Chuikov of the 8th Guards Army was detailed to supervise the reduction of the fortress with four of his divisions and two from the slower-moving 69th Army that was following behind. The siege of Posen was to last until 23 February, and it proved to be an important delaying factor for the Germans.[1]

The armoured vanguards of each corps consisted of a reinforced brigade operating 30 to 40 kilometres ahead of the main body, while the infantry armies formed similar vanguards from their own integral armour and motorised infantry units to operate up to 60 kilometres ahead of the main body. These were flexible distances, of course. As the fighting was done almost exclusively by the vanguards, the main body followed in column of route and only deployed when larger enemy forces were encountered, thus enabling the infantry armies to maintain virtually the same pace as the armoured ones.

The Soviet advance, however, was hampered by the limited quantities of fuel, ammunition and supplies it could carry with it, for its basic supply system depended almost exclusively on the railways with local distribution by trucks, and, as the following accounts reveal, the depots were still east of the Vistula. The Soviet railway gauge was wider than the European, and the German invasion of the Soviet Union had therefore entailed adapting the tracks to suit their trains; the Soviets simply reversed this process as they reconquered lost territory and advanced into Poland and Germany. As Colonel-General Chuikov put it:

> The logic of combat is inexorable; it accepts neither justifications nor plausible excuses if during the fighting the logistical services fail to supply the frontline troops with everything necessary.
>
> We can find any number of valid explanations and excuses why on reaching the walls of Posen we did not have enough heavy guns to pulverise the enemy fortifications. But the fact remains that the assault on Posen dragged out for a whole month instead of the several days allotted for the operation by the Front Command.
>
> It was not a simple matter to adapt the logistical services to the troops' heightened rate and depth of advance. The Front Commander's orders and his determination could not solve the problem. Within a few days the advancing troops had consid-

erably outdistanced their supplies. Motor vehicles had to make longer runs. As a result fuel consumption increased. And there was no magic to turn 100 trucks into 300. You've got to have them, man them and provide the maintenance for them, which means additional repair shops and whole repair complexes. In a word, combat operations demanded that the logistical services perform their functions faultlessly, for a miscalculation or blunder in the transport operations could cost thousands of lives.

But the closer we approached the Oder, the deeper we penetrated into Germany, the more complex became the supply system.

Here is an example. Railways were a constant source of worry. The absence of a standard railway gauge during the initial stage of our advance into Germany adversely affected the supply of the advancing troops. The oversight was put right eventually, but time was lost.

In order to save fuel, half the motor vehicles making empty runs from the front were towed to their destination. All captured fuel was registered and distributed under strict control. Captured alcohol was mixed with other components and used as fuel, and all serviceable captured guns and ammunition were used against the enemy.[2]

Colonel A.H. Babadshanian, commanding the 11th Tank Corps of the 1st Guards Tank Army, wrote:

Our tank troops attacked without pause for breath by day and night, in fog and in snow. Only the lack of fuel and ammunition could check our attack. The communication routes had extended to almost 400 kilometres, the supply depots having remained on the east bank of the Vistula. The railways were not functioning and the road bridges over the river had been destroyed. There was petrol for motor vehicles in the captured German camps but no diesel. Often combatant units were stuck for days.[3]

On 26 January, the day his troops crossed the 1939 German border, Zhukov submitted a plan to the Soviet High Command, which was approved the following day. It stipulated that the 1st Byelorussian

Front's forces were to reach the line Berlinchen/Landsberg/Brätz by 30 January. It should be noted, however, that the Soviet High Command warned the 1st Byelorussian Front that in order to provide reliable cover for the Front's right flank against possible enemy attacks from the north or north-east, one army augmented by at least one tank corps had to be kept in reserve behind the Front's right flank.[4] Zhukov went on to say:

> By the same day the tank armies shall gain control of the following areas:
> The 2nd Guards Tank Army: Berlinchen, Landsberg, Friedeberg; the 1st Guards Tank Army: Meseritz, Schwiebus, Tirschtiegel.
> Upon reaching this line, the formations, particularly the artillery and the logistical establishments, shall halt, supplies be replenished and the combat vehicles put in order. Upon full deployment of the 3rd Shock and 1st Polish Armies, the Front's entire forces shall continue the advance on the morning of the 2nd February, 1945, with the immediate mission of crossing the Oder in their drive, and shall subsequently strike out at a rapid pace towards Berlin, directing their main effort at enveloping Berlin from the north-east, the north and north-west.[5]

In Zhukov's orders issued on 27 January he stated:

> There is evidence that the enemy is hastily bringing up his forces to take up defensive positions on the approaches to the Oder. If we manage to establish ourselves on the western bank of the Oder, the capture of Berlin will be guaranteed.
> To carry out this task each army will detail one reinforced rifle corps . . . and they shall be immediately moved forwards to reinforce the tank armies fighting to secure and retain the position on the west bank of the Oder.[6]

Zhukov continued his forward planning and the next day further details emerged. Once across the Oder, the 5th Shock Army was to thrust towards Bernau, north-east of Berlin, the 8th Guards Army towards Buckow, Alt Landsberg and Weissensee, and the 69th Army towards Frankfurt-an-der-Oder, Boossen and Herzfelde, all three armies operating between the water boundaries formed by the Finow Canal in the north and the Spree River in the south.

No mention of Küstrin was made in these orders, yet it had the only road and rail bridges across the Oder for a considerable distance

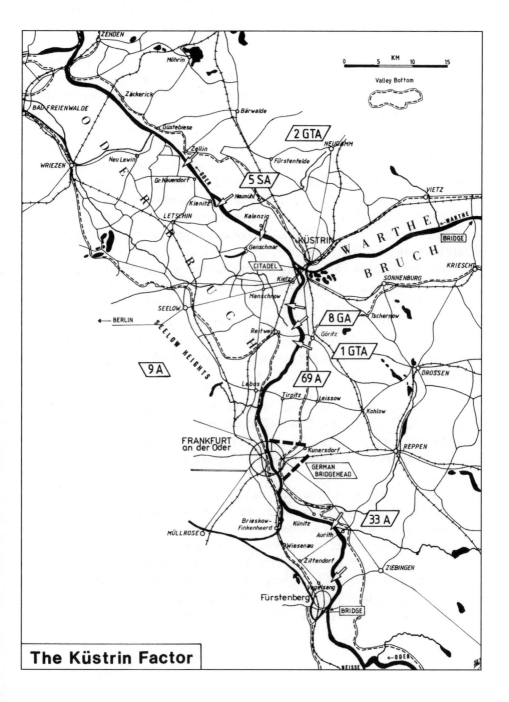

The Küstrin Factor

in either direction. The only available alternatives to the Küstrin bridges were the road bridges at Frankfurt, 27 kilometres to the south, and at Hohenwutzen, 46 kilometres to the north, and the railway bridges at Frankfurt, 30 kilometres to the south, and at Zäckerick, 38 kilometres to the north. Presumably Zhukov expected these bridges to be blown in the face of his advance, thus obliging his men to use their own resources to cross the river.

In accordance with Zhukov's instructions of the 27th, the 1st Byelorussian Front's armies widened the arc of their advance towards the Oder, sending strong vanguards ahead of each army, corps and division. The prospect of rising temperatures forced them to quicken their pace even further in the hope that the ice would still be holding when they reached the Oder, thus simplifying their crossing. A medal that had been struck the year before for commanders who gained bridgeheads no doubt acted as an added incentive. However, in this approach across a wide arc, the Front was uncomfortably split by the Warthe estuary (Warthebruch), while the southern element also had the handicap of the gap in the lines of communication caused by the stubbornly held Posen fortress.

The 1st Guards Tank Army and those elements of the 8th Guards and 69th Armies not involved in the siege of Posen fanned out south of the Warthebruch, with the 33rd Army even further south on the Front's left flank. Colonel Babadshanian described what happened when his troops reached the Tirschtiegel Riegel with its Maginot-like defences that had long been stripped of their guns for the Atlantic Wall:

> On the evening of the 26th January, the vanguard of the 11th Guards Tank Corps, Colonel Morgonov's 45th Guards Tank Brigade, reached the town of Tirschtiegel and the former German–Polish border. Before us lay the Obra River, beyond began Germany.
>
> How long we had yearned for this day, and now it was there. We just had to take one more step and we would be standing on German soil. Our spirits rose. The vanguard tried to take the river on the move, but it was not so easy, as the enemy had blown all the bridges in his retreat and offered bitter resistance.
>
> The 45th Guards Tank Brigade attacked Tirschtiegel in vain on the 26th January. On the night leading to the 27th January, Colonel Gussakovski's 44th Guards Tank Brigade circum-

vented the town to the north, forced the Odra and thrust on to Hochwalde without encountering any resistance.

At 0300 hours the brigade's vanguard, Major Karabnov's 3rd Battalion, came up against a barricade across the road. The engineers made a reconnaissance. To the left and right of the road were ranged anti-tank ditches covered by minefields and concrete obstacles. The engineers pulled out the girders supporting the barricade, and the tanks were able to continue.

Gussakovski had reached the so-called Oder Triangle, the fortified area of Meseritz, a strong and difficult-to-take obstacle on the way to the Oder that began on the west bank of the Obra. This main line of defence strip extended between Schwerin, Meseritz and Schwiebus about 20 kilometres further west.

The Oder Triangle formed a massive defensive installation. It consisted of numerous reinforced concrete bunkers, so-called armoured works, incorporating the latest technical measures and echelonned to a depth of up to 6 kilometres. These armoured works went down two or three storeys into the earth and were mounted with armoured cupolas with artillery pieces and machine guns that could be exposed or retracted. The walls were up to 2.5 metres thick and the cupolas had 350 millimetres of armour. These armoured works were connected by underground passages, had their own power and air filter systems, water and drainage systems, ammunition and food stores. They were further reinforced with field works, anti-tank ditches, barricades, barbed wire and minefields. In front of the main defensive installation was a chain of lakes running from north to south.

As quickly as possible, our corps regrouped north of Schwiebus and entered the fortified area from the rear without encountering strong resistance. Once the enemy realised that he was surrounded, many of the garrisons surrendered to our all-arms armies following up behind.[7]

North of the Warthebruch, both the 5th Shock Army and the 2nd Guards Tank Army, less one corps already detached to cover the Front's exposed northern flank, passed through Landsberg on the 30th, heading for the Oder. The ice on the river was still thick enough to take trucks, but a tank fell through the ice when it tried to follow them across. The troops crossed over to the west bank taking anti-tank guns with them, and occupied the village of Kienitz at 0400 hours on 31 January. They found six German officers with 63 young Reichsarbeitsdienst gunners asleep in a train at the village station and captured their six flak guns. A couple of the villagers managed to get away to warn the authorities in Wriezen.[8]

The southern Soviet vanguard continued on its way, pushing forwards along the axis Tauerzig–Polenzig–Göritz. The main body was unable to take advantage of its vanguard's success and had to fight its way through the old German border defences, which took the whole of the two days of 30 and 31 January to achieve, but resulted in the complete destruction of the 21st SS Mountain Division 'Skanderberg'. It arrived opposite the village of Reitwein on 2 February and immediately started crossing the Oder, even though the ice was already beginning to break up.[9]

Meanwhile General Theodor Busse had been given command of the German 9th Army as part of Army Group 'Weichsel' (Vistula), which was taken over on 22 January by Reichsführer-SS Heinrich Himmler, whose practical military experience was limited to basic training as a teenage volunteer towards the end of the First World War. Following the attempt on Hitler's life on 20 July 1944, the Nazi leadership had become highly mistrustful of military commanders and Himmler's appointment was a direct consequence. Himmler immediately set off in his luxurious personal train to Deutsch-Krone in Pomerania but he had neither a direct communications link to the Wehrmacht command network nor any maps, apart from one which the newly appointed operations officer happened to bring along with him four days later. No sooner had Himmler issued his first orders than the Soviet advance forced him to withdraw westwards again. The ineptness of this appointment system was underlined on the 27th with the appearance of Himmler's Chief of Staff, SS-Brigadier Lammerding, who proved to have no staff experience.[10]

Himmler then ordered the Vth SS Mountain Corps based in the Frankfurt-an-der-Oder area to try to block the Soviet advance on Berlin. This was a mixed formation that included the Panzergrenadier Division 'Kurmark' and the 21st SS Mountain Division 'Skanderberg'. The latter was immediately dispatched eastwards to take charge of the Volkssturm units meant to be manning the Tirschtiegel Riegel defences and to absorb any German troops withdrawing in that direction. The 'Skanderberg' had the misfortune to reach Zielenzig simultaneously with the Soviet armour, and its commander was wounded and taken prisoner. The armoured reconnaissance battalion of the 'Kurmark' set out by rail on 22 January to relieve the Posen garrison but was stopped short of its destination and eventually had to fight its way back, reaching the Oder near Grünberg at the end of the month after many adventures.

Another German infantry division, the 'Woldenberg', was apparently meant to form up and fight in the path of the Soviet advance, as this account by Lieutenant Rudolf Schröter indicates:

In 1942 I was badly wounded in an attack in the woods in the Voronesh area east of the Don and lost my lower right arm.

In January 1945 I was a lieutenant commanding a company in an infantry replacement and training battalion under the command of Major Shellack and based on the Strantz Barracks in the East Brandenburg town of Landsberg an der Warthe.

At the end of January there was a sudden alert. I had to see off my wife and little son who were visiting me in the barracks and put them on a truck going west. Then I received orders to form a line of defence against the expected Russians hard east of Landsberg. My sector began on Reichsstrasse 1 at the Oldenburg Experimental Farm (inclusive) and extended some 1.5 to 2 kilometres south to the village of Lorenzdorf. My left-hand neighbour to Irrenanstalt was a unit under Second-Lieutenant Clemens in a situation similar to mine, and my right-hand neighbour an inserted unit of Hungarian Honveds.

I had about 400 recruits at my disposal, some of whom had yet to be sworn in, i.e. mainly youngsters who had just completed their pre-military Hitler Youth training and were at the beginning of their barrack training. Sergeants and NCOs were completely lacking, so these functions were undertaken by recruits with some military knowledge and whose appearance seemed the most suitable. I had no information about our own forces or the enemy.

The temperature on the 28th January was minus 15 degrees Celsius with a thick and frozen blanket of snow. There was great movement to the rear on Reichsstrasse 1 of men on foot and in vehicles. The enemy situation remained quiet, unknown and uncertain, but attacks by advance units could be expected at any time.

A makeshift occupation of the defences was made in and around the farm but there was no infantry for this. However, in front was a twin 20mm flak gun with its crew, its second lieutenant having disappeared. There were also two Hetzers.

That afternoon of the 28th January I administered the oath to those recruits who had not yet been sworn in, in the cover of the farm.

On the morning of the 29th January a sergeant-major of the Waffen-SS reported to me with two Königstigers, two heavy recovery vehicles, a tanker and an amphibious jeep, as well as plenty of ammunition. There was a third Königstiger of his 500 metres from my position that had broken down. My youngsters had to help with the recovery of this vehicle, as the Russians had already probed Lorenzdorf. The recovery succeeded and my escorting infantry were not only highly praised by the tankers, but the sergeant-major decided to support me with his platoon for our cooperation.

Once the vehicles had refuelled in Landsberg, the two recovery vehicles towed the twin 20mm flak gun into a well-covered firing position behind our sector, as well as the two Hetzers and an 88mm flak gun on its trailer that I had acquired from the fleeing columns. Thus all the heavy weapons had taken up secure positions and had good fields of fire in depth in front of our sector and our neighbour's. My unit was now ready, quietly and confidently awaiting the enemy attack.

During the second half of the 30th January the Russians attacked and took Lorenzdorf. The Hungarians withdrew without concern for us, their left-hand neighbours, without orders or even a 'good-bye', but with the fire of our heavy weapons into the flanks of the enemy, we stopped his advance. Then we forced him to withdraw and abandon Lorenzdorf with the reserve and a Königstiger, during which a captured recruit from my company was released.

I still did not know what my superior formation was or who its commander was. Since receiving my orders in the barracks I had not received any further instructions and had no communications with any staff whatsoever. No officer or messenger had sought me out. I only knew that the Russians were attacking and that, since the flight of the Honveds, I now had an almost 3-kilometre-wide open and unprotected flank to the

Warthe over which the Russians could renew their attack.

An appreciation of the situation showed that we were surrounded by the enemy, forgotten and lost.

As it was suspected that the town commandant of Landsberg had fled in panic, and that Soviet infantry could infiltrate the town by bypassing us, I decided after consultation with my neighbour and the SS-sergeant-major to withdraw [to] preserve lives and fighting ability . . . the untrained recruits would also be spared possible house-to-house fighting at night and Landsberg bypassed to the north. This succeeded during the night in deep snow on field and woodland tracks without enemy interference. Clemens's unit also used the same route to evacuate its position. For the heavy weapons, especially the mechanically incapacitated Königstiger and the recovery vehicles, the only route was by road through Landsberg, if necessary fighting through. The SS, flak and Hetzer crews therefore combined and arranged a rendezvous for the next day between Landsberg and Vietz.

On the morning of the 31st January my unit rejoined the Königstiger SS-sergeant-major about 4 kilometres west of Landsberg in the Wepritz area. As we were still without a superior command or orders, I had us retreat westwards.

Beyond Dühringshof I was met by a car with a general, who received my report. He did not introduce himself, nor did he name his formation. He ordered me to deploy left of the road to Diedersdorf. My left-hand neighbour would be Second-Lieutenant Clemens's unit.[11]

Sergeant Horst Wewetzer was also involved in the withdrawal along Reichsstrasse 1 to Küstrin, as he relates:

On the 28th January 1945, my birthday, we were deployed on the northern exit from Kreuz in artillery support of Infantry Battalion 'Schulz'. As we were about to fire our guns at about 0600 hours, the sentry reported to me that the infantry had already withdrawn. That seemed unbelievable to me, as there had still not been any enemy movement. I thought that they had perhaps seen runners, food carriers and wounded. The sentry was convinced, however, and as it appeared, he was correct.

We opened fire without having any infantry protection in front of us and without having been told of this withdrawal. Naturally the Russians fired back and we had one man wounded.

When the tanks rolled through the rows of houses on the parallel street, we could only beat a hasty retreat. We got away from the Russians, crossed a still intact bridge over the Drage and reached Dragebruch, which consisted of only a few houses. Our vehicles stood on the roadway, while the soldiers looked in the houses for something to eat, but the civilian inhabitants had gone, taking all their food with them.

Our troop leader drove off to re-establish contact with the vanished infantry battalion. Then at about 1000 hours the enemy tanks caught up with us. They were as surprised as we were and did not open fire immediately. They first pulled back a little to open fire from a covered position. Our drivers and some of the men jumped into their vehicles and drove about 200 metres on to the edge of a wood to take cover. The other men who had been searching the houses for food ran across the snow-covered open plain, offering perfect targets, to reach the woods, where there was a prepared position already occupied by our troops.

Among our vehicles was a furniture van, whose driver had not made the dash in time. The tanks fired at our retreat and there were some dead and wounded, of whom the last could not be recovered for hours until the tanks withdrew.

We assembled at a forester's lodge deep in the woods behind the front line and waited there until evening.

In the darkness some officers of the unit occupying the position gathered and talked quietly among themselves, completely ignoring us. I wondered about this behaviour, which was contrary to normal army conduct. We also discovered that they had been given orders to withdraw towards Woldenberg. The enemy had apparently broken through north of our position, but it must have been far away for we had heard no sounds of combat. The infantry assembled at about 2200 hours and marched off.

We still sat there! Our troop leader was still looking for the Battalion 'Schulz'. It was possible that he would not return. Russians, military police or an energetic commander could have arrested him. Meanwhile we had recovered the furniture van that had been stuck between the lines with its engine still running. Its radiator was leaking and had to be provisionally repaired. As the forester's pump was frozen, some snow was melted on a stove.

In front of us were the Russians, our own troops had vanished, and we were in the middle of a wood with no idea of the place or surroundings. Apart from this, when we moved out that morning, our second gun had driven off with its commander, crew and vehicle and had not been seen since.

Our troop leader reappeared at about midnight. We decided to follow the route taken by the infantry, but soon lost our way in the woods in the dark, especially as the infantry had used footpaths and tracks. Following an adventurous journey with the furniture van and other 'combat vehicles' through loggers' and woodland tracks, at dawn we eventually reached a road with a kilometre stone with an arrow pointing towards Woldenberg and, in the opposite direction, to Driesen. At last we had hit the route to Woldenberg. But from there through the morning stillness came the sound of tank guns. It made no sense for our troop to drive into a rolling tank attack with no idea of the place or the situation. We therefore decided to drive towards Driesen, although it could already have been in Russian hands, as from there it was only a few kilometres from Kreuz, which we had abandoned. On the road to Driesen and in the village itself all was dead quiet. Only a few civilians were standing around, apparently foreign labourers awaiting the arrival of the Russians.

We drove on to Friedeberg, hoping to bump into our own troops. The civilian population had almost completely gone and there was no trace of the army. We stayed all day in Friedeberg. Our anti-tank team looked for a garage as their vehicle was not functioning properly, and one of our men tried to bake some bread in an abandoned bakery.

Finally we needed something to eat. Our troop leader was once more away trying to make contact, and returned that evening. Then the Russians rolled into the town from one side while we left from the other. If I remember correctly, the tanks were firing as they entered the town, otherwise we would not have noticed in time and would have been wiped out.

We drove during the night to Landsberg, always with the feeling that we might be overtaken by the tanks at any moment.

At Landsberg we caught up with the Wehrmacht for the first time and drove into a barracks complex. Mounted troops were deployed on the barrack square, all spick and span, feeding their horses. Everything was peaceful with no sense of the Russian spearheads approaching.

We found a headquarters staff in one of the barracks, reported and asked to be allocated. An adjutant wanted to know all about us, especially from where we had come. When our troop leader said that we had belonged to Emergency Battalion 'Schulz', the doubts vanished from his face. That is how one can innocently arouse suspicion of lying. He vanished and we had to wait a long time. We had the impression of being unwanted. We still had the feeling that live firing could begin any moment. It was a strange feeling.

Finally the adjutant reappeared with the order: 'Drive to — and deploy!' This was naturally as unmilitary as the withdrawal 'towards Woldenburg'. The order should have read: 'Drive to —, report to command post X and deploy in support of their troops.' I still believe that they wanted to get rid of us and were sending us out no matter where. There was no sign of any defensive organisation.

In any case we had the bad experience of Dragebruch behind us, where we had also been left in the dirt. Instead of driving to —, we drove towards Küstrin, and were not the only ones. The road was full of vehicles. That was on the 30th January 1945.

We reached Küstrin on the morning of the 31st January. We immediately got the feeling of a more orderly establishment.[12]

Also caught up in the Soviet advance were the German civilian refugees from as far away as East Prussia, usually organised in treks, but invariably clogging the roads in their desperation to flee the enemy with their horse-drawn wagons and push carts. Many left their homes too late to reach safety, for the local Nazi Party officials were reluctant to permit their leaving for fear of being branded as defeatists. However, the towns they had to pass through were generally organised to provide overnight accommodation and food before moving them on.

Hans Dalbkermeyer related:

On the 1st January 1945 I was 15½ years old, a pupil in the

5th Class of the Deutsche Heimschule in Birnbaum in the Warthegau. This chain of senior schools educated us up to Arbitur level. We were called 'Jungmann', were boarders, and wore Hitler Youth uniform and a narrow armband with the words 'Deutsche Heimschulen' on the left forearm. The pupils came mainly from bombed cities or, like me, from the countryside. My parents' home was in a small village about 30 kilometres east of Birnbaum. Birnbaum itself, a small town of some 15,000 inhabitants, lay 90 kilometres east of Küstrin on the Warthe. From 1919 to 1939 Birnbaum was located just beyond the old Reich boundary on the then Polish side.

The Christmas holidays ended during the first days of January, after which the whole boarding school was back, but only Class 4 and below had school classes. We pupils in the 5th Form and upwards were given warlike organisational tasks in the town. Our 5th Form was still at full strength, but the 6th Form was reduced to half and the 7th Form down to about three pupils, and the 8th Form ceased to exist as they were assigned as Luftwaffe auxiliaries or conscripted into the Wehrmacht.

Our task in the town, equipped with horses and carts, was to do as much as possible for the German people flowing through the town. At first we were dealing with only small and individual groups, but this changed. As helpers for the Red Cross, NSV, Party and other organisations, we distributed food, warm drinks, arranged schools and gymnasiums as overnight accommodation and looked after them. There was much to do from morning to evening, so much that we would gladly have exchanged it for normal school classes. But we had to do our duty.

On about the 20th January the situation became serious and threatening. Russian troops were getting closer and were unstoppable. Wehrmacht units were mixed in with the treks, moving west. There was snow on the ground and the temperature dropped to minus 20 degrees Celsius.

Now schoolwork also ended for the younger classes. A Luftwaffe transport unit moved the school in closed transport, including most of the staff, to Cottbus. From here they went on by train to Thuringia. For us older ones the situation altered for us correspondingly. With the school dissolved, we were attached to the local Volkssturm but still accommodated in the school. The police gave us carbines of all types. In a second issue I acquired one of the desirable short Italian ones. It looked good but often failed later in action. One of my classmates was given among other things a muzzle-loader, possibly from the 1870/71 war, with three rounds of ammunition. We tried it out in a pit behind the school from behind safe cover. From fear of a bursting barrel or false action, we tied the gun to a post and fired it using a long string. A big bang relieved our tension and established that the old weapon still worked.

I was detailed as a messenger and even given a light motor-bike. The fuel lasted for three days, long enough in those temperatures. During this time my Volkssturm chief sent me late one evening in an easterly direction to Zirke, some 20 kilo-metres away, to find out where the Russians were. Over snow-covered roads, devoid of humanity and in icy tempera-tures I rode in total darkness, every so often stopping and restarting. Right on the edge of Zirke I turned round. I had carried out my task and could ride back in an easier frame of mind not having seen anyone.

On the 25th January we left Birnbaum and moved about 2 kilometres west to the Vorheide forester's lodge. As a messenger I had to maintain contact with the organisations in Birnbaum and travelled to and fro. On one of these trips between the lodge and town, partly by footpath through the woods, I saw the first dead German soldiers. As the Russians had not got so far forward yet, they must have been shot by Polish partisans.

On the 27th January while on duty in the town I saw Russian tanks arrive. The town was cleared virtually without a fight and the bridge over the Warthe leading to the west was blown. On the same day we left the Vorheide lodge and marched about 10 kilometres to Waitze, where we accommodated ourselves in the local school with the veteran Volkssturm men.

On the morning of the 29th January, while being allocated to the defence of an imaginary front line, we received our first artillery or tank fire. Our Volkssturm veterans with their ex-perience of the First World War gave us some very helpful rules that later were life-saving. No one was injured and so we took up our positions along the road to Birnbaum. We could hear the noise of tanks all day and once saw a group of Russians in the distance.

At nightfall our comrades to the west came back to join us bringing the news that the Russians had entered Waitze, and that we were cut off. Led by our old Volkssturm men, who were familiar with the area, we went in single file in a wide curve to the north of Waitze through deeply snowed woods.

Unmolested we came to the Waitze–Schwerin (Warthe) road leading west, which we followed all night. Dead tired, with blisters on our feet, we reached Schwerin at dawn. There the barracks offered us the chance of having a shower, breakfast, a change of clothing and sleep. We felt safe, let the relief overcome us, but were hardly asleep before we were woken up again at noon by enemy artillery fire.

The whole, but nevertheless meagre garrison appeared to have been completely taken by surprise. Disorganised, they fled the barracks and town and, from necessity, we joined in this disorder with the proviso of reporting to specific offices in Küstrin, 65 kilometres away. In view of our previous strenuous journey and the varying individual abilities to march, there was no question of marching in formation. We would have to see how we would get to Küstrin. So, we were on the move once more, now on crowded roads among the fleeing civilian population with and without horses and carts, and among them groups of Wehrmacht stragglers, some with vehicles. The clear thunder of the guns drove us forward.

Here we lost sight of some of the Birnbaum schoolboys. I only met five of them again. Whether the remainder reached Küstrin or were overrun by the Russian armoured spearheads, I cannot say. I have not heard of any of them, and the same applies to the old Volkssturm men. I never saw them again.

After marching a few kilometres, there came an opportunity of riding on the back of a slowly moving Wehrmacht truck for my fellow schoolboy Manni Roeder from the 6th Form and me, as we were marching along together. At first the crew tried to stop us jumping on, but then saw how young we were and let us on. Unfortunately this truck only went as far as Kriescht, 30 kilometres from Küstrin. There we were able to obtain some food. Looking for another means of continuing we found a train about to leave Kriescht station. Although it was packed with refugees, we managed to find places to sit and reached Küstrin late in the afternoon.[13]

Others were less fortunate, as Councillor Staercke of Güstebiese, downstream from Küstrin on the east bank of the Oder, reported:

I had been in communication with both [the village mayor] Habermann and [Ortsgruppenleiter Fritz] Lorenz about the evacuation until the last moment. I was also in communication with the young commandant during the German occupation. All three said that the civilian population would get the news in time. When asked about the alleged or actual Russian presence near Bärwalde all three were uncomfortable and said that the departure of the population was only possible with their permission. No information or instructions then resulted, as both the Ortsgruppenleiter and the mayor fell into the hands of the Russians.[14]

Chapter Three

Defence Preparations

Küstrin was declared a fortress on 25 January 1945. At that time the garrison consisted of depot, training and convalescent infantry, plus engineer and artillery units with a few anti-tank weapons but no air defences. The newly named fortress commandant was 50-year-old Major-General Adolf Raegener, holder of the Knights' Cross and a soldier since the First World War. He began by incorporating the local Volkssturm and police resources into his garrison, having nothing else to fall back on. Above all, General Raegener needed heavy weapons. Flak guns had been assigned to him from the Berlin area, but would they arrive in time?

Under the circumstances, the most useful role for the fortress, which Clausewitz once described propitiously as a 'place of refuge for a weak or unfortunate corps', was to provide secure river crossings for those army elements still east of the Oder and not withdrawing upon Frankfurt. Raegener's men would have only a few days in which to prepare if the Soviet advance was not delayed by the old border fortifications 70 kilometres east of the town. This was in any case a very vague hope, as all the troops that had been sent there were of equally limited fighting ability, such as the Volkssturm companies of the first levy from Küstrin, Neudamm and Königsberg/Neumark that were being transported by rail that day to Trebisch, 15 kilometres south-east of Landsberg.

Preparations for any sort of defence of the town appeared almost impossible with the existing materiel and personnel available, especially for the Neustadt. In contrast to the Altstadt, it was unhindered by walls and ditches and within a few decades it had developed into a significantly important part of the town, extending over a kilometre beyond the 75-year-old Neues Werke, the small fort that had been built to protect the railway station. Housing and industrial buildings had long since extended along the river as far out as

31

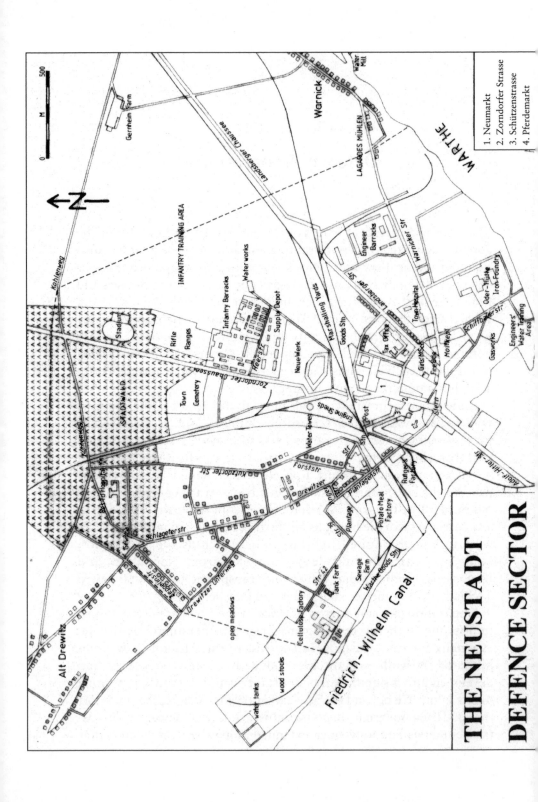

THE NEUSTADT

DEFENCE SECTOR

1. Neumarkt
2. Zorndorfer Strasse
3. Schützenstrasse
4. Pferdemarkt

the boundaries of the Drewitz and Warnick villages. A town bus service had connected the districts until the fuel supply began to run out, and then the buses were fitted to run on town gas supplied from tanks fitted on the coach roofs.

This extension of the Neustadt, with its new infantry barracks, a country pub and its sports stadium erected in the late 1920s, came up against dense woodland in the north-east. Here the land began to climb steeply and the Zorndorfer Berg, the horror of all cyclists, led over 2 kilometres to a high plateau above the Oder-Warthe valley bottom. This plateau exceeded the town in height by about 50 metres and offered, together with a fort in the centre on the road to Zorndorf, an outer defensive ring if only it could be adequately manned. But the garrison was not in a position to do this from its own resources. It was indeed doubtful if the Neustadt bridgehead would be able to hold up to the first energetic attack, however wide or short the front line stretched. Military necessity therefore required that it be held only as long as the railway station and Warthe bridges were needed for the withdrawal. Beyond that there were no reasonable grounds for keeping a considerable proportion of the troops in an unsuitable position. A sufficiently strong Altstadt garrison to bar the river crossings to the enemy would suffice with less risk. But decisions of this nature were no longer to be made according to tactical and strategic considerations.[1]

Back in Küstrin there was concern over the state of the ice on the Oder and Warthe rivers, which showed little sign of movement. During the first winter of the war the ice had formed metre-high barriers and in the subsequent thaw giant lumps of ice released from the flooded Warthe meadows had crushed the pontoons of the bathing stations. Damage to the bridges had only been avoided by some risky explosions with concentrated charges. Now attempts in several places to dislodge the ice with explosives proved ineffective, as the ice floes quickly froze back together in night temperatures as low as minus 20 degrees.

The cold and snow also made digging difficult. Firing positions and anti-tank ditches were prepared on the roads leading into the town from the east and south, from where the first attacks were expected; mines were laid and barbed wire obstacles erected. On the Landsberger Chaussee 14- and 15-year-olds tackled the deeply frozen earth, having to bring their own tools from home, under the direction of a few grumpy soldiers. Even the few picks passed from hand to hand were inadequate. Only when fires were lit over lines marked in the snow to warm the ground a little were they able to make small holes in the frozen earth and then laboriously extend them, but this took hours. Then someone forbade the lighting of fires for fear of attracting aircraft, although locomotives at the nearby goods station were sending thick smoke up to the low-hanging clouds.

When the work was abandoned at dusk, only a few shallow depressions showed the run of the planned position. The boys marched back to town frozen through and hungry, and were dismissed with orders to return to the position next morning. Even the prospect of further days without school failed to raise their spirits. Those born in 1928 and not already conscripted as Flak or naval auxiliaries had stopped attending regular classes since the last summer holidays. Until September they had worked on defences near Kalau, between Meseritz and Schwiebus, then had to assist with the root harvest near the town. This task was considerably pleasanter as they could sleep in the barns, were given good food with supplementary ration cards, and did not have to train or mount guard after work. They might even earn a few pennies. By this time, the schools had been concentrated into just a few schoolrooms, partly because the buildings were needed as hospitals or to house refugees. A few hours of tuition were given in shifts well into the afternoon, to which the teachers and pupils reacted only half-heartedly. And now this too was coming to an end.[2]

Panzergrenadier Johannes Diebe, who had only been a soldier since 15 January as a member of Panzergrenadier Replacement Battalion 50 in Küstrin, reported being employed on a similar task:

About six days before the end of the month our basic training was interrupted and we were sent to various locations to build defences. Our platoon had to go to Schlageterstrasse, beyond the entrance to Zeppelinstrasse, to dig foxholes near the GEWOBA buildings, one section to the left and one section to the right of the street. The distance between foxholes was about 2 metres.

Along the road from Alt Drewitz to Küstrin came an endless stream of refugees, civilians with horse-drawn wagons, handcarts, prams and packed bicycles. Among them were wounded soldiers, often with bloody bandages. Civilians, soldiers, officers, all had one aim, to cross the Warthe and the Oder and reach the west bank.

The people going past constantly asked us to go along with them. Fighting was useless in view of the Soviet superiority. Within us the sense of honour competed with the temptation to clear off. Flight seemed a possibility in this confusion, but one's sense of honour was stronger.

While we were digging, a squad of Feldgendarmerie [military police] appeared from the town and established a control point in Schlageterstrasse. They began to ruthlessly comb the soldiers out of the stream of refugees, registering them and lining them up and sending them marching off to other destinations. Those who refused were either shot or hanged. Those hanged were given a label: 'I am a coward'.

These events depressed us. The view of the four hanging soldiers along the street was unbearable. We therefore asked our superiors and the Feldgendarmerie to cut down the bodies of the comrades. The answer from the Feldgendarmerie was: 'You lads can practise your shooting and shoot through the ropes, but your aim had better be good, or you can watch yourselves being hanged.'

We begged our section leader to agree to this proposal and the sergeant agreed. So we shot our dead comrades down from the trees. It was awful, but much better than having this view in front of our eyes. For the civilians, above all the children, this must have been a terrible sight.

The Feldgendarmerie moved their control point further back into the town. We noticed that from then on soldiers came to us, asking for our company command post. In doing so they remarked that nothing made sense any more. This way we acquired a staff corporal and another corporal in our section. The first wore the ribbons of both Iron Crosses next to his Close Combat Badge. He had got as far as Stalingrad and only being on leave from the front had saved him from encirclement, death or imprisonment there.

We learned a lot from the staff corporal and were always asking him what he made of the situation. He reckoned that there was not much chance of a Russian attack as long as refugees and German soldiers in the present numbers were still coming through.[3]

Corporal Hans Arlt was also involved in the preparations for war:

> Following my successful conclusion of a course at the Army
> NCO School at Arnswalde, I was sent to the front together with
> some other comrades on 26 January 1945 as an RUB [Potential
> NCO of the Reserve] corporal. We were driven in open trucks
> to Küstrin-Neustadt in winter temperatures of minus 15 degrees
> Celsius.
>
> We were assigned to the 2nd Company of Captain von
> Oldershausen's combat team [battalion] in Stülpnagel Barracks.
> A considerable proportion of my platoon consisted of old
> soldiers who had been on guard duty in Denmark until then.
> They made themselves welcome to our group with their rich
> supplies of butter and cheese, but they were not really suited to
> the coming fighting.
>
> I recall that there was a Feldgendarmerie company in
> Stülpnagel Barracks.
>
> There were some garages at the rear of the barrack complex
> that contained large quantities of spare parts for various hand-
> guns, and we were all able to improve our personal arsenal by
> helping ourselves. I too acquired a 7.65mm pistol and obtained
> the necessary ammunition from the Feldgendarmerie company
> in exchange for cigarettes. Later a sentry put an end to this self-
> service.
>
> Our steel helmets were coated with toothpaste for the winter
> fighting. On 30 January the 2nd Company deployed. Our
> platoon was located in deep woods outside the northern
> boundary of the Neustadt near the railway employees' conva-
> lescent home. The position consisted of a row of rifle pits in
> which we spent the day and night. The frozen earth made
> digging in hard work.[4]

One early reinforcement to the Küstrin garrison was 17-year-old
Luftwaffe-Auxiliary Fritz Oldenhage:

> I was born in Stettin on the 7th April 1928. I was conscripted
> as a Luftwaffe auxiliary on the 5th January 1944, and soon
> afterwards my schooling came to an end. I was sent to the 3rd
> Battery, Light Flak Battalion 850 in Berlin and received my first

training with the simple 20mm and 20mm quadruple flak as a gunlayer.

Following action in Stettin and its surroundings, for instance with 20mm quadruple flak at the goods station, protecting heavy and medium flak against Anglo-American aircraft, I was sent to Anklam to guard a flying field. There I was trained on the 37mm flak, telephone exchange operating and telephone line construction.

At the end of January 1945 there was a rush to load everything on railway wagons. The over-hasty securing of the guns resulted in one case of the gun barrel coming loose and starting to swing, hitting something like five wooden telegraph poles alongside the track. Only after sending a written message forward by a level crossing keeper were we able to stop the train.

The order to stop came beyond Stargard. The train was diverted under light snow showers and in full darkness. On the 30th January we reached our new goal, Küstrin-Neustadt, and had to unload immediately.

The guns were allocated to various positions within the town area. The first took up position in the Neustadt, immediately north of the extension of Plantagenstrasse. This was shortly behind the entrance to Anger Strasse, where Plantagenstrasse turns 90 degrees south-west as Strasse 39 towards the sewage farm and from there 90 degrees north-west to Strasse 42 and the Cellulose Factory. The second gun must have been positioned in the Neustadt between the goods station and the Engineer Barracks. The third gun went across to the Altstadt and was positioned on the Island north of the Mittelhöfel between Lunette B and the weir of the Vorflut Canal. Its forward observer sat on the southern point of the Mittelhöfel not far from the point where the Vorflut Canal and Oder separate. All three guns had wide-ranging fields of fire. The fourth gun was unserviceable after the railway journey.

I moved into the Cellulose Factory with the battery headquarters. Within a short time I was telephonist on a 20-plug switchboard, runner and cable-layer, which entailed maintaining communications to the forward observer.

I can only describe the factory premises sketchily and with some reservations. It formed a rough rectangle next to the

Warthe. Its tall chimneystack was a well-known landmark. The only access was opposite the Warthe. Coming along the river from the direction of the Plantage, as one approached the Cellulose Factory one passed two housing blocks on the left-hand side of the road, the first on the premises of a petroleum company and the second already in the Cellulose Factory complex. A wall about 2 metres high began here separating the factory from the road. Here too was the main entrance with the factory gate. Parallel to the road was a long extended building in which I sat as telephonist at my switchboard. Parallel to this was part of the factory yard, then came a hut and behind, parallel to the Warthe, the big factory building. Another part of the factory yard stretched beyond the eastern gable of the already mentioned building on the access road. Between the Cellulose Factory and the neighbouring ground I can remember a drainage ditch and an open pipeline running towards the Warthe, but I cannot recall the exact details. A hut stood to the right facing across the end of the road. Last used to accommodate prisoners of war, the hut now stood empty, as the prisoners had been marched away. In the short time we were there we saw no strangers, either soldiers or civilians, apart from the refugees on the access road.[5]

Other reinforcements arrived in the form of Panther tank turrets with 75mm guns and their crews. The German forces were struggling to cope with an acute shortage of fuel for their tanks, so the idea had arisen of using turrets on prefabricated wooden frames sunk into the earth to reinforce defensive positions. Officer Cadet Corporal Hans Kirchhof reported:

We were Fortress Gun-Turret Company 12/11 and together with other companies were dispatched from Fallingbostel to the Weichselbogen, Bromberg-Thorn-Graudenz area. Our company consisted of three platoons each of four turrets, each turret having a crew of five men. Our train was stopped at Vietz, as our destinations were no longer attainable with the Russians already operating in these areas, and we were then detailed, a company of twelve turrets each, to Frankfurt, Küstrin and Stettin.

Tank turrets of the Panther series were to be fitted in earthen bunkers with wooden frames and linings previously prepared by the Organisation Todt. The earthen bunkers, however, had first to be built.

One of the turrets had slid off its sledge during the move and had been so badly damaged that it was no longer usable. The remaining eleven turrets went to their allotted positions around Küstrin but even before they could be installed eight fell into the hands of the Russians.

Only three turrets went into action. One was built south-east of the Kietz Gate at the junction of the Chaussees to Göritz and Sonnenburg right on the Oder dyke. The second turret was destined for the Island, between the Artillery Barracks and the road bridge over the Vorflut Canal. The main task of both turrets was to stop enemy tanks that had broken through. I never saw the third turret, so cannot give its exact location, but I think it must have been in the north of the Altstadt.

Following the loss of so many Panther turrets even before going into action, we later received two German 37mm anti-tank guns and a captured Russian 45mm anti-tank gun.[6]

Another new arrival was Officer Cadet Alfred Kraus:

Having been born in 1926, I was conscripted into Infantry Regiment 29 at Züllichau on the 23rd May 1944. After 14 days of basic training, we were sent to Denmark, from where I returned in November to join an officer-cadet company in Küstrin, where my field post address was 'Officer-Cadet Company Küstrin, Stülpnagel Barracks', counterstamped with 'Panzergrenadier Replacement Battalion 50, HQ Company'.

On the 29th January 1945 runners called us back from a night exercise to our barrack huts in the Stülpnagel Barracks. Next day I received a visit from my mother, who returned to Berlin that night. As we were not allowed to leave the barrack grounds, I could only escort her to the barrack gate. This was a farewell forever, for both she and my father were killed in an air raid on Berlin in April 1945.

If I remember correctly, on the morning of the 31st January we moved to a country road south of Reichsstrasse 1 and north-west of the Warnick position. The east side of the road was lined with tall poplars. We had to dig a hole for a tank behind one of the trees with our field spades. As the ground was frozen rock hard, we could not get down deeper than 10 centimetres. Our platoon and company commanders were not with us. Towards noon a Russian officer, whose battalion was fighting on the German side, appeared with an interpreter and threatened to have us shot if we did not complete our task. When he checked us later, he found that none of us had done so.

For hours disorderly groups of soldiers were streaming along the nearby Reichsstrasse 1 from Landsberg towards Küstrin. They said we were crazy waiting to take on the Russians on open fields with only 1898 carbines and machine guns. That evening we heard that the Russians had forced their way into that part of Küstrin on the right bank of the Warthe.[7]

Fifteen-year-old Hitler Youth Hans Dalbkermeyer and his fellow schoolboy Manni Roeder eventually arrived in Küstrin early that morning:

Duty-bound we reported to the collecting point in one of the two barracks in the Neustadt. Which one it was I can no longer recall. I remember, however, an Army officer taking us in a Volkswagen Jeep with a great 180 degree skid in the snow to a canteen in the Potato Meal Factory in the Neustadt. As we were the first from Birnbaum, we were to wait here for our comrades and orders. For once we felt safe. It was heated and there was food to eat. The whole building had been organised as a reception centre for members of the Wehrmacht and other soldiers. As part of the 'full pension' was naturally included the Führer's speech on the 12th anniversary of his assumption of power on the 30th January 1933.

We both listened reverently, convinced we must give everything asked of us by the Führer and Fatherland. As the only youngsters among the many soldiers we remained exactly like the others after the speech, only our thoughts following a different path. I still believed in final victory, which for me had never been in question.[8]

Fortunately for the Germans, the 25th Panzergrenadier and 21st Panzer Divisions had already been extracted from the fighting against the Americans and French in Alsace in preparation for switching to the Eastern Front, and the 25th Panzergrenadiers were actually on their way to Küstrin by rail with the intention of blocking the Soviet advance before it reached the Oder. Orders for the 21st Panzer Division in the Southern Pfalz to entrain for the same destination were issued at 1835 hours on 31 January. These latter orders, however, would take twenty-seven trains and another four to six days to fulfil.[9]

Orders too were given for the formation near the town of that name of the 'Müncheberg' Panzer Division from the remnants of experienced units, under the command of the highly decorated Major General Werner Mummert. Considerable priority was given to the equipping and manning of this new division, and later to the replacement of its casualties in vehicles and manpower, but, unlike the other deployed divisions, the 'Müncheberg' was kept intact in reserve on the main approach route to Berlin until the beginning of March before being committed to action.[10]

Chapter Four

The Russians Are Here!

Streams of vehicles wound their way through Küstrin on the morning of 31 January, coming along the three main roads from the east, their speed being determined by over-laden farm wagons and horse-drawn sledges taking up the whole width of the roads and giving others no chance of overtaking. The snow that had first been packed by thousands of wheels and horses' hooves had since been churned into dirty, ankle-deep mush, which dampened down the noise of their passage.

Even on the bridges there was no drumming, no stamping, only pushing and shoving. Whenever a driver blocked the road through exhaustion or clumsiness, it evoked loud abuse. The passengers required neither special attention nor accommodation. The refugee camp quickly emptied, its inhabitants scattering to the railway station or to the main street, looking out for a wagon or truck driver to persuade with money and the right words to take them along.

All had only one goal: to cross the Oder! The dream of finding some respite from the war at last resulted in many men running straight into the arms of the waiting officers of the Feldgendarmerie or SS. Himmler's appeal was stuck on all the advertising pillars: 'Show no pity to all those shirkers who attach themselves to evacuation treks! Chase these brazen cowards to the front with your dishcloths!' Those caught at the Oder crossings by these groups found that their release papers, leave passes, doctors' certificates and other documents were of no account. They would be examined later to see if they were really unfit or otherwise incapacitated – or so it was said. Any soldier taken from the columns in civilian clothes was not detained for the moment, but special notice was taken of such men and they would not be forgotten, they were strongly assured; meanwhile they were 'warned'.

It had long been clear that all organised resistance had collapsed between Küstrin and the Soviets advancing from north of the Warthe.

Even the 'Woldenberg' Division at Landsberg could no longer pose a serious obstacle. Then at noon came the not so surprising news of enemy tanks approaching Neudamm, only 20 kilometres away. Orders were given for the bridges to be prepared for demolition, and the police and fire brigade were put on alert. Their vehicles had been closely guarded ever since the town omnibus, which had been reserved by a senior member of the town administration for his own flight, vanished without trace with its driver and his family.

The crowds at the railway station were dangerously crushed together, the people not knowing whether there would be any more trains. The railway police withdrew to the goods station, where a so-called evacuation train for the railway personnel waited under steam. The train moved off, although it was hardly full by current standards, and passed the waiting crowds. Then soldiers appeared with Panzerfausts on the railway premises as the last train rolled in from the east, packed to the running boards.

Apart from traffic on the main road, the village of Drewitz was virtually undisturbed by the comings and goings in the nearby town. The village NSDAP chief's telephone rang at about 1400 hours and an acquaintance in Neumühl some 10 kilometres away reported that Soviet tanks had just rolled through towards Drewitz and Küstrin without stopping. The NSDAP chief was struck speechless with disbelief. Eventually he calmed down the caller, saying he would ask the Küstrin authorities for an explanation. He had just put down the telephone receiver when the first Soviet tank came down the village street. He grabbed his emergency pack and ran through the garden into the woods.

Some 15 or 20 tanks of the 219th Tank Brigade, 2nd Guards Tank Army thrust almost unopposed into the town. Their first shot on approaching Küstrin wrecked a light 75mm infantry gun that had been deployed on the town boundary next to an unfinished anti-tank ditch. In fact the shot had been unnecessary, for there was no ammunition with the gun. The main body of 10 to 15 tanks clanked along the Drewitzer Unterweg, where some remained while others continued down Drewitzer Strasse. One of these diverted towards Strasse 42 but turned over while making a tight turn and was abandoned, two men escaping unhurt. The smaller group of tanks approached Schlageterstrasse, where they encountered two platoons of Panzergrenadiers, wiping out one platoon for the loss of a tank and the infantry riding it.[1]

Sergeant Horst Wewetzer, who had arrived in Küstrin that morning, was probably one of the first of the garrison to see the Soviet tanks:

A sentry directed us to the Stülpnagel Barracks, from where we were sent on by the artillery chief of staff, Captain Langenhahn, to the Fortress Company, which was deployed in the north of the Neustadt in the Reserve Field Hospital area. As we arrived, the last nurses, medical orderlies, etc., were already leaving the hospital. The town's streets were full of men and vehicles. Our troop leader was off looking for an observation post. Telephone cables were laid out and we deployed our guns in position. At this moment the first enemy tank rolled into Küstrin. I had the impression that the leading Russian tank was racing ahead.

Subsequently we made our observation post on the roof of the empty hospital. From here we had to direct the fire not only of our own mortars, but also that of the two light infantry guns belonging to another unit deployed close to our mortars.[2]

Panzergrenadier Johannes Diebe and his platoon were still trying to dig foxholes on Schlageterstrasse as the Soviet tanks went past:

At lunchtime a tank with infantry seated on top raced past us at an incredible speed on the street leading into town. No one could have stopped it. Even our sergeant was struck speechless. It was not long before other tanks, again with infantry aboard, raced past in the same direction. The same thing occurred twice more. That they were not concerned about us came as something of a shock.

When there was a break our sergeant shouted: 'There are more coming. I am going to take a Panzerfaust and see if I can knock one out.' With my comrades I had gone behind an almost collapsed wall to find firing positions for our rifles. This was necessary as our whole bodies were shaking with excitement.

It was not long before another tank with infantry sitting on it followed and stopped near us. The Russians jumped off and went to the foxholes of our neighbouring section on the far side of the street. Their sergeant opened fire and shot one of the attackers. We were petrified when we saw the sergeant fall to a burst of machine-gun fire and our ten comrades fall to shots in the neck.

When the tank was about to move off, there was an explosion and a track came off. Our sergeant had made good what he had said. However, he was unlucky, as he had been standing in a doorway between two doorposts and the blast from the Panzerfaust had rebounded off the doorposts behind him and burnt his back. The Russians jumped off and fled towards the town, but a brave machine-gunner cut them down.

An ambulance came and took away our wounded sergeant. We laid him down on a stretcher on his stomach. The medical orderly thought that it was a wound that would get him discharged from the service. Our section was then taken over by the staff corporal.

When we wanted to cross the road to the dead on the other side, we could not believe our eyes when the tank turret turned and a shot came from the gun. The shell went through the wall behind which I was standing with my comrade from Guben. Our staff corporal jumped on the tank, pulled out a hand grenade and threw it in the turret. After the explosion it was quiet.

We buried our fallen comrades. It was our first mass grave. A simple cross with a steel helmet indicated that here a sergeant and his Panzergrenadiers had found eternal peace. So that was a hero's grave!

On the company commander's orders we all received a cup of schnapps. This was to calm us and let us think about other things. We all became tipsy from it.[3]

Meanwhile Flak Auxiliary Fritz Oldenhage was manning his field telephone exchange in the Cellulose Factory:

A group of enemy tanks drove along the Drewitzer Unterweg towards the town. I cannot remember the exact number, but believe it was between 10 and 15. We could see them quite clearly across the open terrain. Some of the tanks drove into the town while the others stood still. Several tanks turned their turrets with their guns in our direction, but only fired with their machine guns.

The firing was not directed at us in the Cellulose Factory, where we remained hidden and quiet, but at the area in front of the premises where some of the fleeing civilians with their horses and carts fell victim to the enemy fire.

Our section leader, an experienced Austrian sergeant, radiated confidence, conveying it to us and showing us how to behave cleverly.

As one of the enemy tanks left the rest of the group on the Drewitzer Unterweg and steered across the meadows towards the factory gate we withdrew to another industrial property and the Warthe goods station. In this hurried, short retreat we left our packs and personal belongings behind in the Cellulose Factory. Even I was almost forgotten as I was sitting at my switchboard again.

It was grotesque as the tank climbed the rising exit from the meadows to the road in a curve and tipped over sideways. Two Russians climbed out and ran safely back across the meadows, leaving the tank lying there. We did not fire so as not to betray our position and because the stationary tanks on the Drewitzer Unterweg had a good field of fire in our direction.

At the Warthe goods station we took cover among the installations and goods wagons standing there. More important, however, was the presence of a small but experienced infantry unit who accepted us with kindness. Under their protection we felt able to sleep deeply and securely that night while they, unnoticed by us, repelled a Russian attack from the Cellulose Factory.[4]

Fifteen-year-old Hitler Youth Hans Dalbkermeyer also saw the Soviet tanks going past from his location in the Oder Potato Meal Factory:

Next morning, the 31st January, two close friends from my class, Fred Chmilewski and Helmut Blauberg, appeared, as well as two other students from the 5th and 6th Forms, Erdmann and Specht. It was a great pleasure, but sadly none of them returned from the war.

After lunch we six were sitting together at the table when suddenly firing was heard. Startled, we ran out on to the factory yard and saw Russian tanks going past the factory gate. We quickly left our quarters and headed towards the Warthe. Which road we took I no longer know, but our way took us over one of the Warthe bridges, through the Altstadt and over the Oder. On the streets a column of pedestrians, some with handcarts, refugee treks with horse-drawn wagons, as well as soldiers with and without vehicles, rolled forward.

In this confusion we lost our school comrade Erdmann. Finally the shooting died down. The Russian armoured thrust ended between the Warthe bridges and the Stern in the Neustadt. Four tanks were destroyed. One of them on Plantagenstrasse directly under the railway bridge was smoking all day long, emitting a frightful stench.[5]

It was only in the middle of the Neustadt that the tanks came up against any resistance. Even they could not get through the Stern, the intersection of the most important streets, where wild panic had created an impenetrable barricade of cars, horse-drawn wagons and sledges blocking the exits and obstructing the only street leading to the Warthe bridges about 400 metres away. The tanks had to turn back out of the unexpected cul-de-sac they found themselves in. Without local knowledge and prior reconnaissance, the tank crews were unaware that they could turn into Plantagenstrasse just before the level crossing gates and from there thrust through to the river crossings across undeveloped land. It was at this juncture that the tanks lost contact with their infantry escort. One of them stopped and fired at the traffic jam in front of the bridges. Then, annoyed and frustrated, the tank crews withdrew the way they had come. Meanwhile, behind them the Germans' surprise and initial confusion were overcome when it was realised that this group was operating well ahead of the rest, and the tanks came under hefty Panzerfaust fire in the streets. The first one to fall was a Sherman. Eventually only two of the tanks got away. It was said that the remains of their infantry escort had withdrawn to Loeber's restaurant in the woods.[6]

The town hospital had been cleared during that morning, bed-ridden patients being driven to the goods station for loading on a train, while the others had to walk there escorted by some nursing sisters. But it was too late. The Oder bridges were already under enemy shellfire, so the sick had to be taken off the train again. They were supposed to return to the hospital but on the Pferdemarkt (Horse Market) their allocated bus, marked with a Red Cross, was suddenly confronted by Soviet tanks. The emergency stop caused its engine to fail and the bus had to be towed back to the bus depot, where the patients were hastily accommodated, unmolested by the Russians. It was late evening before the patients could be taken back to the railway station and early the next morning before they finally left the town on a hospital train that was already laden with many wounded. The train was repeatedly diverted and eventually the Küstrin patients ended up in Straubing, where they were unloaded and provisionally accommodated in an auxiliary hospital set up in a monastery.[7]

Sapper Ernst Müller saw the Soviet tanks arrive at the Stern. He had only been in Küstrin since the day before, having just endured a six-day rail journey in open wagons with 150 other members of Armoured Engineer Replacement Battalion 19. Müller had been seriously wounded in Russia and was not yet fully recovered, but had been ordered back to active duty. He reported:

> We were attached to Engineer Replacement and Training Battalion 68 in Lieutenant Schröder's company, in which I remained in Second-Lieutenant Schröter's platoon. The company command post was at the Küstrin Rowing Club.
>
> On the morning of the 31st January we were supposed to take up positions in the Neustadt. In the late morning Second-Lieutenant Schröter called out to us: 'Gentlemen, it's getting serious. Take up positions in the cellar window pits immediately!'
>
> At this juncture I was standing with a comrade on Adolf-Hitler-Strasse between the Warthe bridge and the Stern crossroads. In front of a bicycle shop, about 70 metres from the Stern, we went into a cellar window pit as ordered. A woman saw us out of a window and called out to us: 'You can't get in there! We have valuable things in there!'
>
> Meanwhile the artillery fire had increased. The street was still full of refugees when I saw the first tank. Mad confusion reigned. The refugees were whipping up their horses to get forward faster. Only when a senior paymaster was hit by a burst of machine-gun fire did I realise that enemy tanks were involved.
>
> My comrade had vanished. I sought cover behind the nearest building. I then realised that I had an Italian rifle but German ammunition. This example shows how bad our hasty equipping had been.[8]

Just arrived from the western front, the leading train carrying elements of the 25th Panzergrenadier Division immediately came under attack at the congested railway station in the Neustadt. As the wagons carrying the guns were shunted into the adjacent goods station for unloading, one of the division's anti-tank sections used its Panzerfausts to good effect, as Colonel Professor Erwin Boehm's history of the division relates:

> Thus upon the arrival of the train carrying the 1st Battalion of the 25th Artillery Regiment, the first in action was an anti-tank section, which under Sergeant Sommer shot up three Soviet tanks with Panzerfausts before unloading could begin. There was general chaos in the station area. The guns had to be off-loaded from the wagons by hand. They then went straight into action. Once the German resistance had stiffened, the Russians withdrew to the north-eastern edge of the town. That evening the elements of the division that had detrained in Küstrin withdrew in accordance with orders to the west bank of the Oder.[9]

Artillery Second-Lieutenant Erich Bölke was a regular soldier and holder of the Iron Cross First Class who became caught up in the retreat from the Vistula. He too was involved in repelling the Soviet tank attack:

> I reached Küstrin ahead of the Russian spearheads and remained there for the whole of the siege from the first to the last day, apart from a courier trip to the OKH.
>
> At first I was on the fortress commandant's staff as an ADC. Once I had to take orders to retreat to Küstrin to a major commanding an infantry battalion on the approaches to the town between the Oder and Warthe rivers. I believe it was a motorised unit. I do not recall the date, but there was snow on the ground when I reached them by car.
>
> On the 31st January Soviet tanks penetrated Küstrin-Neustadt as far as the Stern. Among the damage inflicted there by tank shells, I recollect a hit on a shop and a refugees' horse-drawn wagon that was shot up towards the Warthe bridge; there were two dead horses. Under the railway overpass in Plantagenstrasse was an enemy tank that had fallen victim to a German Panzerfaust. During the course of this day I was deployed with some men to counter this Soviet penetration and the crew of a shot-up tank surrendered to me in a garden area. I cannot recall the exact place.[10]

Luftwaffe Officer Cadet Sergeant Helmut Schmidt was a section leader in a motorised flak unit that had lost its guns in the retreat from the Vistula and was now operating as infantry. Having arrived in Küstrin the previous night, he recalls how his unit became involved in the aftermath of the tank attack:

> I cannot remember where we slept in Küstrin, only that we slept the whole night through without being disturbed. In the early morning we drove along Reichsstrasse 1 a bit towards Tamsel, a village on the northern edge of the Warthebruch. We posted sentries inside the place where the road took a bend to the north. It was an unfriendly morning, foggy and cold, with poor visibility. We had orders to wait for a Königstiger unit reported to be coming from the direction of Landsberg and provide the tanks with infantry support.
>
> We waited for hours, straining our ears listening out for the tanks and frozen to the core. The traffic from Landsberg gradually dried up and there were no Königstigers. Those of us not on sentry duty disappeared into a house north of the road where an old man lived. He was friendly and took us in and put a jar of honey on the table. Real bee honey! I don't think the man was oversupplied with it, either.
>
> If I recall rightly, it was about noon when we heard sounds of combat from the north or north-west, rifle fire. Somewhat later a man on a bicycle arrived in a hurry and told us excitedly that a swarm of Russian tanks had driven through his village. We asked him if he was not mistaken? Perhaps they were the expected Königstigers? But no, he assured us that he had seen the Russian tanks with infantry sitting on them from his window. There had been half a dozen tanks passing quickly through his home village, and the place was only a little north of Tamsel.
>
> Somewhat later we heard renewed sounds of fighting from behind us to the south-west. This time it was not only rifle fire. Now flak, anti-tank or tank guns were firing.
>
> We reported to Lieutenant Kühnel, our chief. But he did not take the continuing noise of combat as important. He believed we should remain quiet and tried to tell us that Hitler Youth or Volkssturm were undergoing training on the Panzerfaust. We were of a different opinion. We could easily distinguish between

the explosions of Panzerfausts and the hard crack of tank guns. We were angry that our chief failed to react and would have preferred to return to Küstrin, but Kühnel kept us waiting for the Königstigers.

Meanwhile the sounds of fighting from the direction of Küstrin had become weaker and finally died out. We were convinced that the Soviet tanks had been able to penetrate the town and had raised hell. We puzzled only over whether they had been driven off or wiped out.

At dusk we abandoned our position on Reichsstrasse 1 and drove back to Küstrin. The expected Königstigers had not turned up. Our jeep was the leading vehicle in our little convoy. A few minutes later we reached the town, following the Landsberger Strasse to the centre of town. The street was wide and it was pitch dark. I stood next to the driver looking over the windscreen to see better. This was necessary as along the right-hand side of the street stood a long row of refugee wagons packed together, fully loaded with cushions, baskets, boxes and cartons, with feather beds and bundles of straw. The refugees seemed to have found accommodation.

We had no maps. None of us knew the town. The road took a turn to the right and became considerably narrower. It occurred to me that the line of wagons here appeared more disorderly. Wagons stood in the roadway or across it with baggage lying on the ground, bundles of clothing and bedding covering the pavements. We followed a street of shops and approached a crossing point of several streets, the Stern. The shop doorways and windows were shattered. Dark figures flitted quickly out of the insecure businesses taking things away. Glass splinters crackled under their feet. We saw that the windows of the buildings, even on the upper storeys, were broken. Roof slates lay in the roadway and the wheels of our vehicles rolled with a crunching sound over shards of glass.

It was obvious to us that Russian tanks had caused this damage. Although the event had taken place hours ago, apart from obvious plunderers there were no people about, either soldiers or civilians. Küstrin was in a state of shock. The people had either been wiped out or were in hiding. It was now early evening, perhaps 1800 or 1900 hours. One would have expected the refugees to be seeing to their wagons or putting them somewhere safe, but no one was attending to them.

We crossed the Stern, which looked especially bad, although the place had been made passable. We went along Plantagenstrasse, where the destruction continued. A little later we drove up to a railway bridge across the street. A few paces from it our vehicle drove over a large obstacle that we had not seen in the dark. It looked like a bundle of clothing. A torch was switched on. A dead Russian soldier was lying on the ground. On the shoulder straps of his brown field blouse was a narrow red stripe. A second lieutenant of the Red Army?

We left our vehicles behind and walked on. Under the bridge we came across more dead Ivans on the left-hand side, about ten men. All seemed to be unwounded, as if asleep. Some lay noticeably one over another. A few paces further on we came across a shot-up tank. It stood on the right-hand side of the street, right against the embankment with its rear to us. When it was hit it was already through the underpass and had stopped a few metres beyond. I could not quite identify the tank. We had had nothing to do with this type before. Then it slowly came to me. It was an American Sherman from the Lend-Lease pact of the western Allies with the Soviet Union. The strongly rounded turret bore a five-pointed star, and a long-barrelled 76.2mm gun projected from the turret.

We went back to our vehicles and I reported the situation at the underpass to my chief. He immediately gave our company the order: 'Anti-tank section get ready!' I was to take my section along the high railway embankment to the left of the underpass, i.e. to the south-west, reconnoitre and possibly clear and occupy it. We took our hand weapons, our machine gun and quite a few Panzerfausts, and set off, leaving our jeep behind at the underpass.

We climbed up the railway embankment and tiptoed along the southern track south-westwards. If only we had had a map! We did not know that we were approaching the Warthe. Every few steps one of us stumbled swearing over some wire or other. We also did not know that our legs catching in the shot-up tensioned signal or points wires caused them to ring. These were real foot traps.

We were unable to go along quietly. We were shot at, at first individually then en masse, the shots zipping past uncomfortably close to our heads. They came from a northerly direction and the firers could not have been far off.

I directed my men down from the embankment and we trudged along the foot of it, safe from the firing. We had not taken the noise seriously at first and cursed the Volkssturm whom we thought must have mistaken us for Russians. After we had gone about 500 metres the steel structure of a railway bridge over the Warthe appeared. I stumbled on a sapper sergeant-major preparing the demolition of the bridge with a few men. He was pleased to see us and even more so when I assured him that we would provide him with cover for his work. As we talked in the lee of a steel girder, sparks flew around us from the structure every few seconds. The sergeant-major took the firers to be Russians who had crept forwards to try to secure the bridge.

I went across to the north side of the bridge to take up position with my men immediately behind the northernmost track of the many-tracked station area. We had to lie flat and keep our heads down as the firing intensified with sub-machine guns. It was raining lightly. We lay on the railway gravel, which was covered with the remains of snow.

Perhaps five or ten minutes had passed since our arrival at the bridge when immediately in front of us a green Very light whistled up, spreading a pale light for two or three seconds. The weak light was enough to show some 25 Russians or more forming up to attack the bridge. They were no more than 20 or 30 paces away from us, right in front of the embankment. They gave a shout and ran to the embankment firing their sub-machine guns. We immediately fired back and fired some Panzerfausts at them. Unfortunately, we had no grenades.

While we were quelling the Russians' surprise attack, train after train rolled past behind us southwards over the Warthe bridge, taking numerous wagons, mainly goods wagons, to safety. The engine cylinders hissed barely a metre from our boots. The trains left Küstrin close together, without lights and almost without sound. We could not concern ourselves with them and did not know what they were taking: wounded, refugees, military or civilian goods?

We fired wildly from the embankment for about a quarter of an hour without being able to recognise a precise target. Finally

I shouted my order above the noise: 'Hold fire!' Once I was heard, peace was restored, but it was several minutes before we could hear properly again. From the other side of the embankment individual shots could still be heard but at a great distance. The attackers had disappeared. We had urgently needed Very lights!

I checked my group; none had been wounded. We had been very lucky. We had lacked hand grenades to reach the dead corner of the embankment. Had the Russians had some, they would have had the advantage, and none of us would have survived the attack. We did not know how many trains had got away safely during the fight. The sappers emerged from their shelter with relief, and the company sent us reinforcements.

We checked out the ground in front of us. To our right, about 50 paces from the bridge, there was a building at the foot of the embankment. We carefully examined the ground on this side. The Russians had in fact withdrawn under cover of darkness. We found neither dead nor wounded. Had the Russians taken their comrades with them? Only a Maxim machine gun recalled the event. It stood on a flat bit of land in front of the embankment and the Russians had not been able to bring it into action. With its outdated two-wheeled carriage it looked like a toy. We found no ammunition near it. Presumably the Russians had taken shelter in the dead corner of the embankment and had then pulled out along the Warthe.

The Russians had certainly pulled out but we suspected they were still close. At the moment they would be busy re-assembling, seeing to the wounded and reloading their sub-machine guns. We had to prepare for a second attack in case they came again.

Our chief wanted to do something about the Russians. He ordered Sergeant Max Langheinrich to form a storm troop to track down and destroy them. I was included with my section. We numbered about 20 men. Langheinrich took the lead and I was to cover the rear with René and Hans Hof to prevent the Russians finishing us off. As a base, as well as the start and return point for the enterprise, we had picked a primitive, empty, corrugated-iron hut at the foot of the north side of the embankment. It was 4 x 4 metres in size, with a man-high shrapnel-proof wall around it, and it lay within 100 metres of the bridge. Before setting off, we held a short council of war. We would first go a little way towards the street underpass and then turn and comb through the land north of the embankment in a half circle, finishing at the bridge and the corrugated-iron hut.

It could not have been very late, perhaps 2000 or 2100 hours. After a half-hour pause in the hut, we set off towards the underpass. In spread-out file we tramped along the north side of the embankment. It had long since given up raining, but the night was quite dark and one had to take care not to lose sight of the man in front.

After a few minutes Langheinrich gathered the storm troop together. We left the embankment and began circling round to the north. We came to some railway sidings. Were these factory sidings or a goods station? We stumbled over heaps of coal, then knee-high points control wires again. Every few minutes someone fell flat on his face, every time with much noise and swearing.

On the left-hand side, still near the embankment, a large black cube appeared out of the darkness. It was a corrugated-iron hall, a store about 20 metres long. I told René that I would check the hall and that he should wait for me. Inside it was completely dark. I found a large store of empty petrol barrels. I carefully climbed over the barrels and found no Russians, but at the far end of the hall in a small room between the barrels and the corrugated iron I found some stacks of books. I took some with me with the intention of returning to the hall in daylight if I could.

René and I then hastened to rejoin the group. We could not see our comrades, only hear them. They were not creeping across but trampling through the terrain. Before we could join up with them there was a sudden burst of sub-machine-gun fire from up ahead. Russians! I saw sparks of fire apparently ricocheting off a roadway.

I pulled my head in and waited about ten minutes until the Russians quietened down. When I got up again, my comrades had vanished. I carefully crept on towards the Warthe. It was lighter near the river with weak light reflected from the west. I caught sight of a small railway hut in front of which several men were standing. I took them for Russians at first as they were wearing Russian steel helmets, but as I got closer I could hear German being spoken loud and clear.

I quickly made myself known. I had stumbled across a group of Volkssturm men, old men unaware of their careless behaviour. They could not answer my question about my comrades. They had not seen them. Then they recounted the events of the day to me, the shock of which they had yet to overcome.

While we were talking, about 1 or 2 kilometres off to our right a Russian tank fired across the Warthe and the Oder and scored a direct hit on an electricity transformer or high voltage cable. There was a fantastic blue-yellow arc of light and then the few lights on in that part of the town west of the Oder went out as one. A little later a Stalin-Organ to the north of us fired a salvo to the west. I saw the fire trails, heard the well-known howling, and clearly heard the aftermath.

There were four or five Volkssturm men that I had met in front of the little corrugated-iron hut. They were wearing dark overcoats and had rifles dangling from their shoulders. Why they of all people should have been stationed at this position remained unclear to me. They had not taken cover, despite the firing nearby.

They told me that during the day the Russians had overrun a 37mm flak position and killed the crew of Luftwaffe auxiliaries. I asked about the penetration by Russian tanks into the town centre. Everyone had been surprised and it had happened without warning. Several tanks carrying infantry had taken part and three of these tanks had been destroyed by Panzerfausts.

In the opinion of the Volkssturm men, the Russians had withdrawn to the Cellulose Factory, which lay a bit to the north of here. I could see the buildings as dark shadows. With this new information I carefully made my way back to the Warthe bridge without encountering either Russians or Germans. About an hour after the exchange of fire I returned to our base. I was greeted with 'Hello' by my comrades. After me appeared 'Max' [Walter Schulz]. He too was unwounded.

But our storm troop undertaking had cost some wounded, including René. He had already been taken to a dressing station. No one could tell me what kind of wound he had, nor could I discover where he had been taken. I was angry and sad. My best friend! I would miss him a lot. I did not know then that I would never see him again.[11]

This Soviet attack encouraged the work on the defences, as the following account shows:

When Russian tanks reached Küstrin on the 31st January 1945, my father, Johannes Dawidowski, and his brother Otto had to follow orders and do their duty with the Küstrin Volkssturm. Until then both men had been free of military obligations. They were rated as 'exempt', as both of them worked in an important war industry, the Küstrin Oder-Hütte iron foundry.

Until the first penetration of the Neustadt by enemy tanks only a few measures had been taken to prepare for an effective defence, so the Volkssturm were first put to the construction of defences of every kind. While the Wehrmacht dug in and fought along the curve around the Neustadt and near Alt Bleyen, the work of the Volkssturm was in the Altstadt, digging foxholes on the old Oder fortifications from Bastion Philipp to Bastion König. Other Volkssturm dug positions on the Gorin and on the edge of the glacis. A deep anti-tank ditch with bulwarks was constructed at the crossroads in front of the Kietz Gate. At the southern exit of Kietz anti-tank barriers were erected out of all kinds of agricultural machinery driven together and felled trees.[12]

In order to block the Soviet view from the Sonnenburger Chaussee of the high dyke between the Altstadt and the Neustadt, screens made of tarpaulins and sacking sewn together from air raid shelter bedding were strung from tree to tree on the south side of the road. The red thorn trees on Friedrichstrasse were felled to make a landing strip for a Fieseler Storch, but none ever came. Anti-tank barricades were erected at the southern exit of Kietz, and an anti-tank ditch was dug in the middle of February from Warnicker Strasse to the Jungfern Canal right across the yard of the engineers' water training area.

The main front line ran from the Oder through Alt Drewitz (half of which had been lost in the previous fighting), through the Stadtwald woods, across the Stülpnagel Barracks exercise ground and ended in Warnick. The huge tanks of the Spiritusmonopol company lay outside this perimeter, and the 3,000,000 litres of drinking spirits and 4,000,000 litres of invaluable aviation fuel they contained had to be sacrificed.[13]

According to SS-Grenadier Oscar Jessen:

In January 1945 came the order to pack up and we moved to the Alt Drewitz sector of Küstrin. The front line lay only 40 metres in front of us. The place formed a half circle around a large meadow. Opposite us were the Russians. They must have had an observation post in the church, as they kept going in and out. We could watch them and occasionally raise a hand in greeting to each other.

The whole time in this Drewitz position we could hear German music and were called upon by fellow Germans to desert to them. It seemed very strange to us that the Russians or their German assistants knew the names of our superior officers.

There were several cows still wandering in the meadow and bellowing loudly to be milked. Our anti-tank guns stood between two houses. If I remember correctly, the row of houses opposite was of newer construction. We kept close to one house in which we ate and slept and in which the owners still lived. They did not want to leave their old and very sick mother behind and had made an encampment in the cellar out of a lot of bedding. The other houses were already abandoned and many of them had a notice attached to the door bearing the request not to plunder the house.

Once I was a witness when three ragged figures, whom we took to be Russians, came to plunder. However, they were expected by our headquarters and went into the house next door. I then discovered that they were in fact our own people who spoke Russian and had been spying behind the enemy lines in Russian uniform.

Enemy soldiers also took cover behind dead animals. Sometimes we received shots from the houses behind us, an indication that Russians or their German allies must have got through.

The occupier of our house asked us to bury her husband's corpse. He still had all his documents and papers with him. The Russians had shot him on the street from part of the village opposite.[14]

Dramatically embellished reports about events on the other side of the Warthe sped from mouth to mouth in the Altstadt after the sounds of fighting had died down. Those who had heard the tank cannon fire and the explosions of Panzerfausts believed the noise was ice on the river being blown up or some other harmless event, for there was no official warning – even the sirens were silent – nor were there any instructions or recommendations to leave the town. Now hundreds broke out, joining the treks that were coming in along the still open roads from Landsberg and Sonnenburg. Many wanted to await the next developments in Kietz on the west bank of the Oder, or to try their luck at the railway station. The town administration had collapsed and the town hall was virtually empty. Consequently no one knew that Soviet troops had already crossed the Oder near Kienitz 20 kilometres from Küstrin in the early morning.

The fortress staff had received the news about the Soviet tanks too late to take action and now expected to see them rolling over the Warthe bridges, and were contemplating whether to blow the bridges and abandon the Neustadt. Now they also had to attend to the problem of securing the west bank of the Oder.[15]

Those elements of the 25th Panzergrenadier Division that had unloaded in Küstrin during the day returned to the west bank of the Oder later that evening as ordered. In view of the changed situation, the 9th Army had given the division the new task of driving back the Soviet bridgehead at Kienitz and preventing any further bridgeheads from forming. The divisional headquarters then withdrew to Gusow, committing the divisional units into action piecemeal on the west bank as they arrived.

Two batteries of the divisional artillery regiment and the 2nd Battalion of the 119th Panzergrenadier Regiment off-loaded with considerable difficulty in Golzow, for panicking supply troops had set light to the tall army store depot standing immediately next to the track, attracting Soviet artillery fire. The railway personnel fled and the train driver had to be caught and forced to take the wagons through the flames one at a time to be unloaded by the troops at the only ramp available. The battalion commander had to order the immediate occupation and defence of the village, leaving only a few men to finish the unloading at the station. Soon afterwards orders arrived for them to move to Letschin without delay.

Meanwhile the 1st (APC) Battalion of the latter regiment off-loaded in Werbig, where it was stuck for lack of fuel until the following evening.[16] When the Soviets first crossed the river at Kienitz earlier that day, no German troops in units of any size were prepared to meet them on the west bank. It was not until 1300 hours that Major Weikl, commanding a North Caucasian infantry battalion in Küstrin, was ordered to take his 345th Provisional Battalion and connect with the 203rd Provisional Battalion from Berlin. He was to form the two battalions into a combat group, and then report to Colonel Schimpff, who was establishing a command post in Letschin. The roads west of Küstrin were choked with refugees, so it was 1600 hours before Major Weikl came across Captain Bohl's 203rd Battalion in Zechin. Only assembled that day in Spandau, this unit had been brought out in Berlin city buses. Both battalions then deployed under cover of darkness, with the 203rd taking up a defensive position along the line Sophienthal–Sydowswiese and the 345th covering the west bank of the Oder between there and Küstrin.

At 0100 hours orders came from Colonel Schimpff for the 203rd to attack at 0400 hours up both sides of the Letschin–Amt Kienitz road and to push on to Kienitz itself. For this they would have the support of some driver-training tanks from the NSKK (National Socialist Motorised Corps) school at Wriezen. The German attack happened to coincide with a Soviet thrust from Kienitz, resulting in the German battalion, none of whose members knew each other, and armed only with rifles, being driven back to their start point in Sophienthal. Within the next six days the battalion lost half its manpower, either killed or wounded, but the survivors continued to hold out until relieved on 17 February, when they were reallocated to other units.[17]

Officer Cadet Corporal Hans Dahlmanns:

Upon promotion to captain at the beginning of 1944, my father was posted to Küstrin, where he commanded a company of Territorial Rifle Battalion 513, which was responsible for the security of the bridges in Frankfurt/Oder and Küstrin, as well as the canal ship lift at Niederfinow. In July 1944 I took my annual leave as a flak auxiliary [and went] with my mother to stay with my father in the Engineer Barracks in Küstrin and got to know a little about the town as a visitor. Due to the increasing air raids, my mother moved residence from Dinslaken to Küstrin, while I did my Reichsarbeitsdienst in the Pfalz Mountains. My father suggested in a letter that when I finished my labour service I should check out with the police in Dinslaken and re-register in Küstrin. This was possible as I could defer my military service for the first month and we were able to be together as a family for a short while.

So at the end of October 1944 I travelled to Küstrin as my labour service came to an end, registered with the police and was conscripted and posted to Engineer Replacement & Training Battalion 68, which was in the same Engineer Barracks as my father's company. I could thus visit my parents almost daily during my training without having to leave the barracks. However, on the 30th January 1945 my mother left Küstrin at my father's insistence and went to stay with her sister-in-law in central Germany.

The soldiers in my company were split up and sent to various places, but this did not apply to the 21 officer cadets of the reserve, of which I was one. We remained in the barracks for the time being and came directly under the Army High Command, as I heard.

On the 31st January tank shells suddenly burst on the parade ground; the Russians were there. That night we 21 young soldiers received orders to go to the village of Tamsel, where a nervous second lieutenant had lost his gun. We tried in vain to drive back the suddenly attacking enemy and recover the gun. After the attack, we gathered alongside a building. I went into the building, saw someone standing there and asked: 'What unit are you?' He said something that I did not understand. It sounded like: 'Ruki werch!' I saw in the darkness that he had no steel helmet, but a fur hat, and thought for a minute that he might be one of the Vlassov soldiers that were fighting along-side us in Küstrin. Then I suddenly realised that he was a Soviet soldier, that he had a sub-machine gun pointed at me and was calling on me in his language to put my hands up.

We were at the most 5 metres apart. I had my rifle slung over my shoulder and knew that I had no chance of getting out of this situation scot-free. So I was to become a Soviet prisoner, something that we all feared. I therefore had to do something unexpected. I slowly turned around and without a word slowly strode to the corner of the building. The Russian's killer instinct matched mine. He shot first as I rounded the corner. Under cover of darkness, all of us got away from this first brush with the enemy. Only one had a shot right through the heel of his boot that did not hurt him and raised the astonishment of the others in the barracks next morning.[18]

Despite the thick cloud, Colonel Hans-Ulrich Rudel's famous tank-busting squadron of Stukas, flying out of Neuendorf-im-Sande, immediately north of Fürstenwalde, attacked the Soviet positions in Kienitz that first day with bombs, cannon and machine-gun fire to such effect that the Soviets hastened to bring forwards anti-aircraft guns and get them across to the west bank.[19]

Meanwhile in Küstrin the flak was arriving piecemeal, some of the gun crews, including Hitler Youth auxiliaries, being ferried in by Berlin's double-decker buses. Some crews with 20mm and 37mm guns on carriages were allocated to the Altstadt's Warthe bank and others were sent to support the main battle line that was being formed. By nightfall there was no sound of combat anywhere, and the first continuous front line could be formed undisturbed on either side of the Warthe, running in a half circle around the Neustadt from the Oder via Drewitz and the Stadtwald (town woods), and across the training grounds in front of the infantry barracks to Warnick on the Warthe.

Late in the evening the Volkssturm men who were believed to be missing returned from the direction of Sonnenburg, some of them on the last train from there, which gave up at the trek-jammed junction with the chaussee at the Kietzerbusch Halt. The troops had already been on their way back when the car was sent off to find them after the battalion commander had sought vainly for four days for weapons for his men. In a last call on the morning of 30 January he was informed by a telephone operator that the staff had already left and would not be coming back, whereupon he had given the order to withdraw. Even the fortress was at first unprepared to arm these unexpected reinforcements, but gave them leave until the next morning. So for just one night they would enjoy the illusion of having survived.[20]

Chapter Five

The Siege Begins

Küstrin now adjusted into a state of siege. Even though the Soviet forces confronting the garrison were still relatively weak, the garrison was in no position to assess this. However, before examining the siege at this stage in some detail, it is necessary to review some of the outside factors governing the conduct of operations.

From 2 to 8 February Stalin and General Antonov, the Soviet Chief of the General Staff, were totally tied up with the Yalta Conference, leaving a yawning gap in the control of the forces entering Germany. Stalin had effectively demoted Marshal Zhukov from being the commander of a group of Fronts to being the commander of a single Front when he assumed command of the 1st Byelorussian Front on 16 November 1944. Stalin's assumption that with fewer Fronts in operation he would be able to effectively coordinate their activities himself had not taken into account this distraction. In addition, Stalin refused to fly, thus adding at least two days' travelling time by rail to his absence from the Kremlin.

As Professor John Erickson wrote:

A certain confusion began to prevail both within the Front commands and at the centre. There were unmistakable signs that the Stavka [the supreme high command], was no longer entirely abreast of the pace and extent of the Soviet advance: Koniev's 1st Ukrainian Front had speedily outstripped its Stavka directives, while Zhukov's Front was almost five days ahead of schedule when it reached the Kutno–Lodz line, yet no great thought seems to have been given to re-examining rates of advance and possible objectives. As they outran the Stavka directives, so also the Soviet armies overreached themselves in terms of supplies of food and ammunition; in the onward armoured rush, Soviet tank crews would fill up from one or two vehicles, leave them stranded and press on with the remainder of the battalion or company, but this could not solve the problem of ammunition. At the same time Marshal Zhukov was looking with growing anxiety at his northern flank – and yet again at his southern flank, where he depended upon Marshal Koniev.

On 31 January he sent an urgent signal to Stalin stressing that

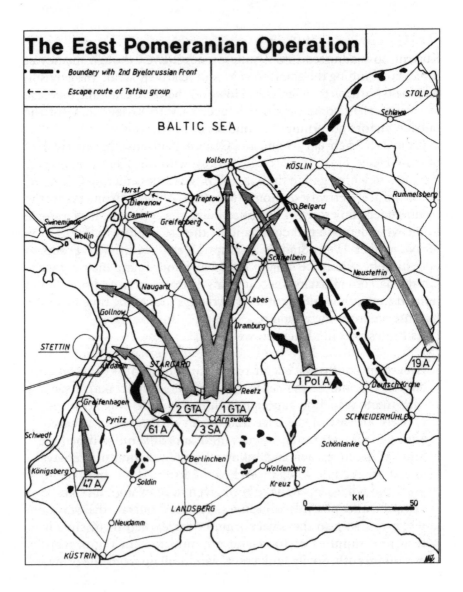

the frontage of the 1st Byelorussian Front had now reached 500 kilometres, that Rokossovsky's left flank was lagging appreciably behind the right flank of the 1st Byelorussian Front – Rokossovsky must push his 70th Army forward – and Marshal Koniev should gain the Oder line as soon as possible. Marshal Zhukov received no reply to this urgent signal, and thus was faced with the dilemma of buttressing his outstretched right flank and at the same time concentrating all his armies for the advance on Berlin.[1]

It is no good looking in Zhukov's memoirs for an informative account of the East Pomeranian Operation, for he barely mentions it. It seems that this was merely an annoying distraction from his main aim, the taking of Berlin, and therefore this episode is almost entirely covered in his memoirs by a counterattack against Chuikov's allegations that the city could have been taken earlier. He summarised:

Initially, the task of routing the enemy in East Pomerania was supposed to be the sole responsibility of the forces of the 2nd Byelorussian Front. However, their strength proved to be totally insufficient. The offensive of that Front, begun on the 10th February, proceeded very slowly; its troops covered only 50 to 70 kilometres in ten days.

At that moment the enemy launched a counterattack south of Stargard and even succeeded in pressing our troops back, gaining some 12 kilometres southward.

In view of the situation, the Supreme Command decided to move four field and two tank armies from the 1st Byelorussian Front in order to liquidate the East Pomeranian grouping, whose strength by then had grown to forty divisions.

As is known, joint operations by the two Fronts to knock out the East Pomeranian grouping were completed only towards the end of March. You can see what a hard nut that grouping was.[2]

The sheer speed of the 'Vistula–Oder Operation' had brought with it problems that made the conduct of this next phase extremely difficult. The railway bridges over the broad expanse of the Vistula were still in the course of reconstruction, a broken link in the essential chain of supply. Consequently there were serious shortages of ammunition, fuel and lubricants. The troops themselves were battle-weary, the units depleted and no reinforcements were coming forward. In addition, the weather conditions were particularly bad with snowstorms, rain, sleet, fog and mud impeding movement. Nevertheless, the East Pomeranian Operation, which had arisen out of Stalin's failure to award Rokossovsky's 2nd Byelorussian Front an additional army to help close the expanding gap between Zhukov's troops speeding westward to the Oder and Rokossovsky's pushing northward to the Baltic, was an important development. Not only had Zhukov to drop off troops to cover this flank as he advanced, but it gave the Germans the opportunity to bring forward reserves to mount a counter-operation from the Stargard area.[3]

Operation Sonnenwende (Solstice) was the idea of Colonel General Guderian, part of a wider plan that would tackle the Soviet forces from Stargard in the north and from the Oder between Guben and Glogau in the south. This, however, depended upon reinforcements from other fronts being allocated to the task, but as Hitler sent them off to Hungary instead, it was only possible to mount the northern thrust, and that with limited resources. In order to ensure the operation was properly conducted, Guderian managed to persuade a reluctant Hitler, who was outraged at the suggestion that Himmler and his staff might not be competent, to appoint Guderian's chief assistant, Lieutenant General Walther Wenck, to take charge.[4]

Aware of the German move across the Oder into Pomerania, Zhukov now had the 2nd Guards Tank Army and the 61st Army deployed across his northern flank from east to west, with the 1st Guards Tank, 47th and 3rd Shock Armies in reserve.[5] The clearance of East Pomerania would tie down these forces until 21 March, a full seven weeks before they could be redeployed opposite Berlin, and those elements of the 8th Guards and 69th Armies besieging Posen would similarly be tied down until 15 February. This left Zhukov with insufficient forces along the Oder, so that he could do little more than hold the existing line of advance for the moment.

However, the leading elements of the 8th Guards and 1st Guards Tank Armies arrived on the Oder at the Reitwein ferry point on 2 February and forced a crossing over the breaking ice against a few Reichsarbeitsdienst sentries posted there to assist with the flow of refugees. A quick thrust forward secured the village of Reitwein and the even more important tip of the Reitwein Spur, a projection of the Seelow Heights where General Chuikov was eventually to establish his 8th Guards Army's command post. Seven tanks were ferried across in support of this operation, only to be recalled when the 1st Guards Tank Army was detailed to assist with the East Pomeranian Operation.[6]

The ineptness of Heinrich Himmler's appointment as commander of Army Group 'Weichsel' is clearly demonstrated in his handling of the so-called 'Woldenberg' Division, a random assembly of troops taken from convalescent and training units stationed on the north bank of the Warthe, with which he expected to block the Soviet advance. Major-General Gerhard Kegler later wrote of this:

> On the 30th January 1945 I received orders from Himmler to take command of the 'Woldenberg' Division without being given any orientation on the subject, nor the division's task. I had to find the division. I found the division's command post east of Friedeberg. It had no signals unit and there were no communications with a superior headquarters. I took over command at about midday as I found this recently established 'division' in the course of disintegration as it retreated to Landsberg. While I was busy in Landsberg on the morning of the 31st January with the organisation and deployment of the available units, I discovered that the 'division' had no anti-tank weapons, no ammunition or food supply arrangements and no signals unit. Neither was there a divisional medical officer. The artillery consisted of two horse-drawn batteries. The 'division' was not a 'strong battle group' nor were the troops battle-worthy.
>
> The population of 45,000 inhabitants were still in the town and no preparations had been made for evacuation.
>
> I received Himmler's orders from the commander-in-chief of the 9th Army to defend Landsberg as a fortress over the tele-phone. Russian tanks were already north of the Warthe–Netze sector. I had the Warthe Bridge demolished. After some consci-entious consideration, I decided to disobey this order [to defend Landsberg], which I considered senseless and whose compliance would serve no purpose other than great loss in human life.[7]

Landsberg was abandoned by the 'Woldenberg' Division that same night. Major-General Kegler had set the withdrawal for 1 February, as the Soviet spearheads had already reached Küstrin some 40 kilometres to his rear, but his demoralised soldiers would not wait and abandoned their positions in the dark. The headquarters staff were only able to stop these demoralised units with difficulty some 3 kilometres west of the town.

Kegler reported by telephone to the 9th Army commander, General Busse, who had meanwhile established his headquarters in the Oderbruch village of Golzow. Busse demanded that Landsberg be retaken and defended, threatening Kegler with court martial in accordance with Himmler's orders. Nevertheless, Kegler stuck to his decision to withdraw to Küstrin by stages over the following nights. Even this, in view of the state of his troops and his open flank, was risky, and depended to a large extent upon their not being attacked as they withdrew along the northern edge of the Warthebruch on Reichsstrasse 1.[8]

Lieutenant Rudolf Schröter, whom we last encountered west of Landsberg on the morning of 31 January, was completely unaware that he and his 400 recruits were part of the 'Woldenberg' Division,[9] as he related:

> On the morning of the 31st January my unit rejoined the Königstiger SS-sergeant-major about 4 kilometres west of Landsberg in the Wepritz area. As we were still without a super-ior command or orders, I had us retreat westwards.
>
> Beyond Dühringshof I was met by a car with a general, who received my report, did not introduce himself nor did he name his formation. He ordered me to deploy left of the road to Diedersdorf. My left-hand neighbour would be Second-Lieutenant Clemens's unit.
>
> When we stopped a Russian armoured reconnaissance vehicle with infantry fire, the soldiers jumped over the sides with a blanket that was supposed to protect them from our fire. That night the first Russian attack occurred with more on the 1st, 2nd and 3rd February. Small enemy breaches were driven back with counterattacks by the exemplary fighting recruits.
>
> On the 3rd February I was summoned to a conference by the divisional staff in Vietz town hall. Here for the first time I discovered that my unit belonged to the 'Woldenberg' Division. The divisional commander, Major-General Kegler, described the situation.
>
> The division was surrounded by Russian troops. Vietz station

on the south-eastern edge of the town was in enemy hands. Blumberg was also occupied by the Russians. Two enemy infantry regiments were at Gross Cammin. Communication with Küstrin was severed. Re-supply was only possible by air. His decision was to leave.

The orders handed out by the divisional chief of staff for my unit and that of Second-Lieutenant Clemens were not possible of execution or would entail heavy losses. I therefore rose to protest and suggested that we should first disengage ourselves from the attacking enemy so that the immovable heavy weapons and especially our infantry could get out of the difficult terrain and deep snow.

As the general declared to the chief of staff that this was also his opinion, the following radio message arrived from headquarters 9th Army: 'Report situation and intentions. Hold Vietz.'

Major-General Kegler promptly rescinded his orders for the division's withdrawal.

Back in my position and after speaking to my left-hand neighbour, both of us fearful of having pointless high casualties among our recruits, I decided to convince the divisional commander that he should stick to his plan to withdraw, and that in any case I would decide according to my conscience. I returned to Vietz.

I had to overcome the resistance of the staff officers to get through to the general. Major-General Kegler was astounded but open to my arguments:

1. Once an order had been given it must be adhered to in order to keep up the morale of the troops.

2. The Army Headquarters' radio message 'Report situation and intentions' unusually left open the decision. If this was not so, the message would have read: 'Report situation. Hold Vietz.' While it was expected that the Army would correctly use tactical language and especially stressed 'Report situation', it meant that it was holding open the opportunity for us to decide for ourselves in this special situation, and our decision was 'Withdraw'.

3. There had also been instances in this war in which troops had withdrawn against orders in recognition of their hopeless situation, had upheld the morale of their troops and the officers had received high decorations.

4. The decisive argument, General, is in accordance with one's own conscience. The responsible officer must, if common sense is to prevail, understand that slavish obedience in a hopeless situation only condemns him to a senseless bloodbath, which he should spare his men.

These arguments, especially the last, visibly moved Major-General Kegler. He then went briefly into an adjoining room. When he returned, he was white in the face. He asked me where I had lost my right arm, praised the discipline and commitment of my youngsters and also my objections at the conference a few hours ago. Finally the following dialogue ensued:

'Do you think that you can withdraw the division in good order in this situation?'

'Yes, if I have your support in doing so.'

'Then I hereby beg you to undertake it on my staff.'

I immediately sent all the staff officers to the units, where they with the sector commanders were to stop the units and individuals retreating and incorporate them into the local defence.

Then I prepared to retake Vietz station with a platoon of my infantry and a Königstiger and while doing so a runner brought me a letter from the general. It read: 'I have given up command of the division. Kegler, Major-General.'

I then asked a colonel to take over command of the division as a matter of seniority, which he accepted under the condition that I assumed tactical control.

The withdrawal of the division was made ready and all sector commanders summoned to an order group in Vietz at 1500 hours.

After stabilising the situation in the town I made a reconnaissance in the amphibious jeep with the SS-sergeant-major and one of my recruits, using Major-General Kegler's map. I discovered that:

1. The road to Küstrin was not blocked by the Russians.

2. There were no Russians in Gross Cammin, the nearest enemy movement being in the northerly neighbouring village of Batzlow.

I stuck to the original plan. A radio message was sent to Küstrin fortress about the division's withdrawal. The order to withdraw was given at 1500 hours and went without problems. When I later went into Vietz with the amphibious jeep to check the enemy situation, the first enemy scouts were already feeling their way forward.[10]

At dawn on 4 February the remains of the 'Woldenberg' Division began crossing the anti-tank ditch that blocked the Landsberger Chaussee at the eastern end of Küstrin. They had already come to within 10 kilometres of the town the previous day but had waited for darkness to get through the area occupied by Soviet forces.

General Busse had sent a young liaison officer to meet them, but without any instructions for Major-General Kegler. When the latter arrived in Küstrin he was promptly given orders to report to the standing court martial in Torgau, thus becoming one of the last to leave Küstrin by the normal road. As the witnesses to the events leading up to Kegler's court martial were now trapped in Küstrin, evidence had to be obtained from them by telephone. Kegler was reduced to the ranks and sentenced to death. He then had to wait ten days for his execution before he was told that it would be delayed until after the war, providing he fought at the front as a simple soldier. He was severely wounded in April, but survived the war.[11]

Lieutenant Schröter concluded his account:

During the night of the 4th February I reached Küstrin on Reichsstrasse 1 as the first of the remainder of the division. The German guard on the town perimeter, the crew of an 88mm gun, were irresponsibly careless.

I reported to the chief of staff at fortress headquarters, Major Witte. When I told him about the lack of security on Reichsstrasse 1 and that I wanted to take it over with my own intact infantry, he regarded this as mutiny and interference in other people's business. 'Your general has already been taken by the Judge Advocate and you "mutineers" can expect a similar fate.' I then handed over the remains of the division to the fortress commandant's chief of staff.

The heavy weapons and the infantry crossed the Warthe and Oder bridges and were attached to the Küstrin garrison. While I was checking in the arriving elements of the division, a runner brought me the following orders from Major Witte. 'You and your division are to clear Russian breaches in Warnick suburb.'

I could not fulfil this order, but in several days of house to house fighting I was able to prevent further penetration by the enemy. After several days SS-Captain Machers took over the sector with myself as adjutant.

Shortly afterwards I received orders to leave Küstrin on the nightly convoy and to report to the Motor Sport School in Wriesen, where I was liaison officer to Colonel Danke, chief of staff of CIst Corps. So ended my short encounter with the 'Woldenberg' Division.[12]

In the cool light of dawn on 1 February Soviet tanks and SPGs felt their way forwards from the north to the Neustadt defences, getting a good view over much of the town from the high ground. The clearly visible industrial sites, such as the Oder-Hütte foundry and the town gasworks, became the targets for a short barrage. One gasometer was set on fire and the electricity supply failed when a main cable or transformer was hit. This was the first effective use of the artillery.

That afternoon a Soviet assault team made a surprise attack along the Warthe on the Cellulose Factory, which was right on the river, halfway between Drewitz and the Neustadt. Not yet ten years old, it was the only strongly constructed building in this area and became valued as a strongpoint by both sides. Like other such places, it was occupied by a Volkssturm platoon consisting principally of workmen and a Hungarian company, but it was relatively undermanned. The Hungarian soldiers, fed up with fighting so far from their homeland, threw down their weapons, and the Volkssturm were overrun. The Volkssturm survivors, having no uniforms and wearing only an armband, were then shot as 'partisans'. (From then on the other Volkssturm units in the town were provided with uniforms.)

The factory was fired at from the Altstadt by the light flak guns and some fires broke out. These had no effect on its modern skeleton steel construction, but the nearby Spiritusmonopol tank farm with several million litres of alcohol and fuel oil was also set on fire. The big tanks burnt like giant torches all night, and in the light from the flames an engine shunted a row of goods wagons out of the railway viaduct workshops next door in order to screen the Warthe bridges from this flank.[13]

The interruption of power and gas supplies gave some idea of what could be expected in the long term. Portable emergency generators were quickly made available for the garrison's most important needs, for the staff and dressing stations, and their fuel requirements could be assured. Nevertheless, the civilian population would have to do without electricity in general. This meant not only no lighting, but also no radio, the only source of information at the time, as the local newspaper had given up. By this sixth year of the war battery radios and accumulators were the privilege of a few wealthy owners and were very rare.

The gas supply was soon restored so that cooking and making coke could be resumed, and brickettes for fires could be taken from abandoned neighbours' houses. There were ample stoves or at least iron ovens in the town's old buildings. The rising temperatures raised hopes that less coal would soon be needed for heating purposes, as was usual at the beginning of February, but a general deterioration in the situation could be expected in motor and household fuel stocks, while supplies of candles and petroleum lamps were already exhausted.

Many of the women, children and elderly people that had spent the night in Kietz wandered back into the town, struggling with their toboggans through the ankle-deep slush created by the thaw over the still-frozen ground. No one warned the people of the dangers now that the town had been declared a fortress and surrounded, and no bunkers or other suitable shelters had been provided for the population. Most had hardly noticed the short bombardment early that morning. If it really was that serious, why had no orders been given to evacuate? Would they be allowed to cross the Oder bridges? But nobody stopped them. The officers and Feldgendarmerie posts had vanished and only a few old Landeschützen (home guards) protected the demolition charges on the bridges.

When the Volkssturm paraded again at 0900 hours, their ranks had thinned out. A considerable proportion of the first levy belonged to the Finance Ministry department that had been farmed out to Küstrin, and these civil servants and some other men had disappeared overnight. Only 300 men were left.

There were hardly any vehicles remaining. The treks had streamed off to the west and no more were coming in. All that remained was a group of civil servants and Nazi officials from Landsberg with the mayor and county Party leader in charge, over whose heads hung the same taint as that over Major-General Kegler for not having either died defending the town or at least not having left it a waste of rubble. So they remained 'at the front', the minority to demonstrate their unbroken determination to hold out, the others out of sheer fear of reprisal, but even those most faithful to the Führer did not pursue their thirst for action as far as purging their guilt in the front line. Instead they found it more convenient to join the Küstrin mayor and county Party leader Hermann Körner in his nearly empty town hall, from where he was still administering the population of some 8–10,000. The Landsbergers were happy to help with the administration, the only hope they had of making a contribution of any significance without becoming involved in bureaucratic complications. Just to show that they were still persons of some importance, a policeman had to stand guard at night in front of the Altstadt town hall, where they had taken over a whole floor for their accommodation.[14]

Luftwaffe Officer Cadet Sergeant Helmut Schmidt gave his account of events on the east bank of the Warthe on 1 February:

> It was shortly after midnight. We had returned dog-tired from our storm troop enterprise, the fatigue overriding our hunger. I quickly sorted out the sentry roster and lay down on the floor with my men.
>
> In the railway hut was an iron stove. The sentry coming in lit it and soon it was warm. There was hardly a minute's peace in our primitive accommodation. Sentries came and went, weapons clattered, as well as the sounds of boots and men attending the oven. With daybreak I was on my feet again, checking the sentries. I heard their reports. The rest of the night had remained quiet. There had been no sign of the enemy.
>
> At last I could see our surroundings in daylight. I had stood on the bridge without realising how close Küstrin station was. Under me to my left flowed the Warthe. I looked across the factory tracks. About 800 metres away began the prominent Cellulose Factory complex.
>
> We had positioned our machine gun immediately north of the bridge, where there was a ready prepared machine-gun position, a long breast-deep hole from where one had a good field of fire up to the Cellulose Factory. The sappers appeared to have completed their job without a fuss during the night.
>
> Our immediate frontage made me restless. I took a couple of volunteers from my section and went to reconnoitre it. We went a bit towards the Cellulose Factory but kept a respectful distance from the factory premises. In front of us was a long, two-storey building with many pipes and rails leading to it. Its

windowed front was facing us, the windows painted blue. This was no place for caution. If the Russians were inside, they could see us through scratches in the paint.

About 150–200 metres from the railway bridge we came across a little half-timbered hut between the railway lines. We took it for a signal box at first, but this turned out to be wrong when we entered it. The building had two storeys with a tiny ground floor. Here the marshalling yard personnel had perhaps formerly taken shelter in bad weather, but lately it had been used for private purposes. Why had this little house been built so lavishly when it was only intended for railway personnel? I was particularly curious.

The entrance door stood half open. As I entered I immediately realised that the Russians had been here. Several drawers from the few bits of furniture had been torn out and the contents barbarically searched. The whole floor was covered in items of female underclothing of the finest quality and dirty soldiers' boots had trampled all over them. On a low table stood a gramophone in a wooden box such as was to be found in many middle-class homes before the war. Most of the gramophone records were scattered broken on the floor. A narrow spiral staircase led to the upper floor, where there was a square wicker basket, a wash basket secured with a lock with clean labels attached, ready for despatch, also some suitcases. The Russians had not penetrated here. I especially remember the basket in the middle of the room, heavy and undisturbed, waiting for collection.

I went back downstairs and collected some stockings. Fresh underwear, even if dirty, was always useful and the feminine aspect did not worry me. I asked myself what kind of people these were that in the sixth year of war would have such feminine underwear. The owners could easily have taken them with them, but presumably it seemed too dangerous for them.

Meanwhile my men had inspected the gramophone. It was still working. Fortunately the Russians had not touched it. Only two of the records were still largely whole. Triumphantly my comrades carried the box back to the start point at the foot of the railway embankment. While my comrades were returning to our railway hut base, I had another look at the books in the shed with the petrol barrels. I came across wonderful leather-covered books from a German publisher, with a dozen copies of each. Apparently someone had put them there in great haste. Even in daylight the shed was quite dark and I had difficulty making out the book titles. As far as I could make out they consisted of Party-acceptable literature, morally correct novels, the usual lying idylls of a healthy world. For me it was reading material for a week, should I be left in peace.

I could hear the gramophone music at quite some distance from the base. My comrades were happily trying out their acquisition. The gramophone was wound up and soon the steel needle was scratching the tracks in the shellac disc. I think it was Richard Tauber, whose hit 'Schön ist die Welt' blared out triumphantly from the walls of our hut. The disc had a small gap and was also lacking a bit from the edge, but that did not bother us much. The second piece that Richard Tauber sang was an evergreen, his unspoilt 'Sonny Boy'. Tauber's voice sounded tinny and had a slightly nasal tone through the loudspeaker. The gramophone played all day long. Star tenor Richard Tauber had to keep on singing. The defect in the disc did not matter. Our little Küstrin world was not perfect either.

I took my books with me to the machine-gun position at the bridge. I was able to read and smoke undisturbed. The railway traffic over the Warthe had terminated the night before. Although we were unable to leave our defensive position, an opportunity arose during the day to visit the underpass. I wanted to look over the American Sherman in Russian service.

My impressions of the previous night were confirmed. The American tank in comparison to the trusty Russian T-34 was unusually tall and narrow, despite its rounding on all sides. Especially conspicuous were the narrow tracks. I doubted that they were much good for cross-country work, better for roads and reinforced tracks. The long-barrelled gun with a thick cylindrical front plate I took to be a Russian 76.2mm cannon. The olive-coloured steel colossus had been stopped here abruptly after passing through the underpass. I found the hole caused by a direct hit from a Panzerfaust on the rear of the turret. It was cleanly curved, round, coloured blue by the heat and with lightly frayed edges. The diameter I calculated as 80mm. The tank was closed. The crew had not survived the fatal shot. The escorting infantry seated on the tank had been thrown off by the explosion and the men lay on the far side of the street, all dead.

I went a bit further along Plantagenstrasse. Near the junction with Forststrasse stood the next steel monster on the left-hand side of the street with its turret turned to the right. The fatal shot appeared to have come from a cellar, but I could not be certain. Where the shot had been fired from was a small square bordered by several storeyed buildings.

I was particularly interested in the question of the type of this tank. I could not identify it. A Russian T-70 looked quite different. It was smaller, flat surfaced and with a gun that I calculated as being 75mm. The small entry hatch was on the left side of the tank. One could see the gun layer at the gun with his back to the hatch and the trigger in his right hand. The exploding Panzerfaust had prevented the gun firing by a few seconds. I also noticed that this tank had been travelling without carrying infantry.

However, a few days later the gun did fire a shot. It hit the building it was aimed at and tore a hole through the wall of the first storey. The furniture of a living room could be seen covered in dust and mortar.

I discovered several years after the war that this was a Mark III Valentine. Although we were often engaged against tanks, the tank recognition service had provided us with no material about this type.

The small tank appeared to have driven ahead of the Sherman. It could well have shot the hole in the façade of the building. In order to be able to be mobile in all directions, it had taken no escorting infantry with it.

Several soldiers joined our little battle group, those that had become separated from their units seeking an intact one. They were also seeking shelter from the military police and fanatical SS officers. One of those who joined our group was Bombardier Horn of the artillery, who was a typical old soldier, quiet, calm and reliable. There were also two Waffen-SS soldiers, tall young lads, whom the war had not yet deprived of the joy of living. These two SS men proved to be a stroke of luck for they were real artists at scrounging. Every day they surprised us with fresh bread, but refused to betray their source.

It was quiet at the bridge at first. Although we did not drop our guard, we could not detect change or movement at the

Cellulose Factory. But we did not trust this quiet. Instinctively, we regarded the factory as not clean. We would gladly have tackled this uncertainty but our group was too small to search or occupy the factory. There were innumerable places of concealment on the factory premises and with the inability to oversee the ground we could easily fall into a trap.[15]

Hitler Youth Hans Dalbkermeyer recalled:

Beyond the Oder bridge and before the Artillery Barracks, Feldgendarmerie and Wehrmacht officers were filtering all men of military age and soldiers out of the refugee stream fleeing westwards and sending them into the nearby barracks. We five schoolboys from Birnbaum were also filtered out, although with our full approval as we wanted to assist in the defence of Küstrin. Either that day or the next we were attached to an officer-cadet company and incorporated in it. Together with three other soldiers and a sergeant we formed a section. We Birnbaumers received 1898 carbines as weapons and a Panzerfaust each. Our clothing was replaced with field-grey uniforms without insignia. Thus equipped we joined a long marching column of several units and marched along the same way back into the Neustadt.

On the edge of Drewitz, or it might still have been Küstrin, our section moved into a suburban house that had been abandoned by its owners. It lay on the outermost edge of town on the west side of a road leading north and was right forward in the front line. In front of us and westwards towards the Warthe and Oder were snow-covered open spaces providing a clear view to the next village, where the Russians settled down opposite us during the next few days.

The property, almost a small farmhouse, served us nine men well as accommodation. Apart from hens, there were no longer any animals. Thanks to our careful and rich feeding, the flock of hens thrived and enriched our menu with their eggs. We never suffered hunger here, nor did we during my whole time in Küstrin. We could almost live in luxury, using only those parts of our rations that we wanted to.

We catered for ourselves with what we could find in our house and a neighbouring cellar. We calmed our thoughts with the well-known belief that stealing food in emergencies is not punishable. In addition we received front-line fighters' packets, which also contained cigarettes. No one protested when we youngsters smoked, but I was not interested and would swap my cigarettes for a bar of chocolate.

The civilian population had completely vanished from our sector. We lived as if on an island and learnt very little of what was going on in the town and on our front line. A radio in the house provided us with the daily Wehrmacht Report. Nevertheless it was said that Küstrin had been almost completely surrounded by Russian troops. I only heard about the publication of a Küstrin Fortress newspaper fifty years later. Nothing much came through to us in the front line. Possibly there was little interest in negative information. We hardly left our position at all, as the central area of the Neustadt was under heavier artillery fire than our north-western sector.

As events were to show, we had been extremely lucky with our allocation of sector of the front and had a better chance of survival than most. First, we were hit far less often in the general firing and bombardments than the remaining parts of the Neustadt, and secondly we were able to withdraw towards the railway station and west to the Warthe when the Russians attacked on the 7th March.[16]

Officer Cadet Corporal Hans Dahlmanns was also caught up in the chaos:

In the following days, to give us something to do in the Engineer Barracks, which were right behind the front line, we had to knock rifle firing holes in the walls while rifle bullets whistled through the windows on the east side. Then came engagements on a small scale. Once we lay the whole night in snow water, the thaw having started, without firing a shot, while bullets whistled past. Following this nature cure, a bad cough that had been troubling me for some time vanished completely.

An 88mm flak gun stood not far from the barracks. It controlled large parts of the north-eastern area to the extent that the gunners did not pay much attention to their cover. However, whoever showed himself at a window on the first floor in the building behind the gun position had to reckon with aimed shots from the enemy. It was an idyll for which the Soviet mortars had prepared a quick ending.

Immediately behind the barrack wall was a wood dealer's yard, where we had to guard the barracks, not knowing where the Russians really were. It was there that I saw the first German dead. On his breast lay a shot-through pay book. I leafed through it and saw my father's signature. This was the first letter he had to write reporting a hero's death. Four or five days later I met a sergeant from my father's company. He told me that my father was fine and that his command post was in the Oder Potato Meal Factory on the riverbank.[17]

Sapper Ernst Müller, recently arrived in Küstrin with other replacements, continued his account:

The ensuing siege saw me next as a number 2 machine-gunner near the Sparkasse Bank. We were lucky and only came under periodic fire from Soviet mortars, guns and rockets. We 'Holzmindeners' were divided into several platoons under Lieutenant Schröder:

1st Platoon	Second-Lieutenant Schröter (later Sergeant Berger), at the Stern.
2nd Platoon	Staff-Sergeant Haubenreiser, at the Warthe.
3rd Platoon	Sergeant-Major Peter Kaiser, Vorflut Canal, command post in the last building before the Altstadt station.
4th Platoon	Battalion Sergeant Major Gleiche, casemate on Friedrichstrasse.
5th Platoon	With demolition squads, Second-Lieutenant Storm, Sergeant-Major Schulz and Staff-Sergeant Kukei for the Oder road bridge, and Second-Lieutenant Lülau for the Oder railway bridge. The latter had a command post in a casemate on the railway.

During the course of the siege, Engineer Replacement and Training Battalion 68 and Territorial Engineer Battalion 513 were combined as the Fortress Engineer Battalion under the command of Captain Fischer. The command post of Captain

Dahlmanns' company was in the Potato Meal Factory. Captain Fischer had his command post in the Law Courts, as did Lieutenant Schröder during the last third of March. (Previously, until the fall of the Neustadt, Schröder's command post was in a casemate on the Warthe and subsequently in a building on the edge of the Altstadt.) In the Law Courts was also Staff-Sergeant Tewes with his men.[18]

Officer Cadet Karl-Heinz Peters, another sapper replacement, related his experiences as a member of the garrison:

Following my time with the Reichsarbeitsdienst, I began my military service at the end of May 1944. After training as an armoured engineer, I found myself in the officer cadet company of Armoured Engineer Replacement and Training Battalion 19 in Holzminden.

In the second half of January we were entrained for the East. It was very cold. We went in cattle wagons with peat deposits on the floor. The rail journey lasted several days and ended at Frankfurt/Oder, from where buses took us to Küstrin. There we had to dig in on the outer defensive line of the Neustadt. Next day we heard the sound of tanks. We were soon withdrawn and deployed at the Warthe bridges. During the first days of February we received massive artillery fire. At this time there were two Königstigers in our sector, an 88mm flak battery and a 20mm quadruple gun. When these were withdrawn we were left with no heavy weapons apart from Panzerfausts from then on.

The Warthebruch was still frozen over. Russian snipers had concealed themselves on the islands and promontories and gave us a hard time. They fired tracer bullets at the swans standing on the ice from the right bank of the Warthe. Before our 20mm quadruple gun was withdrawn, it managed to destroy several of the snipers' nests.

Gradually the Soviet artillery fire diminished. At first we had made ourselves at home on a houseboat in the harbour. There was a gramophone on the boat with the record 'My Golden Baby'. We also found a book, Remarque's *All Quiet on the Western Front*. That was the right kind of literature for our situation. But our time on the boat was not long, for the Russians literally shot off the stern.

When shells exploded in the water many dead or stunned
fish came to the surface, including enormous pike. The Warthe
and Oder must be very rich in fish. Formerly there must also
have been sturgeon, for when I saw a photograph of the
Küstrin Schloss courtyard, I noticed sturgeon on the surrounding relief.

Groups of refugees were still crossing the bridges in February,
moving from the Neustadt to the Altstadt. The Russians deliberately aimed at them and inflicted some casualties. The enemy
had drawn the ring tighter around the town. That Küstrin had
been declared a fortress meant virtually a death sentence for us
soldiers, bringing an enormous emotional strain.

The effect of the Soviet artillery was reinforced by the blanket
barrages of Stalin-Organs that we found frightening. For lack
of our own heavy weapons, we were practically defenceless
against the enemy fire. The Soviet artillery was deployed in open
fields near Sonnenburg and fired at us without pause. There
were some 30 batteries, including 152mm cannon. At first the
enemy fire was directed by an observer on the chimney of a
waterworks until our flak destroyed the chimney.

The Russians must have taken considerable casualties from
the flak at first. One morning I counted 19 burning trucks on
the Sonnenburger Chaussee.

The continuous artillery and mortar fire destroyed all our
cover. We thought that every Russian must have a mortar. The
calibres ranged from 50 to 120mm. As we were getting direct
enemy fire from the Warthe Island and the Sonnenburger
Chaussee, we built a screen at night of interwoven textiles and
paper, but it was shot away again within a few hours.

I had temporarily dug in with my comrade Franz Jürgens in
the front garden of a house standing right next to the railway
leading over the Warthe. We moved some railway sleepers from
a nearby yard on a wagon and used them to cover our hole with
a triple layer. That was just as well for shortly afterwards we
received three direct hits from a 120mm mortar without
damage.

The Russians had such a good view from the Sonnenburger
Chaussee that we dared not let ourselves be seen in daylight.
Once when I was attending to a call of nature outside our hole,
an anti-tank gun fired at me and I had only a shallow dip in

which to take cover. The anti-tank gun fired about ten times at me before I could dive back into the hole.[19]

Luftwaffe Auxiliary Fritz Oldenhage, whose unit had fled from the Cellulose Factory when the Soviet tanks appeared the previous day, continued his account:

Our battery commander had been missing since noon on the 31st January. Perhaps he had been visiting a headquarters or another gun and had been surprised by events with another troop. It turned out that he had stood behind a Panzerfaust when it was fired and had been wounded by the back blast and taken to hospital.

Next day, the 1st February, the battery moved to Lunette B on the Island between the Oder and the Vorflut Canal. One or two days later, on the 2nd or 3rd February, I was under way as a runner looking for our packs. My route took me through Plantagenstrasse. Despite the impressive damage caused by the Soviet tank attack, the shot-up tanks were quiet. One could see from the small holes that they had been victims of our Panzerfausts. Beyond Anger Strasse I came across the destroyed position of our 37mm gun. My school friend Ostermann had been killed. A tank shell had penetrated the thin rampart and killed him on the spot. I do not know what happened to the rest of the gun crew.

Our packs that we had laid out in the open at the Cellulose Factory were no longer there, so I took a blanket from a wagon that had belonged to civilians killed in the fire in front of the factory.

On my way back I was shocked to see a German soldier hanging from a pole on the road bridge over the Warthe. The text of the sign hanging on him read: 'I was a coward', which upset me more than if it had said: 'I was a spy'. Everyone was afraid, but I know of none of my comrades who nevertheless did not persevere. Our basic attitude was: Live decently, but not at the cost of your comrades or the people.

In Lunette B I could once more sit at a telephone exchange with a 20-plug switchboard. It was in a room about 1.5 by 2.5 metres immediately right of the narrow footbridge over the moat. One day a shell stuck in the earth above the door. Thank

God it was a dud. There were many of them among the Russian 122mm shells.

Our rations were good. We also received fruit drops, biscuits, schnapps, vermouth and plenty of cigarettes. The issues were made in the pub close-by on the Pappelhorst. One of its rooms we used during the day as a rest-room and for cleaning weapons. We slept 500 metres away in the Artillery Barracks, where soldiers of various units slept together in a big, high hall. This gave us an uncomfortable feeling in our stomachs at night, because by day we could see Russian soldiers south of the Island and also when they were fired at by our 88mm flak with tracer shells, and should the enemy retaliate our hall offered a good target.

The position of the 37mm gun between the Vorflut Canal and Lunette B was so arranged that it could engage both low-flying aircraft and ground targets or boats south of the Vorflut Canal. In practice, however, it only fired at aircraft. After one engagement came a strong Russian reply with 122mm shells and our cook fled from the gun position to the pub, being fatally wounded on the way.

The day after the death of our cook, a superior handed me the briefcase of my school friend Dieter Gross with the dry information that he had been killed and asking that, as his friend, I should write to his parents in Hamburg. I did this, but beforehand went to see his last position, which was in the Neustadt somewhere in a commercial area between Warnicker Strasse and Landsberger Strasse. The last 200 metres of the way there were particularly dangerous, and my friend had been killed by well-camouflaged Russian snipers. The last 40 metres were outside the trench and could only be crossed by my escorting Luftwaffe auxiliary and myself under covering fire. A steel helmet raised on a stick above cover as a test immediately brought a shot through it. We were not fired at on our return, probably as a result of the firing of a German 'Stuka zu Fuss', which had a devastating effect where it hit.

One day a Tiger – some said it was a Königstiger – took up position near us. It drove from the Artillery Barracks to the road bridge, drove southwards and positioned itself noisily near the road to the alley leading to Lunette B. Its field of fire ranged from Lunette B to the south and south-west, so covering the canal and river approaches as well as the south-eastern boundary of Kietz. It hardly fired at all. At night it took shelter in the Artillery Barracks. This went on for several days.

On the Island we constantly expected an attack by the Russians. This was especially feared by our forward observer on the southern point, who recorded enemy activity either with his own eyes or through binoculars. I could even see this for myself when going yet again to check the telephone cable lying on the ground. Our 37mm gun was so placed as to be able to shoot at the water as well as the ground area.

Sometimes rubber dinghies went along the canal, apparently after specific reports from the forward observer. The paddling was so light and certain that it aroused our wonder. It was said that this was done by selected SS men.

During our Küstrin engagement we flak auxiliaries in our blue-grey uniforms got new photographs in our paybooks and the rank of gunner was stuck over that of Luftwaffe senior auxiliary.[20]

Luftwaffe Gunner Josef Stefanski recalled:

At the beginning of the fighting for Küstrin I was assigned to the Flak unit and dressed in uniform. We were deployed to various places. Our battery had four guns. In the middle of February these stood at the western exit from Kietz. The position was at the Weinbergshof farm. I once got leave from there to see the family off on the last goods train that was leaving Küstrin to take them to safety.

We lost two of our guns when we had to leave the Weinbergshof farm in the middle of February. Dug into the Oderbruch mud and dirt for cover they could not be moved. There were no tractors.[21]

On Friday, 2 February elements of the Soviet 8th Guards Army and 1st Guards Tank Army reached the Oder south of Küstrin apparently heading for those nine places where ferries were already located, although none was in fact operating due to the ice. Those units of the 4th Guards Rifle Corps on the right flank had a shock when they came to the little town of Sonnenburg, 14 kilometres east of Küstrin.

The town contained an old prison that had become one of the first

German concentration camps in April 1933, later reverting to normal prison use. By the end of January 1945 it contained 1,000 prisoners from various countries. In the late evening of 30 January 1945 a twenty-strong special motorised Gestapo commando appeared and within four hours shot 819 prisoners selected from a card index. Five prisoners survived the shooting to be rescued by the Soviets and 150 others were marched off with the prison warders and their families at 0300 hours on 31 January towards Küstrin. Later in the morning a squad of Wehrmacht sappers appeared with orders to blow up the prison but soon gave up their attempts.[22]

At dawn on 2 February aircraft of two Luftwaffe divisions resumed the attack on the Kienitz bridgehead and Soviet units on the east bank of the Oder. Aerial reconnaissance reported that the ice on the Oder was continuing to break up; it was also raining and the day temperature rose as high as 8 degrees Celsius.[23]

Soviet troops managed to get men across at several places, despite problems with the thawing ice as it broke up. The resistance met was minimal as the only German forces in the area were armed Reichsarbeitsdienst personnel posted to assist refugees to cross. However, the crossing points were subjected to repeated attacks by German fighter and ground-attack aircraft as none of the Soviet anti-aircraft artillery had yet arrived. There was no bridging equipment with the forward echelons, except in the case of the 1st Guards Tank Army, which managed to get a few tanks and self-propelled guns (SPGs) across at Reitwein on 2 February, only to have them and the bridging pontoon recalled on the next day for the East Pomeranian operation. Consequently, no heavy equipment could be got across and the bridgeheads were therefore limited to a depth of about 4 kilometres in order to remain within artillery cover from the east bank.[24]

Luftwaffe Officer Cadet Sergeant Helmut Schmidt resumed his account of events at the Cellulose Factory:

> I occupied the machine-gun position with my section from 0700 to 0900 hours. Visibility was good and the temperature comfortable. Only the sun was lacking. We only lay down in the position when Ivan showed himself. First a couple of shots whistled past my ears, and then a Russian machine gun joined in. We could hear the whip of the rounds. Without doubt they were coming from the factory but we could not see the firers.
>
> I reported this to Lieutenant Kühnel, who quickly made up

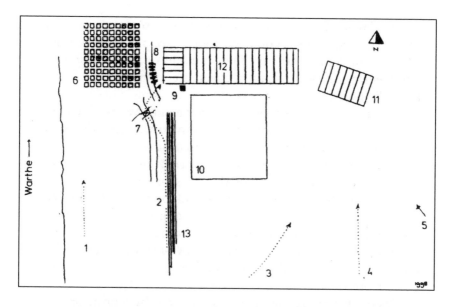

The company-sized attack on the Cellulose Factory, 2 February 1945.

This was drawn by Helmut Schmidt in March 1998. He commented: 'It is almost impossible to draw a sketch of events five decades later, but the situation had such an impact on me that I have dared attempt it. An inaccurate sketch has perhaps far more significance than a detailed description. I may perhaps have distorted the factory area and not shown it accurately, but the topographical features are contained in the sketch.'

1. Finkler's section
2. Schmidt's section
3. Gesterding's section
4. Intemann's section
5. Line of fire of an 88mm gun
6. Stacks of logs
7. Underpass with a small filling station

8. Industrial railway line with dead Hungarian soldiers
9. Small watch tower
10. Water tank with floating logs
11. Building from the cellar windows of which the Russian tried to beat back our attack
12. Big factory building with entrance hall
13. Course of above-ground pipelines

his mind and gave the order to clear the Russians out of the factory complex. It was obvious to me that this was a difficult task. I had the feeling that the Russians wanted to lure us into the factory premises. Certainly they thought they could eliminate us more easily there, as their positions were far more effective than ours.

The attack started early in the morning. Two MG 42s gave us covering fire from the railway embankment as we set off. Sergeant August Finkler and I took our sections along the

Warthe, while Sergeant Werner Gesterding was some distance to my right with his section. As we crossed the railway tracks we came under mortar fire. They must have received supplies. Apparently they were using a covered entrance to the factory from the north.

The firing forced us to split up. Sergeants Martin Intemann and Werner Gesterding went to the right, away from the cover-less ground and out of our sight. August Finkler and his men went to the Warthe somewhat to the right of my section. The deployment should have made the Russian mortar concentrate on one individual target, but our calculation did not come off. The Russians were able to observe us clearly. The mortar was under precise direction. We tried at least to advance quickly and reached a gravelled path alongside a row of raised pipelines. The pipes and a shallow hollow beyond them provided us with some cover from view.

We crawled alongside the pipes, escorted by mortar fire. We wanted at least to reach the factory building that was within striking distance, not 50 metres away. A few paces in front of it stood a wooden watchtower, apparently the perch of a hunter, rising about 2 or 3 metres above the ground. We thought that we had seen some movement in it. Bombardier Horn fired a shot with his grenade launcher at the watchtower. A Russian jumped off in a flash and disappeared behind a corner of the factory as angry mortar fire descended on us. The gravelled path disappeared on the left into a little underpass. We reached safety in short spurts. Unfortunately the protection was a bit pathetic as the mortar splinters also flew in there.

After a short breather I ran to the western side of the factory building, closely followed by my men, getting out of the mortar fire. In front of the factory lay a row of dead men in brown uniforms: Hungarians.

I wrenched open the factory door and came into a sort of lobby, but found no Russians. There was some brown material lying around, as well as some rifles, and along the southern wall was a long table. I ran up an open staircase to the first floor and opened the door to a workroom with a jerk. It was pitch dark inside the room and I could only just make out some machinery. I banged the door to behind me.

Suddenly it was obvious that it was impossible to look for

Russians inside the workroom. We needed light. The windows would have to be shot through. We set about it and discovered that there were no Russians inside the building, otherwise they would have fired at me when I opened the workroom door. Or were we in an ambush?

We searched the high-ceilinged lobby and looked at the dead in front of the building. A few paces from the doorway some six to ten soldiers lay face down on a curved driveway. All had been killed in the most terrible way with an entrenching tool. They had been executed with blows to the neck. The Russians had removed the boots of some of them. The sight of this made us very angry.

The Russians must have surprised the Hungarians eating. There were the remains of a meal on the long table in the lobby: bread, sausage and cheese. Between them were mess tins and long cutlery.

From about the level of the factory building there was a vast store of wood extending to the north with man-high stacks of 2-metre-long round logs. This was the raw material for the factory. The stacks were precisely arranged, row by row and as far as the eye could see, all evenly spaced. My comrades pulled out a Russian from behind one of the stacks. He had apparently become separated from the others. He was not much older than 16. He shook all over and his dark eyes went uneasily from man to man, thinking that he had reached his last hour. We took him back later and handed him over to our company headquarters. He was the only prisoner from our attack.

What had the Hungarians been doing in the factory? The little watchtower showed that they had supervised and guarded prisoners of war working there. Certainly they thought themselves well clear of the firing and thought that they would survive the end of the war here.

The attack meanwhile continued. A Russian tank fired at the roof of the factory in which we were deployed and shot it to pieces. Our next goal was a small factory building to the east of us. I believe that it stood at an angle to the main building. The Russians were firing like mad from the cellar windows. We took ten minutes' pause before attacking, but before we could do so an 88m flak gun shot the building to pieces and thick smoke rose up.

Unexpectedly Senior Officer Cadet Noak and Sergeant Langheinrich appeared with their platoons and relieved us. We set off alongside the Warthe towards our accommodation. Astonishingly, none of us had been wounded.

Meanwhile the attack by Noak's and Langheinrich's platoon continued. Despite the 88mm fire, the Russians fought on bitterly. Finally their resistance was broken by some hits with Panzerfausts. The situation offered them no way out, but none had surrendered, and at the end all were dead.

This successful attack had cost the company some serious losses. Senior Officer Cadet Noak died during the attack from a stomach wound, Sergeant Gesterding had a leg wound and was taken off to field hospital. Less seriously wounded was Sergeant Fritz Wenzig. These losses meant a serious weakening of our company and no replacements could be expected.[25]

Corporal Hans Arlt, now out on the northern edge of the fortress perimeter, continued his account:

Some of our scouts reconnoitred in a north-westerly direction as far as Drewitz Teerofen. Near these crossroads stood two little houses in which we encountered some worried civilians. However, they did not follow us. The woods were a bit thinner to the left of the crossroads area, and in there was a large building, the Drewitz forester's house. My comrade, W. Grunbitsch, with whom I had been at the NCO School, was killed by a shot in the head that day.

Immediately afterwards the advancing enemy were fighting in the wood area around the railway employees' convalescent home. During this we lost all contact with our right-hand neighbour, who had withdrawn. Part of our platoon also left without being ordered to do so. This counted as our first day of close combat.

Looking for other members of the platoon, I went back to the convalescent home again, but without success. Suddenly a bullet struck near me at head level, and through the open doorway I could see the branches of a small tree moving by the fence. That was where my opponent must be. Throwing a hand grenade, I jumped aside, reached the woods and took cover. Quite soon afterwards I was able to meet up with my platoon again. Together we discovered that other members of our platoon, including the platoon commander, were near the level-crossing keeper's hut at the Kohlenweg Hospital crossing. When we met, the platoon commander shook my hand and said: 'Thanks for bringing the section back.' The confidence I had previously had in him crumbled.

Our company commander fell at the beginning of February and Second-Lieutenant Adolf Fleischer took over on 8 February. From about the beginning of February until the beginning of March, our platoon was deployed in the sector south of the Kohlenweg (between the railway and the Zorndorfer Chaussee), and also east of there. Occasionally we could use some earthen bunkers, but these only offered protection from the elements and lacked fresh air. The damp firewood did little in the bunker stoves. Although there was not much trace of warmth, we at least had a roof over our heads in the thaw, and that was worth something.

Even here we had to send out reconnaissance parties of five to six men after first reporting to Captain von Oldershausen. Our task was to bring in prisoners, and three days' special leave was promised for every prisoner brought in. The battalion commander tried to build up our confidence, to rouse our ambitions and called on us to do our duty. (I also passed my probation as a potential NCO.) Then he gave us an account of his military career and the awards of the Iron Cross 1st and 2nd Class. His attitude from then on resulted in our belief that he had 'a pain in the throat' – in military slang a yearning to be decorated with the Knights' Cross – and we had better take care.

In the subsequent patrol we went in the dark northwards through the woods in the direction of the Küstrin forester's house. We came across a deep Soviet trench system that we were able to cross, but were then caught in their flares and hit by overwhelming firepower. Second-Lieutenant Fleischer sympathised with us over our failed attempt. The same had happened to him on his first attempt, and success only came with a repeat attempt. With this kind of assessment our young company commander won our confidence, something that was not always in evidence.[26]

The morning fight at the Cellulose Factory, skirmishes at Warnick on the other wing of the Neustadt, and the first rounds into the Altstadt, had renewed unrest among those of the population still remaining. The news spread with the speed of the wind that a train was about to leave Kietz, even though there was no organised means of passing information, and persuaded many that this was perhaps the last chance to leave. Others appeared still uncertain, or believed the rumours that the Kurland Army had landed in Stettin and would soon roll up the enemy lines along the Oder.[27]

The bulk of the 1st Mechanised Corps (2nd Guards Tank Army) arrived that morning, and a further small bridgehead was established near Genschmar in the Kalenziger Bunst by a rifle battalion of the 19th Motorised Rifle Brigade. The newly arrived 1st Battalion of the 35th Panzergrenadier Regiment immediately attacked, driving the Soviets back to the dykes, but were unable to go beyond and clear the bridgehead completely. The Soviets then mounted several counterattacks towards Genschmar in which they lost four tanks. Further German reinforcements, the 303rd 'Döberitz' and 309th 'Berlin' Infantry Divisions, also arrived in the Oderbruch that day, albeit piecemeal as the trainloads dictated, and were deployed south of the 25th Panzergrenadier Division.[28]

An important event in the fortress this day was the replacement of General Adolf Raegener as commandant by Himmler's nominee, the 41-year-old SS-Gruppenführer and SS-Lieutenant-General Heinz Reinefarth. This appointment was made against the wishes of the 9th Army and the Army General Staff (OKH), for Reinefarth had reached his general's rank not on the military ladder but in the uniformed police in which he had had a meteoric career, although he had in fact been awarded the Knights' Cross of the Iron Cross as an infantry platoon commander in the invasion of France in 1940 when called up for military service. He was known for his role in the brutal crushing of the Warsaw uprising in the summer and autumn of 1944, where his performance as a battle-group commander had earned him the Oak Leaves to his Knights' Cross. 'A good police officer, but no general' was the later comment of Colonel-General Heinz Guderian, the Army Chief of the General Staff. After the war the commander of the 9th Army wrote of him that 'despite the best of will, the difficult task of leading and organising the defence was in no way improved'. Himmler, however, saw in him a man of fanatical perseverance, whom he believed would make a fighting fortress garrison out of the early chaos with his toughness and intellect. Consequently, Himmler would not change him. In like fashion, Reinefarth went on to appoint a colonel of Feldgendarmerie who was totally inexperienced in combat operations to command the Neustadt Defence Sector.[29]

For General Raegener the timing of the handover could not have been more advantageous, for he could leave without reproach, having repelled the first Soviet attack with what at first had been a hopelessly weak garrison and held all his positions, the Cellulose Factory having been retaken that morning. He moved to Podelzig on the Reitwein Spur, where he began organising a division from miscellaneous units in the area, conscripting his staff from elderly local landowners hastily pressed back into their reservist uniforms.[30]

The new commandant was not even allowed to enjoy his lunch undisturbed. Several mortar bombs landed one after another in the Altstadt, some near his command post, but inflicting no great damage. At the same time it was reported to him that the enemy had now reached the south of the town. Here the flooded meadows limited the Soviet troops essentially to the two causeways. The chaussee from Sonnenburg ran like a dyke through the low-lying land and, being visible from the fortress, was virtually impassable in daylight. A bucket elevator standing about 2 kilometres from the town was the only construction on the road for a considerable distance, and had been developed into a strongpoint. The other chaussee coming in from Göritz ran straight through thinly occupied fields and meadows before it joined the Oder dyke at the small Bienenhof hamlet, some 2 kilometres from the town, and continued to the Altstadt. This property had been occupied at the last minute by Infantry Battalion 500, an experimental unit.[31]

Reinefarth's first situation report, issued on 2 February 1945, read:

Enemy attempting to encircle Küstrin from the north and south and to gain river crossings via the main road (railway) with attacks from all sides. The enemy attacked the bridges near the Bienenhof (south of Küstrin) with 5 tanks but were repelled with the loss of 3 tanks. Own counterattack to retake Warnick stalled by heavy enemy fire. Enemy attack from south-west and east on Sonnenburg led to encirclement of garrison. Tschernow in enemy hands.[32]

Officer Cadet Alfred Kraus recalled:

Half frozen and dead tired, one or two evenings later, we were moved towards Alt Drewitz. The road where we were deployed was only built up on one side. Undeveloped land extended to the south-west and beyond it the Warthe could be seen behind the Cellulose Factory.

That evening a young girl appeared from a nearby farm and asked for our help. She had stayed behind alone with the cattle. We warned her and advised her to go to Küstrin and on to the west, but she went back saying: 'I simply cannot leave the cattle to their fate!'

Originally we were meant to attack along the road leading in a north-westerly direction, but our company commander, Lieutenant Schellenberg, received a change in orders. In our place a Hungarian infantry battalion from the Stülpnagel Barracks would conduct the counterattack. A few hours later the poor chaps brought their wounded back crying. We sat on the doorsteps of the houses, knowing what we had been spared.

Entering the houses was strongly forbidden but, after three or four days of being out in the open in heavy frost and without proper sleep, I went into a house with my friend Nils Fauck, where we fell on the beds on the first floor without removing our boots and overcoats. We slept until our screaming sergeant woke us with: 'Stupid! Court martial!' and other threats. This had no effect, as we were still tired. Our company was given a bottle of almost frozen Sekt per man and then was supposed to attack the Cellulose Factory across open fields in the dark and occupy it. No shots were fired and we encountered no Russians. We stumbled across two dead horses at the factory gates. I was sent as a runner towards the south to establish contact with the forward platoon there as dawn was breaking. In unfamiliar territory I came across 200 unarmed Hungarians sitting behind a plank fence. They pointed the way to the factory for me. Suddenly I saw some motionless men lying in a row. When they failed to react to my call, I took courage and approached them. They were about 20 dead Hungarians. A white rag hung from a stick. By the time I reached the factory both our platoons had already linked up without encountering any Russians.

We occupied a position in front of the factory's wood store

with a field of fire to the north-west across open land between the Warthe and Alt Drewitz. There were two shot-up Soviet tanks of American construction on the factory premises. A Volkssturm man, presumably an engineer from the factory as he appeared here several times, had knocked them out with a Panzerfaust. He showed me the way it had happened. Neither tank was burnt out, nor did they contain corpses, but there was a completely flattened Russian nearby. So we were able to help ourselves to cigars, bread and schnapps from the tanks. Further on we found on the premises a 105mm anti-aircraft gun with all its equipment, including numerous anti-aircraft machine guns on tripods, which were slow-firing but used normal infantry ammunition, so that each section got its own machine guns. Gradually with the help of the unarmed but friendly Hungarians we built up our positions and even received some Panzerfausts. The Hungarians were withdrawn once the construction work was finished, but I do not know where they went.

Once the period of frost was over, the soggy soil of the open terrain between the Cellulose Factory and the Drewitzer Unterweg to Alt Drewitz prevented the construction of any positions there. Consequently we were secured at night by having listening posts. During the daytime the open terrain was fully exposed and within our field of fire, as well as fire from the Cellulose Factory and also the Drewitzer Unterweg. Several times the Russians infiltrated behind us but were always driven back.

The company command post was incomprehensibly located not in the Cellulose Factory but far back on Plantagenstrasse near the Potato Meal Factory in one of the modern three-storey housing blocks. As runner, I was responsible for exchanging our radio batteries. Once I encountered our quartermaster-sergeant in a drunken state with the company headquarters troop shooting at empty Sekt bottles with pistols. I was given a rocket for not saluting him properly.[33]

Lieselotte Christiansen later described her experiences as a 13-year-old child:

When the war reached Küstrin, I lived in Warnick.
On the 31st January the first Soviet tanks penetrated as far as

the centre of the Neustadt, but were successfully repulsed and things became quiet again for a while. One day later, on the 1st February, at about 2100 hours it started up again and we heard the first shots. We people from Langardesmühlen decided to move into the cellars of an old villa belonging to Max Falckenberg, in front of which was a spacious park, which would later prove useful to us. The sounds of firing diminished at about midnight, and a German NCO appeared in the cellars and told us that the Russians were in Landsberg. As the distance from Küstrin to Landsberg was about 45 kilometres, we felt safe for the moment. But this was an error, for shortly afterwards we heard Russian voices and the firing started up again. The Russians were lying well back in the park and firing at the villa, which had been occupied by our troops. As well as he could, the NCO kept us informed about the situation outside, where there had been many killed on both sides.

Shortly before 0700 hours on the morning of the 2nd February, a German soldier appeared and told us that the NCO had been killed. There was a short truce in the fighting during which we were advised to leave as quickly as possible, which we did. We came to Schiffbauerstrasse. Near the Bennewitz abattoir a man told us that Küstrin had been surrounded and the bridges destroyed, so we stayed in Schiffbauerstrasse and experienced the siege of Küstrin until the end of February with constant shelling, bombing, dead soldiers and even Stalin-Organs one day. We were sitting in the kitchen when there was suddenly an ear-splitting din. The house next door had been pulverised. My mother and other people from Langardes-mühlen were trapped in the cellar and had to be released through the cellar windows.

From the middle of February we got a daily newspaper called *Feste Küstrin*, reporting important events in the town and including the Wehrmacht Report.[34]

Chapter Six

The Russians Close In

With the arrival of the 16th Anti-Aircraft Artillery Division, the 8th Guards Army was able to resume its crossing operation in daylight on 3 February. The loss of three aircraft in the first attack of the day obliged the Luftwaffe to change tactics from attacks en masse to individual sorties. Consequently, most of the infantry divisions of the 4th Guards Rifle Corps and the 79th Guards Rifle Division (28th Guards Rifle Corps) crossed the river with minimal losses, taking their artillery observers with them, although the guns had to remain on the east bank for the time being, as no bridging or ferrying facilities had come forwards with the 8th Guards Army's vanguard.

That day saw the rapid and virtually unopposed expansion and unification of three small bridgeheads into one extending for several kilometres from Reitwein to Kietz and reaching as far forward as the Frankfurt–Küstrin railway line, which thus became unusable. The 35th Guards Rifle Division went on to occupy the southern part of Kietz and some terrain to the west of the suburb, while the 47th Guards Rifle Division occupied Neu Manschnow about noon and moved on to block the Küstrin–Seelow highway (Reichsstrasse 1) in Manschnow itself.[1] The following day Soviet scouts were seen as far forward as the Golzow–Alt Tucheband road.[2]

Zhukov's eyes were still firmly on Berlin, despite the previously mentioned deployment of most of his forces to clear Pomerania, as the following orders sent to Chuikov show. It is interesting to note that there is no mention of Küstrin, from which one can presume that it was considered too difficult an obstacle to overcome under the immediate circumstances, and that adequate bridging could be provided across the Oder at Reitwein and Kienitz.

On the 4th February we received a Front HQ directive setting the date for the offensive. It said: 'The Front's troops shall

97

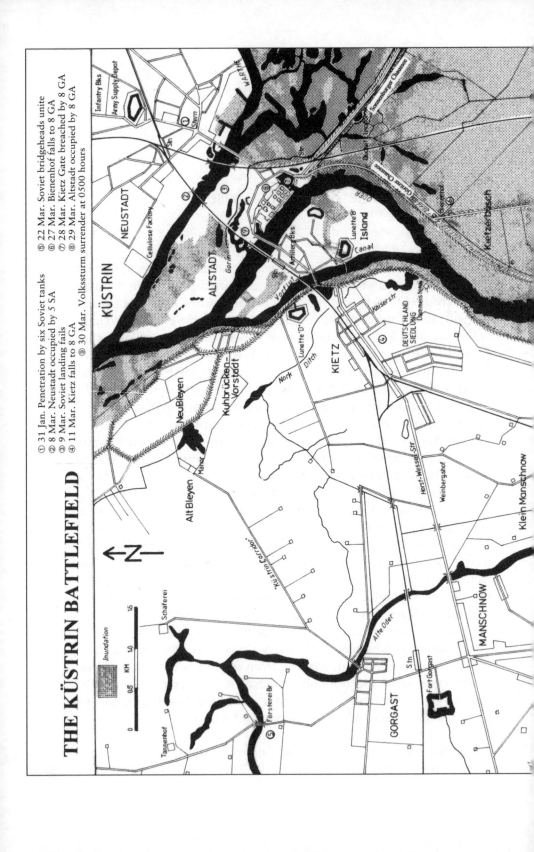

THE KÜSTRIN BATTLEFIELD

① 31 Jan. Penetration by six Soviet tanks
② 8 Mar. Neustadt occupied by 5 SA
③ 9 Mar. Soviet landing fails
④ 11 Mar. Kietz falls to 8 GA

⑤ 22 Mar. Soviet bridgeheads unite
⑥ 27 Mar. Bienenhof falls to 8 GA
⑦ 28 Mar. Kietz Gate breached by 8 GA
⑧ 29 Mar. Altstadt occupied by 8 GA
⑨ 30 Mar. Volkssturm surrender at 0500 hours

consolidate their success by active operations in the next six days, bring up all units that have fallen behind, replenish fuel to two allowances per vehicle and ammunition to two establishments, and in a swift assault take Berlin on the 15th–16th February.

In the consolidation period, i.e. 4th–8th February, it is necessary that:

a) The 5th, 8th, 69th and 33rd Armies should capture bridgeheads on the west bank of the Oder. It is desirable for the 8th Guards and 69th Armies to have a common bridgehead between Küstrin and Frankfurt. If all goes well, the 5th and 8th Armies should link their bridgeheads;

b) The 1st Polish and the 47th and 61st Armies, the 2nd Tank Army and the 2nd Cavalry Corps should hurl the enemy back behind the line Ratzebuhr–Falkenburg–Stargard–Altdamm–Oder. Following this, they should leave a covering force pending the arrival of the armies of the 2nd Byelorussian Front, and regroup on the Oder for a breakthrough;

c) Between the 7th and 8th February it is necessary to complete the elimination of the enemy grouping in Posen and Schneidemühl;

d) The means of reinforcement for a breakthrough shall in the main be the same as those available at present;

e) By the 10th February the tank forces and self-propelled artillery shall complete repairs and maintenance so as to put all available resources back into action;

f) The Air Force shall complete deployment and have fuel on the airfields for not fewer than six allowances per aircraft;

g) The Front's logistical services and the Army rear units shall be fully prepared by the 9th–10th February for the decisive phase of the operation.'[3]

Yet, as Professor Erickson summed up the situation:

For his immediate purposes Zhukov could count on four rifle armies and two tank armies drawn up along 'the Berlin axis', but two of the rifle armies – 8th Guards and 69th – had detached part of their forces to deal with the fortress of Posen, while Berzarin's 5th Shock was besieging Küstrin with elements of that army. On the embattled right flank the 1st Polish, 3rd

Shock and 61st Armies were forced to leave more divisions to reduce the fortress of Schneidermühl and other strongpoints.

Losses and shortages further denuded Zhukov's assault forces. Chuikov could only commit 50 per cent of the 8th Guards for the proposed attack on Berlin (the other half of his army was presently held back at Poznan); battle losses had made heavy inroads into Chuikov's strength, with regiments down to two battalions and the companies reduced to an average strength of 22–45 men. Ammunition was becoming alarmingly scarce and Chuikov had fallen back on using captured German guns with captured ammunition. Berzarin's 5th Shock Army and the 33rd and 69th Armies also reported growing shortages of ammunition and increasingly depleted ranks. Katukov's 1st Guards Tank Army mustered 737 tanks and SP guns at the time of breaking through to the Oder, of which 567 were in working order.[4]

Almost at the same time the Soviet troops in the southern bridgehead launched their first major offensive. There was no longer a secure front line, as the German formations clung on to the villages and isolated farms in the almost coverless Oderbruch. Thus Hathenow – almost 5 kilometres from the Oder on the Frankfurt–Küstrin road – was quickly developed into a strongpoint, as was Rathstock, 2 kilometres to the north, but this was soon lost. A few kilometres further on Soviet troops reached and crossed Reichsstrasse 1 near Manschnow, only being stopped when they reached the parallel-running railway. Over-hastily mounted counterattacks failed. Küstrin's rail and road connections to the hinterland had been severed.

There followed some critical hours during which it was doubtful whether the fortress troops could hold their lines on the southern edge of Kietz and whether they could extend them to the west. However, it was to their benefit that the northern bridgehead remained quiet. The unusually early thaw with its accompanying mud in the Oderbruch valley meant that, with the lack of firm roads, no great counteroffensive could be expected in the near future, and no tanks had appeared in the bridgeheads as yet. The strips of land occupied by the 5th Shock Army to the north and the 8th Guards Army to the south of the fortress were still separated from each other, but at the narrowest point were only 3 kilometres apart, posing an acute and visible threat.

The Soviet occupation of Reitwein attracted considerable harassment from Stuka dive-bombers and from the German artillery, a battery of which was now located in Sachsendorf, where the roads were still congested with refugees, prisoners of war and concentration camp inmates on the move.[5]

For days now the only source of information for the population had been wild rumours. The news that the route to the west was blocked spread more quickly than most. There could be no doubt: there were enough wounded returning to the dressing stations in the town, while all those who had hoped to get a train from Kietz railway station had also returned. No one had been able to leave.[6]

This Saturday, 3 February, however, was the kind of day one sees as a forecast of spring after a long hard winter. The sun was still low in the sky but there was already a pleasant warmth from a cloudless sky, and the last traces of snow were melting away. Some women went out with their babies in prams but kept close to the buildings, aware of the need for flight in an emergency, and, as the only concession to the changed circumstances, never crossing the open squares.

Suddenly there was the sound of aircraft engines and a few heavy explosions marred this peaceful picture for a moment, but the word quickly spread that these were German aircraft and one could see them attacking Reitwein from the Oder bastions. Several dozen people actually gathered on the walls of the Wallkrone to watch a group of Ju 87s and Me 109s flying around and dropping bombs on targets out of sight. Unusually heavy anti-aircraft gunfire filled the sky with sparkling belts of tracer and there were grey-black clouds of smoke from the explosions. Those sightseers busy revelling in memories of Stukas in the 'Lightning War' days suddenly fell silent, and were among the first to flee when mortar bombs ripped up the brittle ice at the foot of the bastion. Soon afterwards civilians were barred from the Katte walls, which had been made into a promenade above the river and were popular for taking a stroll.[7]

Luftwaffe Officer Cadet Sergeant Helmut Schmidt witnessed this air activity on 3 February:

At long last our Luftwaffe appeared in the sky. A squadron of Ju 87s made some dashing attacks on targets to the east and south-east of the town. We could watch the dive bombing of the Stukas well from the railway embankment. Their attacks were followed by heavy detonations and mighty clouds of smoke, while our railway hut shook as if in an earthquake. The Ju 87s did not appear to lack for targets.

There was still no sign of the Russian Air Force. Certainly it had not been idle in the meantime. Presumably it had to prepare and occupy airfields nearer to the front line. In my opinion the enemy fighters and bombers would soon be making our life difficult.[8]

The outpost at the bucket elevator on the Sonnenburg Chaussee was lost to the Soviets that day and immediately afterwards an anti-tank gun started firing from here at the flak positions on the Warthe side of the Altstadt. Then the firing died down in the immediate area, enabling even the most cautious to venture further from their dwellings than they had previously dared. Now that few of the shops scattered around town were open, shopping entailed going some distance, and the older people in particular tried to avoid the risk of finding themselves under fire.

The fortress situation report for 3 February read:

Enemy resumed attacks on Küstrin from north, east and south-east. Early morning a company-sized attack on the bucket lift (1 km south-west of southern Küstrin exit). The strongpoint fell with the loss of almost all the garrison in enemy hands. In a battalion-sized attack either side of the Zorndorf–Küstrin road on Height 63, the enemy gained about 100m ground. Enemy breach south-west of Warnick cleared by counterattack. Enemy thrust from a southerly direction on the west bank of the Oder opposite Küstrin.

The next morning the situation report read:

Enemy thrust in platoon strength south-west of Warnick repelled. Strong enemy reconnaissance activity and lively artillery fire from both sides.

This was followed by a further report later that day:

Attack against southern and south-western front of Küstrin west of the Oder. Attack via Gorgast and Alt Bleyen towards Kietz blocked by Oder Corps.

The anti-tank gunfire from the bucket elevator generated the first official evacuation. Some unauthorised moves had already taken place, such as tenants of an upper storey moving down into vacated accommodation that appeared safer. Most shots had gone over the flak positions hidden by a railway embankment and hit a block of flats near the Catholic church. There were no casualties, but some housing was so badly damaged that alternative accommodation had to be found. This was, as were all such tasks, undertaken by the Nazi welfare organisation NSV, whose local office now took on the roles of supervising housing and social welfare with practically unlimited and only partially defined powers. The emergency administration formed from the fragmented magistrates and NSDAP district offices acted in a similar fashion. Abandoned apartments in the less damaged streets of the Altstadt were taken over, opened by an officially appointed locksmith and the homeless allocated to them.[9]

A combat team of officer cadets named after its commander, Captain Kain, was tasked with retaking the bucket elevator on the Sonnenburger Chaussee and eliminating the threat from there. The Soviet garrison was later reckoned at 103 men with ten machine guns and a lone anti-tank gun, the restricted artillery content of such an exposed position indicating that the Soviets were still short of heavy weapons in this sector. The chaussee, set on a narrow dyke running parallel with the railway line, was surrounded by the waters flooding the Oderbruch and covering the meadows on either side, and was clearly marked by a regularly spaced alley of trees. It was in clear view of a 105mm flak battery that had been deployed in an allotment garden and meadow just outside the fortress walls. Even the distinctive building housing the pumping station was clearly visible from there. On such a narrow approach the attackers had to be aware of the guns behind them.

Heavy Soviet defensive fire inflicted severe casualties on Kain's combat team but, under cover of the flak, the battle group finally reached its goal, a shot-up brick building and a few rifle pits and machine-gun nests that then changed hands for a few hours before the area had to be abandoned once more while it was still visible from the flak position, for without covering fire Kain's men would stand no chance against a Soviet night attack.[10]

The first shots of a firing squad rang out this Sunday when fourteen Ostarbeiter (eastern forced labourers) were executed without investigation, trial or sentence. A two-sentence notice stating that they had been caught plundering was intended to counter public indignation over the increasing number of buildings being broken into and ransacked. The forced labourers still remaining in the town were forbidden to leave their huts between 1800 hours and 0600 hours under pain of the severest punishment. They were having to work all day long on the defences as the businesses they had been allocated to had now come to a halt. However, the plundering continued.[11]

A Soviet thrust along the eastern railway line reached the line Gorgast–Bleyen on 5 February, thus cutting off Küstrin, its last remaining route over the fields being made unusable. The 5th Shock Army desperately tried to get some tanks across the river to reinforce its bridgehead. Several fell through the ice, but four T-34s managed to cross, enabling the Soviets to extend their bridgehead at Genschmar up to a line running through the centre of the village.[12]

Elsewhere on the fortress's front line the day was relatively quiet. Skirmishes that broke out here and there were limited to company-strength actions and were hardly noticed from behind the screen of buildings in the town. At this point there were some 20,000 people – soldiers, Volkssturm and civilians – in the town. Most of the civilian population, including those who had fled here from the Anglo-American air attacks, had been able to leave the town in good time, but some 8,000–10,000 civilians had been overtaken by events and remained surrounded in the town.

On 5 February the NSDAP county office produced its first news-sheet, four type-written pages roneoed on cheap wartime paper. Half of it was devoted to the Wehrmacht Report, followed by statements on the local military situation using the same sort of vocabulary, but there were also announcements such as the addresses of the three civilian doctors still practising, one each in the Altstadt, Neustadt and Kietz, and a request to hand in all battery radios. The latter were carefully guarded by their few fortunate owners, for other sets could not be used for lack of electricity.

Nevertheless, the NSDAP district leadership was determined to take over this unexpected monopoly of information in order to resume its influence over the population. This news-sheet was sent almost entirely to offices, staff and dormitory accommodation, and some were stuck on walls and fences, and there was already a plan to produce a regularly printed newspaper. How many people this reached is unknown; one rough estimate was 8,000. Flight and Volkssturm service had torn apart the block and cell Party structure during the last weeks of January, and in the confusion of the first fighting the last remnants of control over the lives of ordinary civilians had completely come off the rails.

This was of little significance to the population. There were still some basic foodstuffs in a few of the shops, naturally available only with ration cards, and the sewage and water systems were still functioning as normal. Mortar fire was still sporadic, more tiresome than dangerous if one did not go out into the open, and aircraft had still to show themselves. Thus casualties among the civilian population until now had not been due to enemy action. The official deaths register recorded about a dozen suicides under the date of 31 January when the first shots were fired. Some had not been found by chance until much later and no one knew how much more work awaited the undertakers.

Pedestrians and vehicles moved virtually unhindered once the usual midday harassing fire was over. Fortress staff and Party officials were already describing the 5th as a 'quiet day' when at almost exactly 1500 hours a series of heavy explosions shook the town. The few people strolling around hastened to take cover, the threat of the blasts driving them down into the cellars, but then the explosions broke off as abruptly as they had begun. Only those with front-line experience knew what this was: artillery salvoes.

Mushrooms of smoke rose into the clear sky above the Neustadt in rapid succession, distinctly apart at first, then combining as a grey wall at the foot of which a rose-coloured glow quickly spread as the first bright red flames took hold. A number of 130mm explosive and incendiary shells had hit about three dozen houses. Within a few minutes most of them were alight from the roof to the ground floor. Showers of sparks ignited curtains, while broken furniture and rafters were scattered over the streets. A witness to this event reported:

We were sitting down to afternoon coffee, having taken the precaution of going down into the cellar, which I with my war experience considered safer. Suddenly an explosion shook our house, others following shortly after again and again, and whitewash fell from the ceiling. After a short while it was suddenly quiet again, but now there was a frightful sound of burning. We left everything and ran upstairs to be confronted by a horrible sight. Our house on the edge of the Neumarkt, right opposite the water tower, had not been hit, but several neighbouring buildings were ablaze. The tram depot was completely destroyed and there were craters on the market place. Several doors and windows had been torn off their hinges, and the paper was hanging off the wall in strips. All the bottles of conserves in the dining room were broken by the blast. The roof had been torn off and the balcony was only hanging on to the façade as indistinguishable iron rods. The Radio-Helm building was in flames. Except for our house, no building on the Neumarkt had survived the bombardment.

This was not such an unusual sight for most of the firemen, for most had been involved in the air raids on Berlin. Following the first such raids in November 1942, the simple Küstrin fire engines, like others in a wide area around Berlin, had been modernised on a generous scale. Then in the summer of 1944 they conducted an exercise in rescuing trapped people from a narrow street in the Altstadt known as the Wassergasse. Now the route to the deployment site was much closer. The smoke and flame-engulfed quarter was isolated at street junctions and gaps between the buildings to stop the spread of fire to the rest of the neighbourhood. The ruins in the Neumarkt, in the neighbourhood of the town centre around the Stern, and the streets leading to the railway station, gradually cooled down.

Meanwhile the inhabitants of the affected area had taken shelter with friends and relations or had requisitioned empty properties for themselves. No one can say how many people were affected by the explosions, or if all reached the cellars in time. Only two severely injured were reported.[13]

Under General Reinefarth the fortress area was divided into two defence sectors, Altstadt and Neustadt. The larger sector consisted of the Neustadt on the right bank of the Warthe, where the majority of the population lived and most of the military establishments such as barracks, drill squares and exercise areas, hospital, magazine, bakery and supply depot were located, as was the Neues Werke bastion north-east of the main railway station. This sector also contained the town's gas works, water works, a sewage farm, a civil hospital, the cemetery and a large industrial complex.

Despite his total lack of experience in such a role, and in the face of protests from Headquarters 9th Army, Reinefarth appointed fellow policeman Colonel Walter of the Feldgendarmerie as commander of the Neustadt Defence Sector, a decision he was later to regret with the words: 'For lack of relevant previous experience, the situation was consequently not mastered. There was no other officer available as sector commander.' That there was no senior military officer of adequate rank and experience for this role in the garrison is hard to believe.

The Neustadt Defence Sector was overlooked by Height 63, which provided the besiegers with observation over the town. With their backs to the Warthe and Oder, a full two-thirds of the garrison awaited the enemy attack here in positions that ran from the Cellulose Factory, through divided Alt Drewitz, then around a bulge to the north, east via the Küstrin Forestry Office and across the Zorndorfer Chaussee, then in an up and down curve to the south-south-west (about 500 metres east of the water works) to the Jungfern Canal at Warnick.

The remaining parts of the town formed the Altstadt Defence Sector. This included the Altstadt with the Island, Kietz and Kuhbrücken, and for a while also Neu Bleyen and the dyke-enclosed area to Alt Bleyen. The Kietz and Bleyen areas were apportioned between the fortress and the 'pipeline' defenders according to the situation. The sector commander was 55-year-old Major Otto Wegner, in civilian life the manager of the city administration office of Schneidemühl, whose military experience had been in the infantry. He had been awarded the Iron Cross 1st and 2nd Class in the First World War, and the bar to both Iron Crosses in the Second World War during the Polish campaign. In the Russian campaign he had commanded the 1st Battalion, Infantry Regiment 96, of the 32nd Infantry Division, for which he was awarded the German Cross in Gold. At the beginning of 1945 he was given command of Replacement Battalion 4 in Kolberg and, upon release of the code-word 'Gneisenau', went with it to the Filehne area on the Netze River 10 kilometres east of Kreuz, where his battalion became part of the 'Woldenberg' Division and took part in the subsequent retreat to Küstrin.[14]

The spring floods, preceded by the thaw, turned the little Altstadt into an island. In the east the flooded area, several kilometres wide from the Warthe to the Oder, was only broken by the dykes carrying the two railway lines and the two chaussees. Field emplacements on these narrow causeways secured the approaches. Where the chaussee from Göritz joined the Oder dyke some 2 kilometres from the citadel lay the Bienenhof outpost, which became the focus of constant skirmishing. It was defended mainly by members of Probation Battalion 500, whom Reinefarth described as 'Küstrin's best troops'. The Bienenhof was often cited in his morning and daily reports. From here, opposite the Dammeisterei (dyke master's house), the defensive positions ran parallel to and not far from the Oder dyke about 1,200 metres north, crossed the Göritz railway embankment to Kietzerbusch Railway Halt, then went further north curving east to where the road and railway bridges crossed the Warthe.

The Altstadt offered good defensive possibilities provided that the defenders could counter enemy artillery and air attacks with the equivalent weapons and intensity of fire, which was not the case. Further disadvantages for the Germans derived from the crammed nature of the Altstadt and the inflammable nature of many of the old buildings due to their high wood content, as well as the fragility of the century-old casemates that were not capable of withstanding heavy calibre bombs and shells. Keeping the Altstadt, Bienenhof and Kietz in German hands depended upon holding the Island and the two ancient lunettes in the Pappelhorst thickets.[15] The small suburb of Kietz on the west bank of the Vorflut Canal protected Küstrin's precarious supply route to the link with Gorgast at this point. Hard fighting could be expected here, as the besiegers would try to take the road and railway bridges over the Vorflut Canal to separate the fortress from its line of supply. The German positions in Kietz extended from the railway embankment (here connected to the 2nd Battalion, 119 Panzergrenadier Regiment, 25th Panzergrenadier Division) to the western end of Kietz as far as the Dammeisterei at the entrance to the Vorflut Canal.

Throughout the fortress great efforts were made to improve the defensive positions and provide protection from enemy fire and bombs. This involved not only soldiers but also people who had seldom if ever been concerned with the principle 'fight and dig', especially the Volkssturm, civilians, forced foreign labourers from the factories and prisoners of war. The clearing of fields of fire and the reduction of fire risks in the town's narrow streets was conducted by the sappers.[16]

Suddenly permission to evacuate the civilian population was received. Gauleiter Emil Stürtz telephoned it through on the morning of 4 February, stressing the need for action, but the public heard nothing of this telephone call, not even a rumour. It seems that Reinefarth must have suppressed any mention of such an evacuation because of the sheer difficulty of implementing it at this stage. The evacuees would have had to run the gauntlet of the pipeline under the noses of the Soviets to reach the comparative safety of the German front line. Next day a Soviet thrust reached the line Gorgast–Bleyen, thus cutting off Küstrin from the last route over the fields.[17]

Although isolated from the hinterland, Küstrin was not entirely cut off. The Soviet forces from the bridgeheads south and north of Küstrin had acted one after another, but lacked the strength to effect a proper union between Bleyen and Gorgast. Consequently both sides tried to hold on to the positions they held or had reached. The besieged garrison was unable to gain a way out, although the 9th Army was banking on the 21st Panzer Division now arriving from the west to improve the situation in its favour. The Soviet 5th Shock and 8th Guards Armies had orders to dig in on the Oder while most of the rest of the 1st Byelorussian Front was engaged in Pomerania. Consequently the disputed flat terrain of the Oderbruch was ruled by machine guns, anti-tank guns and mortars during the day, both German and Soviet, while at night patrols of reconnaissance and storm troops from both sides tried to prevent their opponents from infiltrating and establishing themselves further forward.

In any case it was obvious that there would be no major attack on the fortress in the immediate future, and Reinefarth could breathe again. The strongest Soviet blows had so far been directed on the town with only some minor subsidiary actions. The German deployment remained substantially unchanged. The troops were a colourful collection, including even the remains of some Turkomen and North Caucasian battalions, and had at best a combatant strength of 8,196 men (not identical to the almost double ration strength), an acceptable potential force. The increased firepower of the flak batteries, now consisting of twenty-four heavy 105mm guns and the same number of medium 20mm and 37mm guns, was the most valuable asset, but in inadequate positions. These batteries formed the backbone of the defence sometimes even in the foremost locations, their crews mainly consisting of the youngest RAD boys and Luftwaffe auxiliaries with no front-line experience.

On the morning of 6 February the commandant unexpectedly issued orders for that part of the Altstadt around the Schloss bordered by the market and Berliner Strasse to be evacuated by noon. The only exceptions were in such establishments as the post office and shops in order to prevent looting. The police were made responsible for informing the inhabitants and meeting the evacuation deadline, the NSV for accommodating those evacuated. No official reason was given for this action, leaving it a matter of speculation. One possible explanation was that Reinefarth's staff believed the smoking chimneys acted as aiming points for the Soviet artillery observers, so the area around the command post had to be evacuated and declared a smoke-free zone.

The townsfolks' reaction to this order ranged from anxious questions about where they could go and how they would find somewhere to live, to angry remarks about the conduct of the war. The police who had to go from door to door were not in an enviable position. They were mainly elderly men, including some with friends and relations among those being evacuated, so none of these adverse comments was reported.

Many evacuees appeared outside the town hall without their baggage wanting to know where their future accommodation was to be; they wanted to see it before deciding what to take with them. In any case they had to take all items of value, for they were instructed to leave the doors of their vacated premises open. Everyone knew what that meant: by the next day there would not be a single drawer that had not been rummaged through.

The allocation to new quarters took hours. The NSV had only two of its normal staff of three, assisted by young messengers. The whole of the remaining Party apparatus, although concentrated in the town hall, remained out of sight, leaving the people to their fate. The lists of available accommodation that had been carefully compiled over the previous days were already out of date in many cases, for the homeless from the burnt-out part of the Neustadt had taken them over, or attic dwellers had moved into less dangerous lower storeys, and many of the beds had been removed from the premises the day before. It was evening before the last people had moved into their new accommodation. Many of the old people had brought with them only the most urgent items, as much as they could carry or pull behind them on a handcart. Nobody had offered to help them. They intended returning to their homes the next day to collect more stuff, but they would only too often find empty shelves.[18]

Reinefarth reported for 6 February: 'Small enemy breaches on northern side of Neustadt. Fighting in progress to clear them. Several enemy attacks in the Kietz area repelled.' The Neustadt once more became the target of an early morning barrage on 7 February from Stalin-Organs. The buildings along Zorndorfer Strasse and some individual houses on the roads leading to the town centre and on the Landsberger Strasse and Schützenstrasse turn-offs to the railway station were in flames. The fire brigade had to defend its own premises when its Neustadt station became flanked by burning buildings, but escaped unscathed.

Tumbled walls, torn-up tramlines and burning stock in the shops made Zorndorfer Strasse impassable as far as the Stern. Shards of glass from shattered shop fronts, broken mirrors, torn bedding and bent chairs lying in the roadway recalled the November night six-and-a-quarter years before when brown-shirted mobs had demolished Jewish premises, thrown the furniture of Jewish citizens into the streets and set light to the synagogue near the railway station. Such recollections were naturally not to be found in the War Diary that the Party officials had ordered to be kept. An elderly civil servant was acting as the chronicler, his task being to record daily the latest information from the Party offices, police and fire brigade.

Totally unexpected was the arrival in Küstrin of about a dozen women, children and elderly people from a village on the east bank of the Oder. They arrived with a few household goods on two horse-drawn wagons. Overtaken by the front, they had been living 'on the other side' for a week. The women had been allowed to cross the Soviet lines to buy food when their supplies ran out, but had been stopped by German sentries who had orders to prevent anyone entering the town. The Soviet commander responsible for the area had ordered them to leave, giving them the choice of heading for the hinterland or going into the beleaguered town.[19]

From 7 to 10 February the 21st Panzer Division, newly allotted to this sector, encountered bitter resistance in its attacks northwards out of Gorgast to Küstrin, but it broke through the Soviet encirclement and opened a narrow passage, and the first supplies were driven through to the fortress that night. This 'corridor', as the opening was called, began in the south near Gorgast and ended in the north in the

Genschmar area, its width varying from 3 to 5 kilometres; it was about 6 kilometres long, running from Gorgast, via the Bleyen manor farm (Gut Bleyen) to the Vorflut Canal railway bridge. It was only usable at night and heavy loads could be carried only by tracked vehicles.[20]

Erich Zeschke described his experiences as a 'pipeline' truck driver:

In 1945 I belonged to 6 Company, Transport Battalion 532. In February and March, until the final surrounding of Küstrin, we were stationed in Mühlenstrasse, Seelow, while the battalion was in Müncheberg. We had about 20 tracked vehicles, two- and four-ton Opels, which the soldiers nicknamed 'Mules'. Our task was conveying supply deliveries from Seelow to Küstrin and bringing back people and materials. We only drove at night in complete darkness.

We collected ammunition and mail from the station in Seelow. Then we followed Reichsstrasse 1 to the crossroads from Alt Tucheband and Golzow, where we turned left and crossed the Berlin–Küstrin railway line, leaving Golzow station to our right. From Golzow we turned right and followed the Oderbruch Chaussee to Gorgast. Here we crossed the Alte Oder and entered the 'corridor' – a narrow land connection to the beleaguered fortress of Küstrin. The length of our route from Gorgast to the railway bridge over the Vorflut Canal in Kietz was about 6 kilometres. At first the route was along a road and led south-eastwards of the Alt Bleyen manor farm over the fields. From Kuhbrücken we then drove south along the dyke road, passed the track junction and then on to the railway bridge over the Vorflut Canal.

In order to avoid Soviet artillery fire, we drove as follows: Stop before the bridge. Each truck crossed the bridge individu- ally. The interval between vehicles varied from half to two minutes and even longer pauses under heavy fire. Then we were on the Island and often across the Oder to the Altstadt. Mainly we went to two places, the Artillery Barracks and another complex in which equipment was stored. The ammunition was unloaded at a park-like place. Often I had mail to hand over to the fortress commandant's staff.

On the return journey we took wounded, six to eight men per truck, and ten to twelve light wounded. When there was still room, we took items of equipment and raw materials, such as leather. We unloaded again in Seelow. Except for a few wounded, we had no casualties to complain about.

Our last trip took place on the night of 21/22 March, after which a Soviet offensive shut off the fortress again, this time for good.[21]

The news-sheet of 8 February reported: 'The army commander-in-chief has expressed his appreciation to the brave garrison of Küstrin for its fierce resistance until now and its considerable success.' The local situation report noted 'lively reconnaissance and assault troop activity' and gave enemy losses as 113 killed. As usual, nothing was said about the extent of German casualties. The dressing stations were still adequate, but the number of casualties they held had increased with every action since the interruption of transportation to the hinterland. The large garrison hospital in the town woods offered excellent facilities as a main dressing station, but this extensive complex had been on the front line since the very beginning, so additional dressing stations had been improvised in two of the Altstadt schools, their old walls giving ample protection against the now dominant mortars. Since the rocket salvoes had started landing on the Neustadt, the wounded had been shaking with every explosion. Some were even lying in the gymnasium of the Boys' Senior School in Friedrichstrasse. This single-storey functional building of recent construction only had a light, flat roof and thin brick walls with wide expanses of window. Nobody went there voluntarily.

When the artillery was relatively quiet, the street traffic livened up. Cars, apart from those bearing the Red Cross, were rarely seen for lack of fuel but horse-drawn carts and tractors were common. Those who begged could, with the right words or cigarettes, according to the mood of the driver, reach their destination more quickly. Because of the extensive flooding resulting from the thaw, there were no other means of conveying people to and from the more distant parts of the town. The trams had given up even before the fighting started and the depot with all its trams in the Neumarkt had since been destroyed by the first salvoes, and there had never been a town bus service except to Drewitz and, for a while, to Kietz.

Even the most fragile wagons were in use transferring civilian and military stocks from the Neustadt into the presumably safer Altstadt. Volkssturm men not deployed in the front line for lack of weapons or on health grounds were ordered to clear the Army Supply Depot, which had been prepared for demolition with explosives. They were in no great hurry, for there were always more difficult and dangerous jobs for them to be allocated to. But neither the willingness of the labour force nor the capacity of the transport was the decisive factor here, for it was the capacity of the almost 200-year-old military barn in the Altstadt that set the limits.

Next Hitler Youth teams quartered in the Hitler Youth office building on the Marktplatz began moving the stocks of abandoned private wholesale and retail businesses into the Altstadt, this being momentarily the main task for those not yet called up for the Volkssturm or military service. The boys often had difficulty convincing their parents of the quality of the household articles, textiles and foodstuffs they were moving from the partly ruined Neustadt, for everything was still strictly rationed in the few shops still open.[22]

Then came a restless night, the most disturbed night since the refugee trains and treks had passed through in January, as windows shook to extensive booms that arose in irregular waves, only to diminish and then resume at full strength. The cannonade was far enough away that one could not distinguish between the firing and the explosions, but too near to enable one to sleep peacefully. The flashes of gunfire and exploding shells were like sheet lightning in the sky. For days there had been talk of heavy Bavarian artillery regiments unloading at Müncheberg. These were only harmless rumours like others that arose daily and often developed into dramatic legends before being quietly forgotten again.

The thunder of the artillery kept soldiers and civilians fully clothed until morning in expectation of having to take shelter in bunkers and cellars. (So far the use of shelters for permanent residence had not been necessary.) After eight days of only candles or paraffin lamps for illumination, it was now possible to enjoy the luxury of electric light. The power plant of the Potato Meal Factory in the Neustadt, which with its 1,000 or so employees was the biggest business in the town, had become the town's power station after all the cables to the outside world had been cut. An announcement in the news-sheet warned everyone to be exceedingly economical in order to avoid overloading the system. Heating appliances and suchlike were not to be used.

The artillery battle died down but in the early morning all parts of the fortress came under harassing fire, the main concentration being on the Altstadt, and Küstrin suffered its first civilian casualties. A man and a woman in a side street near the town hall fell to shrapnel splinters while taking advantage of a pause in the firing to attend to their needs. The roneoed news-sheet that afternoon described the night's exchange of fire. Contact had been made with the formations attacking from the west. This was the first official acknowledgement of the existing encirclement and almost complete isolation of the town. Its restrained formulation and its position at the end of the situation report showed that success was not taken as certain. In fact the 21st Panzer Division had pushed through to the town on the general line of the railway and opened a roughly 2-kilometre-wide aisle in the Soviet encirclement. However, both the railway and the road remained impassable.[23] The fortress situation report for 9 February read:

> Several company-strength attacks north-eastwards of Alt Drewitz repelled. Strong enemy artillery and rocket fire midday on the Altstadt. Lively enemy barrage from heavy weapons on the other sectors. An enemy battery taking up position south of the Bienenhof engaged to good effect.

A new threat appeared on 10 February when Soviet aircraft appeared for the first time, presumably on reconnaissance. The weather was perfect for them, being sunny and cloudless. They circled at gradually lower heights until the flak thickened. There was no sign of any German aircraft, for there was sufficient fuel only for the ground-attack aircraft to engage the Soviet crossing points from the Neu Hardenberg airfield and elsewhere. Once again Fürstenwalde was the base for the almost legendary tank-busting exploits of ace pilot Hans-Ulrich Rudel. In fact he had been shot down the day before by flak over Lebus and severely wounded, but was able to make an emergency landing near Seelow with the help of his air gunner.

In the south Infantry Battalion 500 became heavily engaged on both sides of the Oder. Only a week earlier it had had difficulty holding off an attack by seven tanks supported by two companies of infantry. The little hamlet of Bienenhof on the east bank blocked the approaches to the Altstadt from the south, preventing direct fire from along the river banks, and also covered the flank of the positions in Kietz on the other bank of the Oder, giving good tactical reasons for either side to hold or take it. This time the Soviet tank-supported infantry assault was increased to battalion size and the group of buildings was lost, but the Soviet troops were unable to consolidate their success. Behind the hamlet the passable strip of land narrowed down to the Oder dyke, where the defenders regrouped. One of the attacking tanks turned back on the roadway running along the top of the dyke right in front of the flak, apparently afraid of mines, and exploded. Reinforcements from the town enabled the lost ground to be regained after some costly close-quarter fighting.

The noise of this fighting was muffled in the Altstadt by unusually heavy firing. Hardly anyone dared go out into the streets before midday. In the quarters occupied by the Party officials from Landsberg the birthday of the well-rounded NSV district leader, a former butcher, was celebrated unconcernedly, and there was no lack of drink or food for the table. They had not occupied all the important positions in the supply organisation for nothing, and were getting twice the rations of the people they were responsible for. The celebrations also offered an opportunity to mark the fortunate turn of events that Major-General Kegler had been made the scapegoat for their precipitate breakout from Landsberg.[24]

The 21st Panzer Division, now urgently needed elsewhere, was withdrawn from the 'pipeline' to Küstrin and replaced by Major-General Arnold Burmeister's 25th Panzergrenadier Division, which took over the sector from Neu Manschnow to Genschmar with the task of keeping open access to the fortress, the handover taking place in pouring rain.[25]

Sunday, 11 February was comparatively quiet, the peace disturbed only by the flak opening up from time to time when Soviet aircraft ventured too low. In the news-sheet that appeared in various places in the afternoon there was no mention of the local military situation.

One week after the Soviet advance had interrupted regular rail and road connections with the hinterland there was no chance of these being reopened. The encirclement had quickly solidified, withstanding counterattacks at all the decisive points. The town was now utterly dependent on the track between Bleyen and Gorgast. Heavy half-track vehicles, including the towing tractors for the 88mm guns of Army Flak Battalion 292, were being assembled in Seelow. The drivers were on stand-by in the Drei Kronen pub, waiting to bring the most important loads through the 'corridor'. Tests had shown that the convoys could make the return trip twice a night, but in daylight they were forbidden to go anywhere near the Soviet lines. The approximately 25-kilometre route began along Reichsstrasse 1, turning off as for Golzow, past Golzow railway station and then along the road to Gorgast. The most difficult part of the journey was the 4-kilometre track to Bleyen, where the road on the Oder dyke connected with the road into the town.

The most urgent requirement at the moment was ammunition, particularly for the heavy weapons. The flak batteries that had been thrown in with the utmost haste were not equipped for sustained action, and their ammunition stocks had rapidly diminished. Reinefarth must have been concerned about the fighting capability of the fortress's main armament. The foreseeable end to this scarcity gave him confidence once more. The access route was narrow, but relieved anxiety over the growing number of desertions and the need for an extensive control system. The system of military sentries on the 'corridor' was so dense that no one could get through without permission. No soldier, even when the planned traffic started working, could pass as wounded unless he had a special evacuation label.[26]

Concerned that the 'corridor' might prove to be a trap, Reinefarth had a provisional aircraft landing strip prepared. His choice was the straight and open strip of roadway running across the foot of the Hohen Kavalier from the Altstadt to the Warthe road bridge. Engineers removed the rest of the snow, the street lamps and the posts carrying the power for the trams, levelled fences and the young red-thorn trees lining the street where just four and a half years previously the garrison had held a victory parade celebrating the success of the Blitz wars over Poland and France. The cobbles were smoothed over with gravel but one did not need to be an expert to see that the barely 300-metre-long strip was inadequate for all but a Fieseler Storch, which could only take one passenger, and who would that be?

At the same time Reinefarth required the soldiers and inhabitants to pay particular attention to the words of Hitler's speech of 30 January, in which the Führer had called on everyone to 'exert themselves to the utmost to prevent unnecessary loss and damage'. Reinefarth gave orders that this phrase was to be used in the introduction to the first edition of the *Feste Küstrin* garrison newspaper that day, and finished with the charge: 'We hold to our country and thus grant our leadership the freedom to deliver the final blow.'

The *Feste Küstrin* appeared for the first time on 12 February. It was printed in the old Oderblatt printing premises on Plantagen-strasse in the Neustadt, and the last issue was number 23 of 7 March, the day the Neustadt fell. The first edition contained the following appeal:

> Soldiers and Inhabitants of Küstrin Fortress!
>
> In the defence of our Fatherland fate has decreed a hard task for the old fortress of Küstrin. So far we have succeeded and have already received recognition. We will also succeed in the future and keep the door to Berlin closed to the Soviets. It is only necessary for everyone to give their utmost and harden themselves against unavoidable losses and damage.
>
> To improve information to the troops and the civilian population about military events and all necessary measures, the emergency newspaper *Feste Küstrin* will be produced jointly by the commandant and the NSDAP county office. It will soon be extended if possible. Its regular appearance will, however, depend upon the electricity supply.
>
> Help and support each other! We are guarding the home country and allowing our leadership the freedom to determine counterblows. The Soviets will be driven away from Küstrin again soon.
>
> Hail the Führer!
> Reinefarth
> Gruppenführer and Lieutenant-General of the Waffen-SS
> Commandant of Küstrin Fortress

> Men and Women, German Boys and Girls of Fortress Küstrin!
>
> In the happy years of peace and the build-up [of Nazi Germany] we have often been able to do beneficial work for our town in conjunction with the Wehrmacht. Today Küstrin has become a front-line town. We have to live through difficult times that have brought much sorrow to our families. However, the Wehrmacht, Party and civil administration must today overcome this serious situation together. It is important that every one of us does their duty to the utmost. Under the thunder of the Soviet cannon at the town boundaries, our spirits are stretched to meet this difficult test. Let us always belong to the strong and true. The men and women of the Party and the administration will do everything possible to lighten the lot of

the civilian population. That is why we are here and will remain until the brave soldiers of our Wehrmacht drive the Soviets away.

As so often in Prussian-German history, the old fortresses stand as outposts to the east. Let us show ourselves worthy of our predecessors.

War brings painful scars to this town and individual families, but even if our walls should break, our hearts will remain strong.

Körner
Kreisleiter und Bürgermeister

Gauamtsleiter Westphal added his own contribution to this first edition with: 'It is difficult from the local District point of view to form an opinion whether a sort of evacuation is desirable, expedient, absolutely necessary or even possible. The evacuation of the town has not been ordered and consequently cannot be executed. An "unpredictable military development" just as permission had been given "made its execution impossible".' Interestingly, this was the first public acknowledgement of receipt of the evacuation order.

There was also an appeal in the fortress newspaper for the registration of people living in the Neustadt, by which each household on production of the blue household pass would report the number of family members. Cardboard to replace shattered windows could be obtained from either the town hall or the town savings bank. Finally the newspaper announced, without providing any reason, that going out at night was immediately forbidden for civilians between 2000 and 0600 hours, and for foreign workers between 1800 and 0600 hours. Exceptions required the permission of the local police authority for a special curfew pass.

More important to the Küstrin garrison's future was the Army Order issued this day ordering that the fortress 'conduct the fighting so that contact is maintained with the Oder and that the construction of [Soviet] crossings over the river can be hindered by combat teams to the last'. This was just another formulation of 'fighting to the last man'.[27]

The local situation report for 12 February read:

Infantry combat took place west of Kietz during the last 24 hours, when a lost group of buildings was regained in a counterattack, as well as both sides of the road to Zorndorf. Increased enemy artillery activity against the Altstadt. Enemy guns were engaged by our own flak and infantry guns. Air activity weak.

Luftwaffe Officer Cadet Sergeant Helmut Schmidt resumed his account of events in mid-February:

We were back in our old position on the railway embankment, where we manned the machine-gun position and lived in the railway hut. The gramophone played practically all day long. Whenever I had a chance I buried myself in a book.

We checked the ground in front of us every day without getting close to the Cellulose Factory. To go in did not seem advisable to us. We knew the ambush that awaited us there and were aware of the covered approach from the north. There was an underground channel that had little water in it at the time and served as a loophole for the Russians.

The weather was fine and the temperature rising.

For two or three days after our attack on the factory the Russians left us in peace. Afterwards they made themselves noticeable once more and fired at our machine-gun position at the bridge. These were only single shots, needle-pricks, in order to disturb us. They wanted to lure us on to the factory premises again, but we were not strong enough for a second attack.

More days went by. It was obvious to us that the Russians were occupying the factory. They had settled down there and presumably received reinforcements through the underground channel. Occasionally the Russians fired harassing fire on the town with mortars.

One day I was sitting with a comrade from my section on the south side of the railway embankment not far from the bridge. The air was unusually mild that evening. My comrade, Heinz Tiedemann, was a few years older than myself, married, and came from Swinemünde. We were looking towards the town, watching the rising Very lights and drinking a bottle of vermouth of the cheapest kind. Heinz was talking about his home, his wife and how much he missed her. I listened. Whenever there was a longish break we could hear the Warthe gurgling. Somewhere or other a Russian machine gun was tacking and a grenade exploded. We sat there a long time with our thoughts. It was good for Tiedemann to have found someone who would listen to him. We did not know that this would be our last evening on the Warthe.

The next day began as usual. We mounted sentries and watched the Russians. In the corrugated-iron hut our tenor sang 'Schön ist der Welt' again and again. Who could still believe him? Whenever the spring ran down someone would rewind it. Someone cranked the handle as a metallic crack sounded. The needle was broken. Richard Tauber had sung his last song. A bad omen? Perhaps. Barely an hour later came the order to clear the position. A strange infantry company was relieving us. We set off in the late afternoon with sour faces.

We trotted back to the underpass, where our vehicles were waiting for us. News and words were exchanged. For the first time we heard that Küstrin was completely surrounded. We had already suspected it but had hoped that the Stuka attack would have broken the encirclement.

We left the Küstrin Neustadt by the road bridge. To the damage caused to the buildings by the Russian tanks more had been added by artillery and mortar fire. We crossed the Oder Bridge, drove through the Altstadt and crossed the Oder–Vorflut Canal to reach the south-western suburb of Kietz. We slept while the company commander made a reconnaissance of the new position.

There was an alert before dawn. We went westwards in files. It was very foggy and the damp air made our clothing wet. We stumbled over railway tracks where they crossed the road. The last buildings were passed and we reached open countryside. Our file followed the northern roadside ditch of Reichsstrasse 1. The enemy must be somewhere to the south. Individual shots pinged in our direction and we could hear the slow tacking of Russian machine guns. The road surface offered breast-high protection against shots flying over. Again and again our legs got tangled in the coils of thick wire that had fallen from the telegraph poles alongside the road and lay curled up in the ditch.

About a kilometre west of the level crossing we turned right towards the south. Our guide followed a track. After about 150 to 200 metres the dark shadow of a building appeared. We had reached our destination, the Weinbergshof Farm. The farmyard

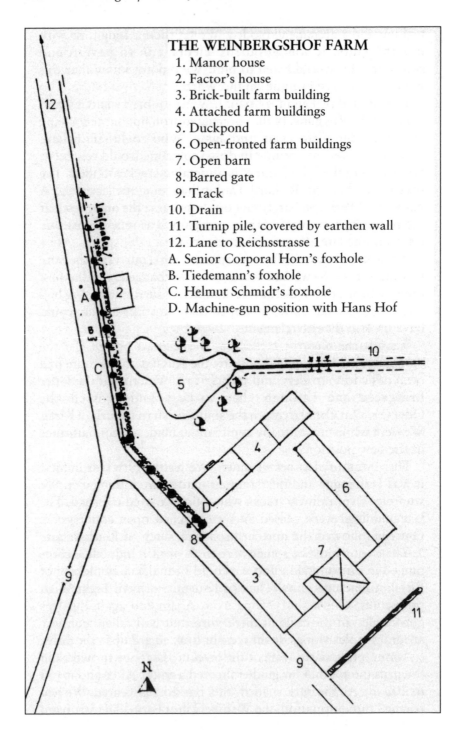

THE WEINBERGSHOF FARM
1. Manor house
2. Factor's house
3. Brick-built farm building
4. Attached farm buildings
5. Duckpond
6. Open-fronted farm buildings
7. Open barn
8. Barred gate
9. Track
10. Drain
11. Turnip pile, covered by earthen wall
12. Lane to Reichsstrasse 1
A. Senior Corporal Horn's foxhole
B. Tiedemann's foxhole
C. Helmut Schmidt's foxhole
D. Machine-gun position with Hans Hof

itself was parallel to the track and alongside a hedge, and we passed by a brick house as the chimes of a Westminster clock struck the hour. Then we passed a duck pond surrounded by old trees and came to a stately building, the manor house. The occupants had fled and the house was empty. Lieutenant Kühnel moved into the cellars with his small staff.

The morning lightened hesitantly. It seemed that the fog would thicken even more. Lieutenant Kühnel ordered me to occupy a position facing south [actually south-east] with my section. We moved off alongside a brick-built barn. Facing the fields, running from east to west, was a breast-high earthen hedge in which we would dig our foxholes. The sandy earth was frozen rock hard. We picked and hacked with our spades. After a quarter of an hour of sweating work we discovered that the fine earthen wall was the covering of a pile of turnips. We could not expect much protection from that.

We had relieved an army unit, whose troops were happy to leave at last. The Russians had given them a hard time. They forecast some uncomfortable days ahead for us.

Our view to the south sank into mist and fog only 200 metres away. The terrain was completely flat without a tree or a house to be seen, and appeared to be devoid of people. We knew, however, that the appearance was false. Therefore, as we dug in, we had several men keeping watch. But nothing unusual happened.

With our morning rations came some bottles of Sekt of a good make. Unfortunately these precious drops were 'served' while we were sweating and were hastily consumed to quell our thirst.

Ivan was keeping quiet. We were able to move about freely between the turnip pit and the farmyard. Only occasional shots came out of the milky greyness. A bit to our left we could sometimes see the shadows of two guns, 105mm flak cannon, that for some unaccountable reason had not been brought in to safety.

We did not only use the day for digging in, we found our way around the farmyard, which did not look so grand by daylight. Its dirty grey façade was unpleasant. The house with the Westminster clock was the farm manager's. It had been damaged. Apparently a shell had ripped off the south-west corner and one could see inside. The clock had not been damaged and could still be heard. Between the manager's house and the manor itself our predecessors had dug a hip-deep trench, most of which was not flooded by groundwater.

The first day and the following night at the farm passed quietly. The Russians did not show themselves, but we mistrusted this quietness and kept silent ourselves. We crouched in our primitive foxholes and kept our ears alert, but there was nothing to see or hear.

The second day dawned slowly. The fog of the previous day had thinned, but a milky ground mist remained. When the daylight eventually allowed a view of several hundred metres, we were surprised to see that the Russians had made good use of the darkness. About 200–300 metres to the south of the turnip pit was an infantry trench, the light-coloured dug-out earth betraying the line of the trench. The Russians had had the same problem in digging as we had, the high groundwater allowing only a hip-deep trench. Presumably the enemy could move around crouched down without being seen by us.

The enemy position was in a straight line from west to east. It appeared to be only a trench beginning east of the Weinbergshof running at an even distance from our position and ending abruptly a little west of the farm. This was a sudden alteration to our position. The trench was occupied and we could no longer move around freely between the pile of turnips and the farmyard. It was wise to keep under cover. The Russians would fire at every individual. It gradually became more uncomfortable.

We dozed all day in our foxholes so that we would be fit for the night. But our legs quickly became stiff. It was still not spring temperatures. Although we kept an eye on the enemy, we were unable to see any Russians. Once again they had camouflaged their observation posts in a masterly way. In our opinion they must have used quite a lot of men for the construction of their position, and they too must have had to get through the hard crust of frost.

With nightfall we were able to leave our foxholes. At about 2200 hours we received hot food, or rather lukewarm food. With it were cold rations, a few cigarettes and a cigar. Bombardier Horn swapped my cigar for several cigarettes.

The next night was as disturbed as the last. There was some

firing to the left of us at about midnight. Some comrades were investigating whether the 105mm guns should be removed or blown up when they surprised some Russian scouts. This skirmish was repeated on the following night. The Russians thus prevented us from either removing or demolishing the guns. Daylight the next day revealed that the Russians had extended their trench to the west. It annoyed us that we could not stop their trench digging, or even interrupt it. Our company was too weak and had not received any reinforcements so far. Apart from this, we lacked a mortar. We did not even have enough ammunition for our machine guns. Especially important would have been a Very pistol, but that was also lacking. We had become a poor lot.

After our third night in the Weinbergshof it appeared that Ivan had extended his trench even further to encompass both sides of the farm. During the night the Russians had dug their trench about level with the manager's house. The Russians could now watch us, and fire at us from two sides. Our situation was critical and we felt as if we had a noose around our throats.

The weather improved inasmuch as the sun showed itself timidly. Then we discovered a digging Ivan some 120 to 150 metres from our turnip pile. That is, we did not actually see him, for he was in a hole, but every few seconds the black blade of a spade appeared and earth flew from it. He was digging himself a listening post at least 100 metres in front of the Russian trench.

We watched this Russian mole for a while and fired with our carbines at his spade, but without evoking any reaction. Then we tried with a rifle grenade, but it exploded uselessly on the open ground. Finally the Russian gave up digging. Had we achieved our aim at last? No. He put up a short stovepipe from his hole from which soon after smoke appeared. Such a cheeky rascal! He wanted to show us and tease us. A man from our section went back to the armoury in the manor and fetched a 150-metre range Panzerfaust and fired at the smoking pipe. There was a loud explosion and the stove was out.

Once the Russians had completed their trenches, they started harassing us. Especially at night, we were fired on from the front and from the side. Our primitive foxholes between the turnips offered us little protection and Lieutenant Kühnel ordered the position to be evacuated. We were not sorry. Our new task was the defence of the farm from the west. We were to occupy and improve our predecessors' trenches.

The allocated sector began in the south at the farm buildings. A closed gate formed the main entrance from the track and a metalled path led to the manor. From the gate a hedge ran north-wards on the right of the track to beyond the manager's house. The trench ran along the east side of the hedge. We occupied the trench to a bit beyond the house. Not much improvement was needed for this trench. One hit groundwater just a few centi-metres below the bottom of the trench. The thaw and the rising water level of the Oder were raising the water table. We had no option but to dig small shelter holes against the hedge. Everyone dug out his hole to his own specifications.

Night-times were hellish. Every few minutes the Russians would fire machine-gun bursts at the farm. Rarely did we get so much as half an hour's peace. The explosive bullets were devilish. They pattered against the asters in the hedge, and we regarded the ensuing splinters as harmless sparks. To protect ourselves from them we turned our holes into little caves. The nights were still cold and the dampness of the earth penetrated our camouflaged uniforms.

Every night was a long one for us. Every quarter or half hour I went along the trench from man to man warning them to be alert. During the hours after midnight we all had to fight against falling asleep. The night was dark and one could only see a few paces. It was important to react to noises. Company headquar-ters had told us that we would be relieved next evening. It was certainly time!

Early in the morning the sound of heavy fighting came from a north-westerly direction. We looked over the edge of the trench. A German attack! We cheered. At last German troops were trying to break out of the encirclement.

At first the Russians were quiet. I saw a German 20mm self-propelled gun break through a bush and tracer flew southwards. I heard bellowing shots and saw German soldiers charging. German machine guns fired burst after burst. The fight was taking place about one and a half kilometres away. The SPG went along east of the Alte Oder to south of Reichsstrasse 1.

We were unable to trace the events exactly. Unfortunately we soon realised that the sounds of combat were dying down. The attack seemed to have been checked. We had cheered too soon. Our disappointment was great. We could not have supported the German attack ourselves for lack of strength, manpower and weapons.[28]

There was more skirmishing activity than usual on 13 February, a rainy day. The Soviet harassing fire increased and the fortress artillery also became more active now that the first convoys from Seelow had replenished their ammunition stocks. The bombardment routine, which was still mainly mortar fire, set the course of the day for the population. Particularly critical in this respect were the hours from 0800 to 1000, 1200 to 1400 and 1500 to 1700. At other times shopping and other business could be dealt with at relatively little risk.

The *Feste Küstrin* described the population enduring this restricted kind of life as showing 'a determined hardness'. However, this assertion was undermined by the increasing number of impatient questions being asked about the possibility of leaving the town. Some emergency measures were introduced to try to curb this growing unrest. Letterboxes in every part of town were regularly emptied, or so it was said, indicating normal postal services were still operating, and an administrative office was opened in the Neustadt to save people having to use the dangerous route over the Warthe bridges, while a deserted building was taken over to replace the closed hospital.

One outcome of the shelling that day was a chance hit on one of the two demolition chambers on the Warthe road bridge, as Sapper Karl-Heinz Peters described:

About halfway through February a shell hit the demolition chamber on the Warthe road bridge, causing part of the bridge to collapse. Afterwards a provisional wooden bridge enabled the passage of pedestrians and light vehicles.

Shortly before the Warthe road bridge collapsed, we had hauled some planks across from the sawmill in the Neustadt with a one-horse cart. But an enemy fighter, an Ilyushin 2, spotted us there and chased us like hares among the stacks of wood, firing its heavy machine guns at us. As he was unsuccessful, he broke off the chase. We used the planks to prop up our position, which kept collapsing in the sandy soil. During this work a shell burst near me and buried me for a short while. However, my comrades quickly pulled me out again. Our losses meanwhile were so high that the number of soldiers was halved within a week by death or wounding.

During the first weeks we could still wash regularly. There was a point at the Warthe–Vorflut Canal railway bridge that was hidden from enemy view, where we could enter the water. Later we had the opportunity to have a proper bath. It was curious. One section was detailed for the preparation. They had to carry water in buckets and fill a boiler on the second floor of a half-destroyed house. The boiler was heated with wood and coal. Eventually each of us in our sector enjoyed a hot bath. It was a strange feeling sitting in a bathtub under artillery fire. I can recall not wanting to get out and thinking a direct hit would put an end to this misery. After the bath we were given fresh socks and underclothes.

Sometimes we had to parade briefly for a head count. These were clearly measures to raise our morale, for we were somewhat depressed.

From our positions on the Warthe bridges we could see how the Neustadt was being systematically destroyed by artillery fire. There were fires everywhere. The biggest blaze came when the railway sleeper depot caught fire, giving the dying town a ghostly light.

We had become used to dead comrades, but it was different when women or children were hit. I had to experience a shell splinter hitting a baby in its mother's arms. I was also strongly moved when a soldier was hanged from an A-mast for plundering. His girlfriend was shot in front of the Catholic church.

Our provisions were becoming more meagre. There was hardly any warm food any more and a loaf had now to be shared between eight of us. The last meat I remember was strips of raw, albeit briefly smoked horsemeat. (When long after the war I read in reports about the siege of Küstrin that the rations were sufficient and assured, I could not understand it.) That is why we sometimes searched the cellars of abandoned houses for food; but always in great fear of being punished for looting.

When American Red Cross parcels from an evacuated prisoner-of-war camp were removed from the Altstadt, I was able to steal one from a passing truck. It contained cigarettes, conserves and other foodstuffs. The most important item was a bar of Lux soap. It was snow white and smelled unbelievably good, and each of us had one wash with it at the Warthe Vorflut bridge. Only those who experienced German wartime soap can understand what this luxury meant to us.

At night we had to prepare the lower Warthe railway bridge for heavy vehicles, that is, for tanks. For this we had to extract the sleepers from the rails. I was so exhausted that I collapsed several times. Afterwards we were given a full day to sleep it off. Usually we had to be awake for four hours and then could have four hours' rest. We immediately fell asleep once our guard duty was over. Often I fell asleep on duty, but was able to report half-asleep whenever a superior checked. A comrade who had been found asleep at his post several times was brought before a court martial. The experience was unpleasant. We were also soon split up and I had to go to help fill another section at the Warthe road bridge that had taken high casualties.

Meanwhile the Soviet Air Force ruled the skies. Their bombers came almost every day and strangely always along the river. They aimed poorly and had many duds – something that also occurred with their artillery. We frequently saw fighter-bombers and fighters overhead. The apparently slow-flying IL-2 fighter-bombers were immune to our infantry weapons with their armour.

At night the PO-2 'Sewing Machines' would appear. Predominantly built of wood and stretched material, these slow, single-engined aircraft were powered by a 110hp engine that sounded like a sewing machine. They dropped parachute flares, switched off the engine and glided while dropping small bombs on us. While we were reinforcing the Warthe railway bridge with sleepers for tank traffic, which went on until the dawn, our sentries were able to shoot down one of these aircraft.[29]

The turmoil of the first days of fighting unsettled the outward routine that made life bearable and in which there were at least some traces of normality, such as acts of kindness. However, anxiety about basic survival remained. Apart from the two salvoes on the Neustadt there had still been no concentrated fire on other parts of the town, but the general increase and effectiveness of the besieging artillery was

unmistakable. Even in the duty-bound optimism of the Party administration it was recognised that the bounds of 'normalisation' had
been reached.[30]

The fortress news-sheet complained that 'despite the statement
included in the first issue' there was still vagueness prevailing about
the evacuation, and that rumours were giving rise to questions and
requests. It declared: 'If an orderly evacuation becomes increasingly
necessary, all necessary measures will be taken to guarantee its execution and the re-housing. In this eventuality, Werbig has been
prepared as a reception camp to which the transport will go. From
there, there will be a prepared move to accommodation in
Westprignitz.'

All the other pages were equally confident about the future. One
example read: 'He who makes his way from Berlin to Küstrin will
traverse no kilometre in which he will not see the lifeblood pulsing
eastwards from Berlin in a current of belief, trust and restless commitment. Along the whole stretch from Berlin to Küstrin many hands are
active and our strength grows from hour to hour to be released at the
desired moment, bringing forth the day of decision and liberation.'
Another read: 'Küstrin fortress is an important feature in the current
military game of chess over our East German homeland. Let us therefore take care we put our utmost effort at the disposal of the Führer,
however and whenever he requires. We are convinced that the Führer
is already in control and that in the foreseeable future the effect of
his handling will be noticeable in our sector of the fighting.'

Events left little opportunity for these exhortations to take effect.
Kietz had come under artillery fire during the night, then in the
morning ground-attack aircraft in large numbers attacked positions
in the Neustadt. At about midday the Altstadt and Kietz were shaken
by bombardment by what was reckoned at about 1,000 rounds of all
calibres. Bitter fighting erupted once more at the Bienenhof strongpoint, involving two Soviet rifle battalions and eight tanks. Precisely
as had occurred four days previously, the ruins of the hamlet changed
hands twice before the old front line was restored at dusk.[31]

Operation 'Sonnenwende' (Summer Solstice) got under way on 15
February when ten German divisions attacked southwards from the
area of Stargard. Their objectives were to break through the
extended flank of the 1st Byelorussian Front in Pomerania, to cut it
off and then destroy the Soviet forces on the Oder, pushing through

to the Küstrin area. In the meantime the besieging batteries resumed their fire on Küstrin and engaged nearly all parts of the front line. The headquarters reported 5,860 hits. Several freestanding houses in Wallstrasse on the edge of the Altstadt, not 500 metres from the front, had to be evacuated. The cellars were flooded, as happened nearly every year in the thaw, and could not be occupied in the foreseeable future. The remaining inhabitants of Kietz were advised to move into the 'less dangerous' Altstadt from their village homes, which offered little protection, especially now that Soviet tanks had been used in the Reitwein bridgehead. However, the fortress staff forbade their acceptance into the Altstadt 'on military grounds', so they had little choice but to head for the Neustadt. Several families moved as suggested. They had heard about the destruction, but now everything was being talked about and exaggerated, both good and bad. Perhaps they really would be safer in these more densely built quarters. However, all illusions fled when they saw the heaps of rubble where once had been thriving streets, and almost all the families returned to Kietz, some slipping unnoticed into the Altstadt.

The fortress newspaper had new reasons for criticising the behaviour of the population, this time because there was some confusion among the men and women about their obligations for labour service. All childless women up to 55 years old were supposed to report for duty. Additionally, all girls from 14 to 21 years old in the Jugendpflicht (Youth Duty Service) were to report immediately to the Hitler Youth offices for employment in dressing stations, kitchens and tailor shops, or to do laundry for the Volkssturm and barracked Hitler Youth.

A group of women had already been mobilised a week earlier to sew enormous screens that the engineers spread like banners from the Altstadt entrance to the Neustadt end of the Warthe bridges. For part of this stretch the trees could be used as securing points, while wooden laths were used on the bridges. Shots and splinters left their mark and at first this damage was quickly repaired, but as time passed either the repair troop became tired of this task or had been given another one. The construction disintegrated, gradually giving the Soviet artillery observers on the Sonnenburger Chaussee a better view of the scanty bridge traffic.

The *Feste Küstrin* published the first Standing Court's actions: 'Corporal Z was sentenced for plundering by the Standing Court on

10.2.1945 to death and military disgrace. The condemned entered damaged business premises in the Neustadt where Hitler Youth were busy saving household goods. He went along with the cart the Hitler Youth were taking to the Küstrin-Altstadt and removed items from the cart to take home with him despite protests. The sentence is to be carried out by shooting on 11.2.1945.'[32] The Wehrmacht Report on the front page of the fortress newspaper of 16 February reported among other things the fall of Budapest, Soviet attacks on Breslau and Golgau, the retreat to Grünberg and heavy house-to-house fighting in encircled Posen; things seemed quieter on the west front, but central Germany, with Saxony, Münsterland and south-east Germany, was suffering, and in particular Chemnitz, Magdeburg and Dresden were named as having been targets for Anglo-American air attacks.

The Standing Court also had a soldier executed for leaving his unit in the front line and hiding in a nearby building for eight days.

Everyday life continued within the fortress. Soviet batteries brought down heavy fire on the Bienenhof and were engaged by the heavy flak guns in return. Low-flying Soviet ground-attack aircraft attacked the Neustadt and a German fighter-bomber attacked Soviet positions near Drewitz.

The electricity supply to the town failed again, but whether this was the result of a direct hit, technical problems or other reasons was not known. Candles and oil lamps came into their own once more, although fuel for the lamps was running out. Here and there a dusty bottle was found in a cellar, but there were no longer any larger supplies. Fuel for motor vehicles was equally scarce. In any case an order had appeared that motor vehicles could only be used with a special pass from headquarters and with a work chit for every journey. Wehrmacht vehicles now carried the letters 'FK' for 'Fortress Küstrin' painted in white on the wings. The only non-military vehicles in use were those of the fire brigade and one belonging to the NSDAP district office.

The provisional delivery station in Roonstrasse reported the first birth of the siege, a boy. Sadly, he would never get to know his father, who had died three months earlier somewhere in the east.[33]

Fighter aircraft from both sides met early in the morning over the town. The harmless rattling of machine guns so high up brought many people on to the streets. They were sure there was nothing to worry about, as long as the nimble machines were so intensively engaged with one another. The planes stayed beyond the range of the light flak and the heavy guns that in any case were holding back from endangering their own aircraft. This new spectacle attracted interest from all over the front. The Soviet batteries were suddenly silent after having been very active since dawn. For a long time the hunting spurts of tracer bullets found no targets in the cloudless sky, then one aircraft suddenly emitted a plume of smoke, lost height and vanished out of sight. This acted on the other pilots like a pre-arranged signal to break off the fight, and in a few minutes there was no trace of this bitter engagement.

The groups of spectators dispersed without saying anything, not knowing whether the downed aircraft was German or Soviet. As people queued in the few grocers' shops that still had provisions, the relative strengths of the machines came under vigorous discussion, and the debate continued until the firing started up again, and most people abandoned their places in the queue to go home before the storm broke in all its fury. It was afternoon before people could go out again. The picture that many streets offered was desolate, with broken tiles and windows, masonry and roof timbers littering the pavements. The Marktplatz area had suffered the most, the façade of a corner building on Berliner Strasse having collapsed from a direct hit. The roof truss hung freely over the ripped open storeys. Volkssturm men who had been accommodated in the pub on the ground floor could not understand how they had survived this horror. They stood around covered in dust and white-faced with shock as firemen and air raid wardens cleared the street of heaps of debris. Headquarters staff calmly summed up the day: 'Harassing fire day and night from all calibres on the whole sector (5,560 shots). The Altstadt and Neustadt suffered heavy damage.'

On 16 February the fortress, which until then had come directly under 9th Army Headquarters, was allocated tactically to SS-Obergruppenführer and General der Waffen-SS Matthias Kleinheisterkamp's XIth SS Panzer Corps. Kleinheisterkamp's head-quarters were located at Neuentempel, 6 kilometres south-west of Seelow.[34]

There was still no indication that an evacuation would take place in the foreseeable future. The information in the fortress newspaper on 18 February, however, gave the impression that those in the know expected some more difficult days, perhaps weeks, ahead. New identity cards were being introduced, with passes for the Oder bridges and special passes for going out at night during the curfew. Anyone who had moved into a different building without official approval had to obtain an official permit immediately; NSDAP cell leaders and Red Cross personnel were requested to report for further duties. The former Landsberg District farmers' leader, now head of civilian supplies in Küstrin, spoke of the efforts being made to provide the town with enough supplies to enable it to withstand a siege of weeks or months. Even tobacco would be rationed for men on ration cards in future. 'The biggest problem is with milk and butter supplies as, due to enemy artillery fire, often milk cannot be delivered from Alt Bleyen and Kietz. Here the NSV is helping out with dried milk. Instead of butter, the same weight in clarified butter or margarine will be issued.' Issues of ersatz milk were actually not made regularly and in any case were limited to children up to 4 years of age. The official rations were set out as follows:

Infants up to 1 year	1 x Dried milk for 8 days
	1 x Condensed milk for 14 days
Children 1–2 years	2 x Condensed milk for 8 days
	1 x Condensed milk for 14 days
Children 2–4 years	2 x Condensed milk for 8 days

The dried items came from the stocks of Küstrin merchants. Canned milk had been brought in from Frankfurt on the night of 4 February in a truck guided along by tracer bullets. The route via Seelow was unknown to either the driver or his companion, and from Manschnow they had been exceedingly lucky to get through the Soviet advance positions. Theirs was the last vehicle to reach the town by Reichsstrasse 1.

Fortress surgeon Dr Weglau considered the state of hygiene in the town 'very good at the moment', commenting that 'infectious illnesses have not appeared to any extent'. Nevertheless, the population had only the Altstadt pharmacy to turn to, in its lightly damaged building on the Marktplatz. The Neustadt pharmacy had been closed since the first fighting, and plunderers had subsequently rendered it unrecognisable in their search for narcotics.

Following a relatively peaceful morning there was an unusually big explosion that afternoon that gave rise to the rumour that the Warthe bridges had been destroyed. The engineer staff who quickly appeared at the site discovered that the situation was not as bad as first feared. The bridge structure had not been torn apart, as only one of the two demolition chambers on the central piers had exploded after receiving a direct hit. However, vehicular traffic over this single road bridge between the Altstadt and Neustadt was now impossible. The roadway hung down at a steep angle into the flooded Warthe. At considerable risk pedestrians could cross on the pathway resting on the remains of the piers, but these had substantial cracks in them. The construction of an emergency bridge over the sagging structure would take time, but meanwhile one could use the railway bridge 100 metres away from Breslauer Strasse. Thick planks were laid over the tracks between street-level crossings in the Altstadt and Neustadt, and by evening the first wagons were able to use the new crossing. Nevertheless it was open to one-way traffic only, controlled by the sentries at either end. The water pipes and telephone and electricity cables that had been ripped apart in the explosion could not be replaced so quickly, and the carefully assembled sightscreens had come to the end of their life.[35]

Major of the Reserve Werner Falckenberg, who owned a sawmill and factory in Warnick that had been taken over by the Wehrmacht during the war, wrote a letter to his wife on 16 February:

> I have written to all the places where you might be, perhaps one of them will reach you. The uncertainly of not knowing where you are, and how you are, is trying. All my thoughts are of you.
>
> We are all right here. Our resistance has strengthened considerably. The Soviets attacked the day before yesterday with 8 tanks, 2 battalions and 4–6,000 rounds of shells from artillery and mortars of various calibres. They wanted to get to the Altstadt via the Bienenhof. Three tanks were knocked out, as was the attack. Yesterday we made several sorties that succeeded, including our own, inflicting considerable casualties on the Russians. Overall the Soviet losses are especially high in comparison to our own.
>
> The following occurred the day before yesterday: a Soviet unit, perhaps a platoon or something similar, approached along the Sonnenburger Chaussee to where the bridge leads to the 'Pilsenweg' – how lovely it would be if we could both go there again! So the unit was there. A car led the way. Apparently orders were issued, then the man who had got out of the car

began to shake everyone by the hand. Of course our people were not asleep, they blasted the unit and the whole business off the chaussee with direct hits from a gun or battery.

Our accommodation is well protected. The Middle School in front of us catches everything.[36]

Officer Cadet Corporal Hans Dahlmanns recalled:

About the middle of February we officer cadets were marched off to the front line. We marched from the Engineer Barracks across the Warthe Bridge to the premises of an aquatic sports club on the west bank, where we took a rest between two parked pontoons. I looked around for a place to sit down. I saw my comrade Günther Franzak, whom I liked, sitting on an ammunition box in front of a building. As there was another box near him, I sat down on it. 'Can you keep that place free for Hans, he's coming back any moment,' he said. I knew that Günter and Hans Priebenow were friends, so I stood up and sat down on another ammunition box two or three paces away. A moment later both friends were sitting together. Suddenly a mortar bomb fell on the edge of our group and killed both of them. They came from around Küstrin, one being a dairyman and the other a postman. I had sat immediately next to them and remained unwounded, apart from a pronounced deafness in my right ear. After the mortar bomb explosion the remainder of the officer cadets were sent back to Küstrin-Neustadt, where we were accommodated in the hospital in the south-west part of the barracks.

Next day I with two others received orders to report to my old company commander, Lieutenant Schröder, whose command post was in a casemate on the small peninsula between the harbour and winter harbour in front of the swing bridge over the Warthe. The other officer cadets, as far as I know, were deployed in an infantry role on the southern or eastern front. After a few days the news came that one or another had been killed or severely wounded. I heard that one had lost his eyesight from a flare coming out of a flare pistol.[37]

Officer Cadet Corporal Hans Kirchhof of the tank turret unit recounted his experiences in the Kietz Gate area:

One day in February we were doing some firing practice with our pistols on the fortress walls near the Kietz Gate and witnessed two guns south of there at the Bienenhof shoot up an enemy tank of the T-34 type that had broken through a long way.

In the meantime, while waiting for the anti-tank guns, we took over the transport of supplies to the Bienenhof and the removal of the badly wounded from there. The Bienenhof was defended by a unit of Probationary Battalion 500.

We were three men that had come from the NCO training school at Jülich to the front line as tank-hunters. A volunteer was sought as a gun captain from the three of us. To avoid any preferment or discrimination, we put ourselves at the disposal of our superiors. This was accepted and a little later all three of us were designated gun captains. This happened because – in contrast to both the other guns, two of which were further back – the location of the third was directly in the front line. Here at the Bienenhof were two relieving gun crews. I led one and my friend, Wolfgang Paul, the other. Each crew remained three days and nights in the position and rested afterwards for the whole time at the company command post.

As there were sufficient gunners available, the gun crews could be picked by their captains with the consent of those selected, which included some experienced corporals. None declined to be selected.

About two-thirds of the way through February we took up our new position. About a week before, the first defenders of the Bienenhof had been so reduced by casualties that a flak unit in the infantry role had replaced them. Shortly afterwards the Bienenhof was lost and men of the Probationary Battalion were called into action once more and the flak troops sent back.

Our anti-tank gun was aimed directly at the Oder dyke and was sited in the infantry position, whose southernmost bunker lay within grenade-throwing distance of the Russians. The latter had posted a sniper who, despite all the efforts of the infantry, could not be knocked out of action. Our 36mm gun, useless against tanks, was a silent gun and only supplied with explosives. We had a good relationship with the infantry.[38]

Luftwaffe Officer Cadet Sergeant Helmut Schmidt wrote of his experiences at the Weinbergshof Farm and in Kietz in mid-February:

We were not feeling good. We were sitting in a trap called Küstrin. It was only a fortress in name, with ancient fortifications and without heavy weapons. The Russians had it firmly in their grasp. (We did not then know that there was a 'corridor' through to the main German front line, but we did know what was meant when Führerheadquarters designated a place a 'fortress' to be defended to the last man and the last drop of blood.) We did not even know our fortress commandant.

The Russians had set up a 120mm mortar. The first bomb suddenly exploded near the Weinbergshof during the course of the day. At irregular intervals they sent over two or three bombs, but none hit the target. We got used to the new situation, becoming alert and keen-eared, reacting quickly to the typical bubbling of the discharges.

It became dark, and after the rations orderly had delivered our food to the trench, we were relieved. Tiredly we shuffled along the communications trench to the chaussee, our legs automatically following the road ditch to Kietz. We ducked our heads whenever the tracers from a Maxim machine gun came our way. Our quarters were in one of the first houses. We climbed up the steep and narrow stairs to the first floor of the wretched building, laid down on the bare floor and immediately fell asleep, some using their helmets as pillows.

Early in the morning we were awoken by noise, shouts and the stamping of boots. I did not react immediately, but at last heard someone shouting 'Alarm!' I jumped up and woke the sleepers around me. We grabbed our weapons and tumbled down the steep stairs. Our group then assembled in a small yard between the buildings. We were urged to hurry and marched eastwards in well-spaced single file towards Kietz.

A fight was going on somewhere to our south-east. We could hear German and Russian machine guns, sub-machine-gun fire and the harsh shots of Russian tanks or anti-tank guns.

We had left our quarters with rumbling stomachs. The morning was cloudy and we trembled from the cold. While we trotted along the road under cover of the houses, we listened attentively to the increasing noise of fighting coming from a short distance to the south-east.

We encountered no vehicles or pedestrians on Reichsstrasse 1. In the middle of the Horst-Wessel-Strasse/Kaiserstrasse cross-roads stood a hunting tank, a Hetzer. Its weak armour was reinforced with concrete panels, its tracks moving it about nervously. It seemed to have found a target, but did not fire. After a short stop we turned right towards the sound of fighting. The road ran south-east and ended in the meadows after about 300 metres.

We hurried to reach the buildings on the south-eastern edge of Kietz. We passed a large block of flats on our left. The attackers could now see us and opened fire with infantry weapons. Moving in bounds we reached the cover of an individual house, one of a row of them extending westwards. When a tank shell hit the roof, we pressed against the wall of the house. There was a frightening bang, followed by a reddish cloud of smoke and a clattering of slates landing at our feet.

I took a quick look round the corner of the house. Two T-34s were standing about 500 metres away. I had just pulled back my head when there was a bang and a tank shell whistled past a few metres away. I had a brief glimpse of its tracer and then saw the shell hit the block of flats. There was a double bang, dust billowed out and there was a jagged round hole in the wall.

We moved over to the next house and crept crouched past the cellar windows. One of my section found a bottle containing fruit in an open window, but when he reached for it, he was rapped on the fingers. We then noticed that the cellar was full of civilians, several families with children.

We divided up among the houses. I went to the end house with several comrades. It was badly damaged, and the occupants had moved next door. I came across some infantrymen in a cellar room. A dead man lay on a laundry table, a sergeant or sergeant-major. The soldiers had a machine-gun position behind the fence in the garden. I climbed upstairs. Broken slates covered the steps of the wooden staircase. I looked through a hole that the tanks had shot in the outside wall. Both T-34s stood front left. They had got stuck in the meadows and the attack had come to a halt. The tank guns were silent, but their engines were roaring, emitting blue exhaust smoke, their tracks digging

deeper and deeper into the ground. Russians were working fran-
tically on the tanks. I could hear shouts, orders and swearing.
The two T-34s were trying to tow each other out, but without
success. They only sank deeper. The tracks pulled cleanly
showering fountains of dirt behind them. More shouts and more
Russians hurried up.

The Russians called off their attack. Without tank support
they dared not get closer to the buildings of Kietz. We watched
their hours-long efforts with malicious grins. The Hetzer did not
attack, although the T-34s offered a suitable target. Our
infantry weapons were also silent. We had received no order to
open fire. Were we saving ammunition, or was it to avoid
provoking the Russians?

The Russians vanished back to their trenches, the T-34s
remaining behind, still offering a threat to us that could quickly
become dangerous. We crouched in the cellars of the unoccupied houses while our sentries concealed themselves in the
foliage behind the fences.

It became dark early on this cloudy day. During the first night
hours the Russians tried to get their tanks out again, setting
about it with the aid of some searchlights. They made a row
with the tank engines running at full speed. This went on openly
for hours, and we were withdrawn before the situation with the
tanks had changed.

We marched back to our quarters. We were pleased that the
Russian attack on Kietz had failed. In the accommodation we
were surprised to receive orders to return to the Weinbergshof
immediately. Our 'day off' had come to nothing. After a short
rest we wandered back grumbling to our old position.

We particularly liked our rest days, especially without alerts.
The first of us would wake up after ten or twelve hours' sleep.
We looked for an opportunity to wash and for a lavatory in the
unoccupied house. Freshly shaved, we ate breakfast together,
the usual spirit having returned. We smoked and had a drink.

The few hours in the old house did us good. Recovered, we
prepared unenthusiastically for dusk and the relief. We ate
something quickly, checked our arms and ammunition and then
at about 2130 hours we set off reluctantly back to the
Weinbergshof.

We were told that in future we would have one day in the

trenches and one day's rest. But on our return to the trenches we realised there had been a worsening of the situation. The Russian mortar was firing frequently, the hits occurring here and there, bracketing the whole of the Weinbergshof. The mortar's short barrages were malicious, as the sound of the shots was easily missed. One night I had a lucky escape. Fritz Wenzig, a Rhinelander with an irrepressible sense of humour, had been lightly wounded in the attack on the Cellulose Factory and returned to us from the field hospital. Every evening we would meet by chance at the north-western corner of the manor and would chat in a low voice, myself in the trench and he above on the edge of the trench. Suddenly we heard a mighty whistling. Instinctively we both made ourselves small as a mortar bomb exploded a few paces away. There was an almighty bang and I felt a blow on my shoulder. Fritz Wenzig had his hands to his face. A tiny splinter had penetrated his right cheek and bruised his tongue. I checked my shoulder, but nothing had happened to me. When I looked the next day I found that the thick wadding of my camouflage suit had stopped about fifty tiny iron pellets. But Fritz had to go back to the field hospital, returning to us a few days later. The new crease in his cheek made his cheeky grin even more boyish. We had both had enormous luck. The bomb had not exploded properly due to a fault in its manufacture.

The relief system did not last long. As the manning of the trenches had to be reinforced, we had to stay forwards for two nights and were only relieved on the third. We cursed the order but could do nothing about it. We knew well enough that our company was not up to a Russian attack.

The first night in the trenches passed mainly correctly and badly. With many checks I ensured that my men were alert, but already by the second night I had to check more often as fatigue was overcoming the comrades. They were often asleep on their feet. I went back again from man to man, prodding them to keep them awake.

Every third day we longed for the time of our relief. At last it became dark, the food carrier appeared and put the canister in our trench. We opened the lid, poked the contents and complained about them. We spooned down some soup but were too tired to eat properly.

Eventually the relief took place. We clapped our comrades on the shoulder, exchanged a few words, and gathered at the manager's house. The route to Kietz was covered by most of us in a daze. Finally we climbed the steep wooden stairs to our night encampment, lay down and fell asleep.

Our rations were getting worse by the day. Smokers especially missed their usual cigarette rations. Instead there were cheap cigars that they did not like. So I kept creeping back to Bombardier Horn. As the last man in my section, he 'lived' at the outermost right-hand end of the defence sector in an 'arbour', having dug himself a fine hole immediately before the hedge and camouflaged it from the side and above with a tight entanglement of twigs. Horn smoked cigars and exchanged mine for a few cigarettes, of which he often had a small stock. We crouched for about a quarter of an hour in his airy arbour and had a chat. Apparently Horn had chosen a good site for not once had a mortar bomb come anywhere near it. He felt quite safe in his primitive 'arbour'.

We thought that because of the distance involved the Russians would have problems with their supplies, and the flooded area around the Oder must also be a disadvantage for them. Then one day a Russian 76.2mm gun started firing at us. It was estimated to be about 2 or 3 kilometres away on the far side of the Oder. It was certainly not by chance that it seemed to hit the brick-built extension of the Weinbergshof barn with precision. The aim was just right. The Russian gunners had only to adjust their settings minimally to hit their targets.

The Russians now fired daily half a dozen rounds at us. The gun could not miss its target. The shells exploded within the yard without exception, coming dangerously near to our communications trench. This insidious, disruptive fire considerably reduced our freedom of movement, and we had to be particularly careful when the mortar joined in. The number of shots increased and the gaps between the firing diminished. Seldom did the gun keep quiet during the night, taking over from the tiresome mortar.

Our situation had clearly worsened. The constant sudden bombardments shattered our nerves. Every night we had to fight our fatigue and still got no rest during the day. We were defenceless against these weapons and could do nothing about them.

There was no German artillery to support us and hardly any sign of the Luftwaffe.

I spent hours trying to improve my shelter hole. I scratched a narrow horizontal hollow towards the south in the sandy earth and strengthened the cover of my mouse-hole. Naturally this digging did nothing to improve my protection from enemy fire, but it made me feel a little safer.

Sunday, 18 February, was a day no different from the rest. The damned gun pestered us persistently. The buildings in the yard suffered further hits and the shell holes spread over the ground. In addition we were dead tired. The gun stopped firing at dusk and even the Russian machine guns were quiet. Lieutenant Kühnel then held an order group. He told us that the Weinbergshof would be secured against sudden attack by the Russians with barbed wire fences and mines. Upon leaving the manor, I saw a punishment unit carrying rolls of barbed wire and defensive mines. All the men were unarmed. They stood silently in the lee of the house waiting for their orders. A quarter of an hour later they shouldered their equipment and moved off in a southerly direction, the darkness absorbing them. We had orders not to fire until the minelayers returned, which was expected before midnight.

For a while we thought ourselves safe, at least until the men of the punishment unit had set up the barbed wire fences and laid their mines. We relaxed and dozed. But the work in no-man's-land could not be accomplished in absolute silence. The rolls of wire clinked and clattered as they unrolled, and the holes for the mines could not be dug without making a noise. Apart from this, everything was being done in a hurry.

The Russians had noticed the noise coming from in front of our position and used it for a surprise attack. Perhaps both actions coincided. In any case the enemy went round the minelayers from the west and approached our position to within a few paces. They opened heavy fire abruptly with several sub-machine guns. I could see the orange flames. There was a hell of a din reinforced by the 'Urräh!' shouts of the attackers.

Now we urgently needed the hand grenades that we lacked. We had to keep our heads down. Once they had got through the thick hedge we could see them off, but the Russians recognised this obstacle. Some of them kept us down with their fire, while a group attempted to get through the gate, which they managed to do. We could see individual shadows flitting about towards the manor but did not know whether they were comrades or Russians.

Here was general confusion. We could only reply weakly to the enemy's fire. We received the order to withdraw and made our way back, finally meeting up with the company on Reichsstrasse 1. Lieutenant Kühnel was swearing, blaming the minelayers. He regarded the whole action with the barbed wire and mine-laying as ridiculous. Then I noticed that Hans Hof was missing. I found out that he had fired at the attackers with his machine gun, thus attracting enemy fire, and had been shot in the chest. Comrades from another section had taken him back to the dressing station in Kietz. In all the noise and confusion I had failed to notice this.

We cursed the Russians and were bitterly angry with them. Our company commander soon gave the order for a counter-attack. Within an hour, before midnight, the Weinbergshof was to be in our hands again.

We set off full of anger. Two sections went east of the duck pond and mine went along the communications trench. As we reached the manager's house we heard a mortar firing and then the bursting of the first bombs. The Russians were laying down defensive fire, but those that had forced their way in remained quiet.

As I went past my shelter hole I saw a dead man lying in the trench in front of me. He was one of the men from the punishment company. I took his pay book from his breast pocket. The poor chap had been unable to reach safety.

While I was seeing to the dead man, a shout went up in the dark from the south-east side of the pond, like an animal's cry. Corporal Schorer had surprised a Russian in the trench near his shelter hole and hit him with his rifle butt on the head. The Russian ran away and disappeared into the darkness.

I was the last section commander to reach the company command post in the manor cellars. I gave the dead man's pay book to the company commander. The retaking of the position had succeeded and by midnight all the sections were back in their positions. The Russians had penetrated the company command post and left an anti-tank mine in a discreet wooden case behind. Presumably they had intended planting it when they had more time.

Unfortunately the counterattack had cost us dear. Both section commanders, Sergeant August Finkler and Sergeant Willi Bohnsack, had fallen victim to the mortar. We were not allowed to bury the dead ourselves, having to give the last services for both our comrades to strangers. A pity. We were not allowed to leave the position even for a short time.

We did not know what had happened to the punishment company. They had not completed their work. Our position remained insecure from the south with neither barbed wire nor mines.[39]

Chapter Seven

Evacuation

By 19 February the nightly passage of the supply convoys had already lasted a week without any significant incidents. Now at last the civilian population was to be evacuated by the same route. Those concerned had been waiting impatiently for this moment, yet very little had been done to prepare for it.

Fearing accusations of defeatism, the Party authorities had caused the subject of civilian evacuation to be ignored throughout the preceding weeks, but now entered a hectic debate about how it should be conducted. There was no hint of a plan for informing the inhabitants or for any sort of organisation at the assembly point. No provision was made for assisting the elderly and handicapped, who constituted a considerable part of the remaining population. Eventually the Neustadt was chosen as the first area to be evacuated, with the square in front of the Boys' Middle School, now the main dressing station, designated as the assembly point at 1800 hours. The fortress newspaper did not appear that day because of the failure in the electricity supply, so leaflets had to be prepared but, for the same reason, these were insufficient in number to convey the evacuation instructions to everyone, and many people had to rely on word of mouth as the means of passing on the official instructions.

Although a large group of people duly assembled for the breakout at the appointed time, they first had to wait for transportation while the route to Alt Bleyen was discussed for hours. The halftracks could only drive as far as Alt Bleyen, and for a regular shuttle service through the 'corridor' some form of intermediate transportation was necessary. The women, children and old people had already walked 2 kilometres to the school and were unable to walk on twice that distance to the front line in the dark. Apart from two tractors with trailers and three horse-drawn carts, there were no other means of transport available from civilian resources, and urgent pleas resulted

146

in two trucks being sent from the fortress headquarters. This for an estimated 2–3,000 people!

Reinefarth's staff suddenly intervened when he suspected that soldiers desperate to escape the war might try to make use of the evacuation certificates. These were typewritten blank forms – three to a page – reading 'On the orders of the fortress commandant, Frau — with — children/Herr — from Küstrin, — Street No. —, is to leave Küstrin as part of the general evacuation. The receiving district is Westprignitz.' Not only was there no master list of inhabitants with names and addresses, but there was also no time to complete the individual certificates, so they were merely stamped and signed, often by young helpers. However, Reinefarth need not have worried, for even if the certificates fell into the hands of soldiers, such primitive documents would never have passed scrutiny at any military checkpoint. His headquarters staff finally dropped their objections to the certificates in order not to endanger the entire operation, but a security police detachment was posted at the assembly point to ensure its orderly conduct.

Mistrustful and cautious from bitter experience, many Neustadt inhabitants were on their way hours before the appointed time. The fortunate owners of handcarts, bicycle trailers and strong children's scooters were envied by those having to carry their worldly goods in suitcases, rucksacks and bedding rolls. The only official assistance was shown by the Volkssturm leaders tolerantly allowing their off-duty personnel to leave their quarters to escort their families to the assembly point. Use of the adapted railway bridge was forbidden to the civilians without explanation, and they had to use the badly damaged road bridge, where the heavily laden handcarts were often hampered by the ripped decking of the narrow side strip that was still passable.

Soon hundreds of people were standing in front of the Middle School on the old chestnut tree-lined Marktplatz, where the surroundings offered little cover. A sudden bombardment would have resulted in a bloodbath, but fortunately the Soviet guns remained quiet all day long. Young messengers handed out the blank evacuation certificates, and then the crowd was left to itself again, with the women and children sitting on their baggage. Others, especially old folk on their own, wandered around restlessly in the hope of finding people they knew to group with. Responsible persons from whom information could be obtained about what was to happen were sought in vain, as were marshals whose job it was to allocate individual groups to vehicles. The Party administrators remained out of sight in their quarters only 100 metres away, providing neither staff, policemen nor Hitler Youth work teams. Certainly a sufficient number of helpers could have been deployed immediately without deflecting them from their responsibilities, even men from the fire brigade or Volkssturm staff, but nothing of the sort occurred. Instead the numerically weakest part of the civic apparatus, the NSV, had suddenly been detailed for the task that morning. When they arrived at dusk, its three staff, 'reinforced' by an adolescent messenger, were confronted by between 2,500 and 3,000 people. Obtaining an exact figure was neither planned nor possible; a rough assessment being estimated from the number of certificates handed out. Women were stamping and signing the certificates in the NSV office as they were run off in the Hitler Youth office on the Marktplatz.

The evacuation took hours. This was foreseeable but no provision had been made for it. There was no handing out of warm drinks, although the evenings and nights were still decidedly cool. Disappointment spread when it became known how limited the transport available for the first stage was. Only a few were prepared to walk all the way to Alt Bleyen so as to keep the places on the wagons free for women with small children, the sick and feeble. The instruction that the vehicles could only take small items of luggage brought an angry reaction from the crowd. Even old people who had given up the chance of a place on one of the trucks in order not to lose the last of their belongings gathered on the approaches to the nearby Oder bridges, hoping for a lift. There were still many hand-carts, as those who wanted to go on the vehicles – and they were the majority – did not need them any more. They began marching off in batches of 20 or 30 in the darkness, with their escorting security guards giving the impression of shepherding prisoners on the march. The armed escorts were explained as precautionary against nervous bridge and road sentries as the evening curfew for civilians, to whom the password could not be given, even as an exception, had already begun. But everyone knew that their presence was really to deter potential army deserters from slinking into the column.

At last the first vehicle moved off and was promptly stormed. A few voices calling for calm could be heard in the trampling crowd, amid the complaining and wailing. Older people dared not enter the turmoil. There were no kind hands to pull them up on to the high truck beds, and there were no stools or mounting blocks to help people climb aboard. Loaded to the limits of their capacity, the wagons drove off, winding their way through the anti-tank barricades of ancient cannon rammed into the roadway before the bridges, and vanished into the night. Ownerless suitcases, purses and prams, for which no room had been found or which had been torn from people's hands in the press, remained behind.

Only half an hour went by before the first vehicle returned, during which time the crowd had quietened down a bit and the second trip began in far less dramatic circumstances. Thus the evacuation went on until midnight, when an officer brought instructions to stop as bright moonlight now made any movement in the 'corridor' risky, and the shuttle service from Alt Bleyen to Seelow/Werbig had to be stopped. However, there were still about 150 people waiting and the dressing station in the school could not take them. A return to the Neustadt during curfew – and crossing the Warthe bridge, which was dangerous even in daylight – was out of the question. So abandoned buildings in the neighbourhood were broken into and used as temporary accommodation. The vacated assembly point bore the depressing evidence of the breakout. Between the old trees were strewn suitcases and satchels, prams and even a bicycle. The NSV people were in no position – and anyway were far too tired – to secure the ownerless items, but stacked them under a tree so the police could collect them the next day; however, when the police duly came they found only a few ripped open and plundered items, the rest having vanished.[1]

Lieselotte Christiansen remembered the evacuation:

On 19 February we received the order to leave Küstrin immediately. We left our cellar in the Neustadt under fire and reached the Altstadt over an almost completely destroyed bridge. We arrived in a hail of fire. It seemed as if the heavens were in flames. We thought it was the end, but it could not be. It became quieter again and we went to the collecting point where the vehicles were standing. Only old and sick people could be taken. The Wiese family, my mother and I obtained a place on a truck that had brought ammunition into the town. We were all squeezed up together, but were happy to get away. The driver drove in such a way as to dodge enemy fire.

We arrived unharmed in Gusow from where in the morning a train took us on to Erkner and then to Woltersdorf.[2]

The inevitable looting started after the first departures and increased during the evacuation of the population, but soon the fortress commandant got a grip on the situation and hanged people for even the smallest offences, both soldiers and civilians. The *Feste Küstrin* reported that the Standing Court dealing with looting and desertion sentenced one soldier for looting on 15 February, another for desertion on the 18th, another for desertion and looting on the 23rd, an Italian prisoner of war for looting on the 24th, and one soldier and a girl for looting on the 26th. Almost all the fortress news-sheets carried in bold letters the notice that 'Looters will be shot!', and later 'Looters will be shot or hanged!' This had some effect on reducing this crime.

Ten German soldiers were shot in Kietz one day. On or around 20 February two members of the Wehrmacht were hanged from the Kietz Gate with a placard saying, 'I deserted'. From then on there was no further absence without leave. It was just about impossible to get out by the 'pipeline' and no one wanted to go over to the Russians. The incident at the beginning of the siege in which the Volkssturm troops captured at the Cellulose Factory had been executed had been discussed by many of the fortress's defenders.[3]

Luftwaffe Officer Cadet Sergeant Helmut Schmidt continued his account of the defence of the Weinbergshof Farm on Monday, 19 February:

> The night was exciting and we remained alert until dawn. Should the Russians have risked a second attack, we would have given them a hot reception. Our machine gun was back in its old position. In the trenches the men chatted about the Russian surprise attack and our counterattack. They spoke concernedly about Hans Hof and thought about the fallen. In the cellar of the manor Lieutenant Kühnel went over the events of the previous hours with his platoon commanders. What had gone wrong? In my opinion we should have provided cover for the minelayers, and they should not have been working in the open ground without protection.
>
> We thought that the Russians had made a spontaneous surprise attack when they discovered the minelayers. We calcu-

lated the attackers at about one or two dozen. They had gone
forward without preparation and counted on surprise. I think
they must have asked for reinforcements but had set off before
they arrived. Support from the mortar had come at the right
time, and its blocking fire had enabled their rapid withdrawal.
The Russians had only been able to hold the Weinbergshof for
an hour, but this had been enough to reconnoitre our positions.
They now knew the exact situation of our trenches, the
company command post and the weakness of our defence. Their
opportune attack had proved a valuable reconnaissance.

We had hardly sat back in our shelter holes when the Russians
started shooting at us again with their machine guns. We
noticed their nervousness and irritation. They were angry. They
put the hedge and my section of the trench under particularly
intensive fire, and the mortar went on firing with the hits
crashing down between the buildings, and at daybreak the
76.2mm gun joined in too. We ducked down in our primitive
holes. The barrage increased and lasted longer. The Russians
wanted to keep us awake. We urgently needed a breathing
space, for we were frightfully tired.

Towards midday we came under an especially bitter barrage
from the 76.2mm gun, most of the shells exploding in the area
of our communications trench. I crouched down in my hole. All
hell was being let loose around me. I began mechanically
counting the explosions to get through it.

It gradually quietened down. My ears were drumming.
Dazed, I crept out of my hole. As I stood up I saw a dud shell
lying on the barely 30-centimetre-thick cover of my shelter hole.
The shell was right in front of my eyes. For seconds I stared at
it like a mouse at a snake. I was unable to react or move. I looked
at this plain piece of slightly rusted iron lying crossways. I saw
the badly dented detonator, the fine threads and the blackened
copper ring that the rifling of the barrel had caused.

Eventually I overcame my shock and quickly left that
dangerous spot. I called out to Tiedemann and crept into his
hole. He gave me my next shock. Tiedemann was kneeling
propped on his carbine with his back to me. He was not wearing
his steel helmet and a shell splinter no bigger than a fingernail
had gone into the back of his head. There was a thin trickle of
blood from the wound. Tiedemann's face was totally altered

and I could hardly recognise him. His face was unnaturally
yellow, waxen and completely relaxed. He seemed to be asleep.
Heinz Tiedemann, the unwarlike soldier, was dead. Why wasn't
he wearing his helmet and lying flat on the ground?

Sadness and anger overcame me. Yesterday Tiedemann had
passed his 31st birthday unnoticed by us all. That evening
Tiedemann's body was taken back to Kietz by two men of my
section, carried in a tent-half. We stood sad and depressed in the
trench and saw him taken away without a word. We were not
allowed to bury him ourselves.

A few days later came some totally unexpected news for Schmidt's
unit:

Like a bombshell came a radio message from the 23rd Flak
Division that the company commander passed on immediately
to the men in the trenches. All members of the division were to
be withdrawn from Küstrin.

At first we took the order for a latrine rumour. Why should
we be selected to leave the fortress? It took a while for us to
begin to believe the authenticity of the news. The company
command post announced that we would be leaving the
position that night. But what would happen to the Army
members of our company? We were actually a Luftwaffe
battery, but without our guns. Could we take the comrades that
had joined us with us? I thought of Bombardier Horn. Could
we leave him behind? We were completely confused.

It became dark early that evening. Our relief appeared, a
mixed bunch. Many young soldiers and with them old corporals
with Iron Cross ribbons. Their arms were not much, just
carbines and a few machine guns. Then things began to happen
quickly. We briefed our successors quickly as the company
commander was calling for us to hurry. Saying farewell to our
brave Bombardier Horn was particularly hard. I stood before
him and gave him my hand and wished him well. Both of us
tried to smile, but it did not come right. We knew that we would
never see each other again.

I did not look back. Even before we reached the Chaussee I
was overcome with weariness. I did not register that vehicles
were waiting for us in Kietz, that we climbed on to the trucks,

An aerial view of the Altstadt showing the Schloss, Marien Church and the Marktplatz with Bastion König and the Kattewall in the foreground.

Bastion König and the Schloss seen from the Oder Island.

The Neumarkt in the Neustadt with the big water tower. Zorndorfer Strasse is on the left.

The Neustadt post office on Schützstrasse with the main railway station and a water tower on the left.

The Cellulose Factory.

Inside the grounds of the Potato Meal Factory on Plantagenstrasse.

The von Stülpnagel Infantry Barracks seen from the Heerstrasse, with the guardroom on the left.

The dry moat of the Neues Werke.

Refugees passing through Küstrin immediately before the siege.

A Mark III Valentine that was destroyed on Plantagenstrasse on 31 January, with the railway underpass and Neustadt town centre in the background.

SS-Lieutenant-General Heinz-Friedrich Reinefarth leaving his command post.

Volkssturm battalion commander Gustav Tamm with a section of his unit on the Gorin at the beginning of February 1945.

The railway bridge to the Altstadt seen from the Neustadt end. Helmut Schmidt's section had a machine-gun position in the hollow in the foreground.

The railway bridge over the Vorflut Canal seen from the Altstadt. A soldier is gathering firewood, while sentries on the right guard the bridge to prevent unauthorised movement to the west, and a machine-gun position is sited on the left.

An aerial view of the ruined Neustadt.

The wrecked Kietz Gate after the battle.

drove to the Alt Bleyen manor farm and left the fortress area from there in a bumping, rocking night journey. I slept on the truck like a dead man. It was daylight when I awoke from my exhausted sleep. I tried to remember what had happened but was unable to. My comrades had also slept through it. The air was fresh and my legs were stiff. I got up from the bench and pushed the tailgate of our little truck down and saw two pairs of boots hanging in front of my eyes. I jumped down from the truck and found two soldiers hanging from telephone wires with cardboard notices around their necks on which was written: 'I was a coward!' The sight was shocking. The soldiers' boots almost touched the garden fence alongside which we had stopped. Everyone found this barbaric, disgusting and idiotic. On the roadside was a shield that read: 'Anyone who is encountered west of the Oder as a straggler has forfeited his life. Any soldier that has become separated from his unit must immediately join the nearest front-line unit. There is no going back from here. The Russian avalanche must be finally stopped at the Oder!'

We were in Seelow. Our truck was alongside a small cottage. A group of men were standing near the hanged men, cursing and swearing at the SS and Feldgendarmerie; they would not be quiet.

In Fürstenwalde we went to a hutted camp. We thought that we had landed in another world, it was so clean and orderly. Signs showed that there was even a canteen. The barrack rooms were large and everyone got a freshly made bed. We could at last have a wash, a shower to scrub away the earth of the Weinbergshof trenches. And we got fresh underwear. What a luxury! A little later we were given a good lunch.[4]

The leading article in the newspaper of 20 February began in encouraging style: 'The garrison and population of Küstrin already have twenty days of fighting behind them. Traces of the fighting have made themselves more evident in the appearance of the town.' Success could be measured in physical terms: 54 prisoners taken, 23 tanks and SPGs destroyed, 3 aircraft shot down and 'several Soviet divisions held up'. There was also a flood of decorations: 28 Iron Crosses First Class, 94 Iron Crosses Second Class, two Tank-Destroyer awards, three Infantry Storm awards, one Close-Fighting award. There was even an award for the population: Reinefarth had given the Party district leader 16,000 packets of fruit drops from the soldiers' supplies as a gift from the garrison to the women and children of Küstrin. These would be distributed as soon as possible.

It was now the turn of the people of the Altstadt to dig out their most valuable and useful items from cupboards and drawers, and secure them in handy bundles. Some had seen the first transports leave and knew what to expect, and so were able to prepare themselves better. They were also spared the long march to the assembly point, but the weeks of anxious waiting made them leave their houses earlier than necessary. The crowd of people waiting in front of the school and nearby grew quickly and soon amounted to another 3,000, including late arrivals from the Neustadt, people who had only just received the order to evacuate or did not want to wait in uncertainty from one hour to the next. Others had not yet been able to make up their minds, although eviction threatened sooner or later. Quite a number of those surprised at the assembly point by the breaking off of the evacuation the evening before and sent into emergency accommodation had gone back to their homes, lacking the energy to become involved in the turmoil yet again.

The Party authorities had again done nothing to make things easier. Not once had they contributed anything, although this time there was some hot coffee prepared by two women in a wash-oven and carried in buckets, as even Thermos flasks and a wagon to carry the container was lacking. (An ownerless bicycle trailer taken for this purpose from the assembly point the night before had been stolen from the NSV cellars during the night.) So the same procedure as on the previous evening was pursued: members of the SD (security element of the SS) escorted the groups on foot, and there was a storm on the first vehicles waiting. Most people took hardly any notice when, one after the other, the mayor and the fortress commandant in full parade uniform appeared. They stood a few minutes talking together and then disappeared equally unnoticed. The people's only interest was in finding a suitable position in the street and perhaps getting a place on the next wagon.

It was already midnight when suddenly the sound of an aircraft engine was heard in the sky. Invisible, but almost palpable, the PO-2 flew several times over the square. Off-duty soldiers who had been watching the evacuation in the absence of any other form of entertainment and some individuals hoping for new loot from the luggage left behind all vanished. They had experience of these double-deckers, which often lurked over the front lines. Most people searched the night sky, bewitched. Where was it? Would it drop bombs? A flare flamed brightly only a little to one side towards the Oder. Hundreds stared as it moved and stopped. There was no movement, no recognisable target, either seen or heard. The light flak woke up. The plane flew off, the light dwindled and vanished. The transport started up again. People relaxed, they had been lucky yet again. But the solders' scepticism was correct. Fire rose over the roofs and, although the explosion was a good distance away, it caused anxiety in the narrow streets. The next shots were even closer. One wagon was already loading, but the driver was nervous and set off before all the places had been taken. Seconds later there was an explosion on the cobbled square in front of the school, bringing the shattering of glass, cries of horror, trampling and flight. Three people were left unconscious, a soldier and two civilians, and were taken injured to the dressing station. After this interruption the transportation continued until two o'clock in the morning. Even before the last wagon was ready to leave, inhabitants of the neighbouring quarter slunk up to the assembly point to fall unembarrassed and unhindered on the abandoned bundles and cases.

The evacuation was more successful once the 'corridor' had been properly established, with the tracked vehicles coming right through to the Altstadt on the nights of 19 to 23 February, all with minimal casualties.

The Mayor of Küstrin and NSDAP County Leader Hermann Körner was also responsible for the security of the considerable supplies stored in the Neustadt. The foodstuffs in the Norddeutschen Kartoffel-Mehlfabrik (Potato Meal Factory) alone were estimated by him to be worth 3.5 million Reichsmarks. When the nightly convoys on the return journey were not required for personnel and wounded, they took these supplies with them.

The 9th Army's eight-day-old operational orders for Küstrin were now enforced in a formal order from the staff of the XIth SS Panzer Corps. This specified that the defence of the fortress area was to be conducted in such a way as to prevent a Soviet attack on the Warthe and Oder bridges, and to hinder enemy traffic over the Oder within range of the garrison's heavy weapons.[5]

Lieutenant Erich Bölke recalled:

I was placed under Captain Langenhahn, who was a liaison officer between the artillery and flak units and the staff, under Major Fenske of the fortress commandant's staff. Captain Langenhahn was a soldier through and through and carried out his oath of duty until his death. He was not especially liked by the simple soldiery, because he sought to be hard and thorough in sticking to orders. I knew him for many years and can personally only speak well of him.

Mostly I was deployed as an observer on the tower of the Marienkirche in the Altstadt. I remember three special events from this time. First, a Stuka attack by part of Rudel's squadron. Secondly, a Soviet bridge downriver on the Oder. Once I called down our heavy artillery fire on it from behind the German front line. Direct hits broke the bridge, but within hours the Russian engineers had repaired the damage. Thirdly, Major Fenske. He had been in the First World War and came from Dresden. When I was on duty as observer on the church tower of the Marienkirche he would sometimes join me. As he was a heavy smoker, I gave him my cigarettes. He would set himself at the periscope and ask: 'Bölke, where are the cigarettes?' and smoke one after another. Major Fenske possessed good military knowledge and also a cooperative attitude. Between ourselves, he said to me: 'Bölke, we are not going to win the war any more. Don't put yourself so much at risk. Let Langenhahn do it. You have to survive.' I believe that his main thought was how to survive this engagement and come out of this shitty situation.

The fortress had two reactive mortars. They were not mobile but fired from racks. Their chief had been promoted from Second-Lieutenant to Major in the course of the events of 20 July 1944 and fell during the siege. One day a war correspondent appeared in Küstrin and wanted to take pictures of the reactive mortars being fired. He misunderstood the instructions by the officer responsible about the danger from the rocket-like tail blast, got too close and scorched his forehead. He then complained to the staff about his destroyed camera and damaged uniform.[6]

Again on 22 February it proved impossible to get all the civilians through the 'corridor' before the moon rose. About 150 people had to wait at Alt Bleyen manor farm, condemned to a 24-hour wait in the immediate front line, accommodated in a barn. After all that had gone before, it was hardly surprising that the fortress staff refused to take responsibility for the evacuees. Even a request for a sturdy vehicle to take the most pressing cases through that morning was not met. So, as the Party administration had grabbed many of the few remaining vehicles, someone had to go to help them. A motor vehicle courageously set off with a driver, assistant and medical orderly, laden with big milk cans filled with coffee, biscuits and cartons of sweets. The road along the dyke was slippery from hours of fine rain. The cold, wet weather appeared fortunately to have affected the alertness of the Soviet observers, for the vehicle only came under mortar fire on its return journey and then suffered only minor damage. When a warm meal had to be delivered to Alt Bleyen at noon, the vehicle became stuck and had to be pulled out by a jeep that was fortunately coming by. The Altstadt people would have to be taken by tracked vehicles from Alt Bleyen that evening before the next batch of evacuees, this time from Kietz, reached the shuttle service boarding point in the farmyard. Only about 300 people gathered in the pouring rain at the sawmill next to the Vorflut Canal that was being used as an assembly point, showing that the majority of this westernmost suburb's inhabitants had already left with the last treks or trains.

For the first time there were no problems with the transport to Alt Bleyen, which had taken about 6,000 people in the previous three days. Those responsible within and outside Küstrin could consider themselves lucky that everything had gone so well and that neither in the previous three weeks nor during the evacuation had there been any big losses.

Nevertheless not all the civilians had left their home town. Consequently, when the Neustadt was stormed, some 500 to 600 of them fell into the hands of the Red Army. In addition, individual inhabitants kept returning to collect belongings they had left behind until 22 March, and some of these became trapped and remained in Kuhbrücken until the very end.

For lack of fresh material – even the local situation report was reduced to four and a half lines of nothing new, with not even the evacuation being mentioned – the *Feste Küstrin* produced just two 'holding-out' contributions. After six days of vain attempts to gain some operational depth in Pomerania following some local successes in Operation Sonnenwende, the attack had been broken off. Küstrin remained a distant goal.[7]

All those living in the Altstadt who had not already taken to sleeping in the cellars were driven down their cellar steps at 0500 hours. Medium calibre guns firing from the south poured a dense volume of shells into the town centre, the main target being Friedrichstrasse between the courthouse and the old army bakery. This lightly built-over terrain along the line of the filled-in fortress ditch, on which Reichsstrasse 1 ran, had hardly been troubled until now, as it was probably protected by the camouflage screen. Several 150mm infantry guns were deployed in the open on the little Rosengarten Park, not 100 metres from the dressing station in the Boys' Senior School.

The firing came at regular intervals of 15 to 20 minutes, then there was a hefty explosion and a chain of lighter detonations in quick succession. A rain of splinters poured over into the Altstadt. A provisional ammunition dump near the youth hostel, in which heavy flak shells had been stacked in open pits, had been hit. The blackened remains of wickerwork baskets used for carrying shells were blown into the water, and the ground was strewn with bits of explosive materials and unexploded shells over a wide area. This dangerous hail came right over the fortress walls and hit the quarters of an engineer platoon in the hostel there.

Although a considerable number of civilians still remained in the town, they had not been hurt. Because of the apparent peace of the past days, some were already thinking about leaving the fortress. Many elderly people found it unbearable to be carted off somewhere else when their own four walls still stood, and many families of soldiers and Volkssturm men serving in the fortress wanted to stay on as long as possible to be with their fathers, husbands and sons.

This barrage and its consequences had a sobering effect, especially among those who lived close to ammunition stores. The capacity for accommodating military stores in vacant or somewhat shellproof rooms in the Altstadt was already about exhausted before the convoys from Seelow started arriving. Since then, however, many truckloads of supplies had arrived in the last ten nights, particularly ammunition. For instance, the shells for the heavy infantry guns had been stacked under the archway of the Berlin Gate, in the last remaining fortress stores, and the adjacent small casemates. But cases of Panzerfausts, together with anti-tank and flak ammunition, had been laid out on the grass under canvas in the immediate vicinity. A nearby garage was packed to the roof with aircraft bombs, being unusable in that role because of the lack of fuel for the aircraft to carry them, but useful to the sappers for demolition purposes. Even the lower-ranking Wehrmacht staff who had taken up quarters in this area were unhappy, and eventually protested when it was proposed putting a petrol canister depot in the open air here.

Towards evening the area around Friedrichstrasse came under a short barrage again when about 300 civilians were gathered waiting for transportation from the nearby Boys' Middle School. One shell hit the new Law Courts. Volkssturm men accommodated there left their supper and took shelter in the passages. Later recorded as the only damage, the swastika over the doorway lay smashed on the ground.[8]

'Artillery activity continues to increase', commented the *Feste Küstrin* of 23 February. The front lines and the town continued to resound to surprise bombardments of varying intensity. There was hardly a building whose roof had not already been pierced, whose façade had not been damaged with shell splinters. There were shattered stones and glass splinters everywhere. Only in the narrow alleys of the inner town, where the buildings provided some shelter for each other, could the ground-floor rooms still be used without permanent danger. But here too rows of windows had been broken. Sappers went from one staff quarter to another to prepare the cellars for permanent residence, putting wooden timbers under the ceiling beams to support them, and sandbags over the rooms above and in front of the windows.

The subject of the mail came under discussion in the town hall, regarding the fate of the packages and packets abandoned by the officials in the Neustadt post office when fighting broke out. There were thousands of items, mostly en route to places east of the Oder, that had only been found by chance. Since then a Volkssturm guard had been maintained on the stores at the station, which already showed clear signs of having been looted. Cut strings, paper strips, ripped cartons and trampled cakes covered the floors of the passages from the stores to the loading platform. Withered sprigs of fir clearly showed that many of the packages had been there since before Christmas. Getting any to their destinations or back to the sender could not be taken seriously under the circumstances, so the post office was ordered to open the parcels and sort out the contents for distribution to the Volkssturm and soldiers.[9]

Of particular significance to the future of Küstrin that day was the fall of Posen after five weeks of siege, releasing those six divisions of the 8th Guards and 69th Armies that had been engaged there and could now be used on the Oder front.

Heavy rain overnight washed away the dust from the road surfaces, making the dirty traces of artillery strikes barely noticeable on the morning of 24 February. The progressive diminution of the population began to have an impact on the town, much to the chagrin of the self-justifying Party administration, whose estimated 1,000-soul domain would vanish within a week at the current rate of evacuation. The local authorities were embarrassed by the idea of having to do Volkssturm service, but the Landsberg prominenti knew how to utilise their special position. The task of managing the civilian supplies, given to them now that nearly all the shops were closed, had become meaningless, but their three-week stay in the beleaguered fortress would be well noted in 'higher places'. The lesser civil servants could be sacrificed to hold the fort, while the close circle around the former mayor of Landsberg could leave the hot seat on the Oder inconspicuously. The gentlemen gathered together in their quarters out of the rain that evening to wait for transport. Some had donned civilian overcoats over their brown uniforms 'because it will be cold in the open wagons'. They could only conceal their unease with difficulty as they puffed away on thick cigars. One of them went to the door from time to time to ensure they would not miss the arrival of the tracked vehicles. For the first time the evacuees were to be taken from the town and not from Alt Bleyen, the rapidly reducing numbers having made the special intermediary shuttle service unnecessary. The refugees' departure time had nevertheless yet to be agreed by the headquarters, by which of the two night convoys – at 2000 hours or midnight – the requisite number of vehicles would be available. The 2000 hours convoy had already gone and they now had to wait another four hours before the halftracks rattled back along the empty streets. This time the gentlemen did not even allow themselves time to button up their greatcoats before plunging outside.

That same day the Fortress newspaper sang the praises of a 76-year-old man: 'He too did not want to be left behind'. He had – possibly simply out of fear of exile in an asylum – tried to be taken on by the Volkssturm for attachment to a fighting unit. However, in view of the volunteer's age, he had been taken on instead as a clerk in a Wehrmacht office.[10]

Officer Cadet Alfred Kraus recalled:

Towards the end of February the enemy brought many tanks and trucks into Alt Drewitz, the noise of which came over to us. Observers established the presence of Stalin-Organs and guns. We expected a Russian attack. Instead, one lunchtime a Stuka squadron appeared, Rudel's squadron, and bombarded the enemy positions.

Although this meant that a Soviet offensive was now unlikely, enemy pressure on the Cellulose Factory increased. It was less quiet in our position on the north-west side of the factory premises. The firing of mortars and Stalin-Organs increased. Since we were not visible from the front, I sometimes had the impression that an enemy observer was located on the chimney behind us and was directing the fire.

When a returning Soviet bomber squadron flew over us, our anti-aircraft gun shot down the leading aircraft, whose tail plane hit a second bomber and the remainder hit a third. All three enemy bombers fell from the one direct hit.

I was wounded by a shell splinter in the right arm while taking a message to the firing position. Nils Fauck brought me back. The dressing station was on the first floor in one of the housing blocks opposite our company command post. It was in the charge of a corporal with a glass eye. He had tended the wounded during a mortar barrage. There was a rumour that he was a degraded doctor. He operated on me straight away. During the night I awoke from my drugged sleep when a 105mm flak gun fired not far from my window. This gun which we had found in the Cellulose Factory had an alternative firing position in front of our dressing station and was tended by former Luftwaffe auxiliaries of our company. While I was detained at the dressing station I saw it shoot up two enemy tanks that advanced over the open land between the Cellulose Factory and the Drewitzer Unterweg at night camouflaged as haystacks.

I was still at the dressing station when I was wounded for a second time. French civilian workers were digging an anti-tank ditch in front of the buildings. The Russians laid down mortar fire on them and a splinter hit my back when I looked out of the window. Until I was fully recovered I was detailed to work in the company's radio position, but this did not happen, as I had a confrontation with the quartermaster-sergeant, who sent me back into the front line. When I arrived at the Cellulose Factory, Second-Lieutenant Thom had already been informed by a runner and told me: 'I've already heard. However, you will remain as a runner as before. The quartermaster-sergeant can come here and see me if he doesn't like it.'

That same evening our company commander, Lieutenant Schellenberg, organised a night fighting patrol as ordered. Nils Fauck, who during my absence had been manning the radio and telephone, went of his own accord. The attack took place on 23 February, supported by flame-throwers, artillery and mortars, the latter firing from the Cellulose Factory. (Whether the mortars had been moved here for this reason, I do not know.) In our opinion the undertaking was senseless and costly. My friend Wolfgang Warner was wounded in it. Nils Fauck was brought back to the dressing station with a shot through the arm. I did not see him again, nor did I find him again after the war. I met Wolfgang Warner again in Munich and we are still in contact.[11]

The first execution by hanging took place on 25 February, the victim being a flak sergeant-major. According to the announcement, he had been living in his allocated quarters with a 20-year-old girl, and they had packed a bag with underwear and clothing with which to leave the fortress. Within the same hour that her boyfriend was hanged from the crossbar of a telephone pole near the Altstadt railway crossing, the girl was sentenced to death by shooting. It seems that the real reason for their planned flight was the actual crime of looting. How could the garrison's flak units, which consisted of so many young soldiers and Luftwaffe auxiliaries under the physical and nervous strain of being in combat, grasp that one of their superiors – for whatever reason – saw nothing wrong in discontinuing to endanger his life? Making a disciplinary example of an officer over stolen property would certainly have a widespread impact. There had been anger for a long time over the increasing looting and malicious damage in abandoned buildings, especially among the remaining civilians and local Volkssturm.

A front-line cinema was opened that day only a few hundred yards from the place of execution. The three cinemas in the town, Urania, Apollo and Küstriner Lichtspiele, had been closed at the end of January and damaged since. A new location was chosen, a former air-raid shelter on the youth hostel plot in the Altstadt. Various containers of household goods deposited there for safety by several families during the evacuation were dumped outside and primitive wooden benches were used to fill the now musty vaults. For the première there was the film *Menschen vom Varieté* and an old news-reel exhorting victory.[12]

Fighting around the town continued to remain minimal on 26 February. The local situation report – as it already had done for days – spoke only of the activity of the heavy weapons, implying the two sides were equally matched:

> Enemy artillery fire especially on the Cellulose Factory and the Oder Vorflut bridges. Lively activity by our own artillery with good success. Our own patrols active against positions north-wards of Alt Drewitz and south of Kietz.

Low cloud interrupted the deployment of Soviet aircraft and enabled work on the fortifications to continue relatively undisturbed. This was concentrated on strengthening the naturally poor defences in the Neustadt along the curve of the front line based on the Warthe. After an eight-day interruption, traffic into this sector over the road bridge was partly resumed, engineers having built a wooden structure over the sunken arch. Nevertheless it was little more than one track wide and was only usable by light vehicles owing to its limited weight capacity. Other traffic had to be directed over the railway bridge.

One of the SD (security service) teams stationed in the fortress had begun combing through the streets one by one, ordering the remaining inhabitants to leave. This team of about 30 men, supported in the Altstadt by a few members of the Party administration, pursued the task with enthusiasm. The end of the evacuation was finally achieved when even the rear area troops were withdrawn. Those civilians who had refused to leave were scattered over the whole town, and short-notice changes of residence following fire or artillery damage was part of the daily routine, so another check had to be made of all inhabitable buildings down to the cellars. But the manpower available was insufficient, as the SD also had to enforce the stricter blackout regulations.

The emergency power station restarted after several days of dis-ruption, but only operated from 2000 hours in the evening to 0600 hours in the morning, partly in order to save fuel and partly to avoid smoke from the factory chimney alerting the Soviet observers. As the power came on during the first evening lights appeared in windows all over the town. The fear quickly arose among some fanatics that this was either sabotage or a deliberate act intended to aid the enemy, but the real connection with the evacuation was soon realised. After five years of enforced blackout, thoughtlessness among those remaining rarely occurred. The problem almost exclusively involved buildings whose inhabitants had left for the assembly point in daylight. Most had not closed the shutters and curtains and in those areas where the power had gone off, light switches had been left on unheeded. Because of the increase in these cases and out of well-founded respect for the PO-2s flying over the town at night, the patrols received orders to shoot through the windows at these light sources when shouted warnings were not immediately responded to.[13]

Corporal Hans Arlt was serving on the Neustadt outskirts:

Another reconnaissance in an easterly direction was made towards the end of February. This time we got stuck in no-man's-land with a similar enemy undertaking. No one attained their goal. Here the greater firepower of the enemy showed itself. This was the first time I had had an assault rifle and experienced a blockage. Nevertheless it ended well.

Our position was in open country east of the Zorndorfer Chaussee. In front of us was a low, lightly wooded hill that was in Russian hands. We lay in partly covered foxholes. Our weapons consisted of carbines, some assault rifles and hand grenades. The enemy was at times only about 100 metres away. Apart from occasional shell bursts, it was quiet all day long, as snipers prevented all movement. At night Soviet double-deckers ('Sewing Machines') flew over us and dropped small explosive charges. A three-man team in a hole 20 metres from us received a direct hit.

One day as we were celebrating the shooting down of a fighter with a lot of noise, the Russian side reacted with a long-lasting hail of shells.

Notices displayed in the town announced the Fortress Commandant's order that coal and potatoes could be taken from abandoned buildings. Everything else was considered as looting and would be severely punished with death. This almost included me, as I took a half-filled bottle of paraffin from the cellar of Siedler's Waldgastätte pub. I wanted to soak the damp wood in our bunker stove with it, but I was caught by Captain von Oldershausen, who was accompanying my company commander. The battalion commander wanted to make an example of me and demanded a statement as the basis for a court martial. Second-Lieutenant Fleischer was able to prevent this, but was himself given a severe reprimand at the battalion command post next day.

While on a reconnaissance of the area at the beginning of February, we had come across some cans of sausage in the cellars of the abandoned hospital in the woods. Each of us three soldiers took a full box of cans. Speed was needed to cross the railway embankment, which was under enemy observation. Anyone moving attracted at least Russian mortar fire. When we returned next day, the cellars had been emptied.

By the end of February our rations were even more reduced. Apart from this, the warm rations were cold by the time they reached us, and our displeasure could be seen on our faces. The paymaster responsible appeared with a drawn pistol, being concerned for his own safety while the food was being handed out.

After four weeks in action our platoon had earned a rest in the von Stülpnagel Barracks. Meanwhile a heavy machine gun was deployed in support of our position in the Kohlenweg-Zorndorfer Chaussee crossing, its crew being Waffen-SS.[14]

Kietz came under fire all day on 27 February, but was not attacked. However, as the OKW report put it, the enemy was able 'to enlarge his small bridgehead south of Küstrin a little with the aid of strong artillery support'. In the town area, mortars and light guns kept the Warthe crossings under fire. The team protecting the bridges withdrew to trenches and earth bunkers on the banks of the Winterhafen (winter harbour) on the west bank. A prominent building here was the boathouse, which stood on a small hillock above the harbour and so became a target for all the shots coming over the roads and bridges. Even this deeply cut bay was not safe from mortar fire. An old steam paddleboat long since withdrawn from service already lay here with its bows ashore, its funnel shot away and its wooden decks and contents long since burnt in the bunker stoves.

A horse and cart trying to take advantage of a pause in the firing had just reached the middle of the bridge when a direct hit tore the horse apart, smashing the cart and injuring the driver, the wreckage momentarily halting the traffic between the Altstadt and Neustadt. However, the Soviets were apparently not intending to destroy the bridge completely, for they could have done so long before with aimed bomb attacks and intensive use of large calibre guns. The assumption was that they reckoned on using the crossing themselves in due course and would also profit from the railway station. Even the *Feste Küstrin* said: 'We still do not know when the storm from the east will be stopped . . .'. Nevertheless the newspaper continued to insist that: 'Every German town, every German village, every small market town, every crossroad must be a fanatically defended bulwark. A German must be waiting for the enemy with a Panzerfaust from behind every cellar window, from behind every bush, and nail him when he comes.'

Gauleiter Stürtz arrived with the first evening convoy, apparently to reassure himself that people in Küstrin were conducting themselves as was expected. He conferred with Reinefarth, Mayor/District Leader Körner, and the former Landsberg district farmers' leader Herr Siedke, who had meantime taken up a kind of chief-of-staff function in the local Party office. A robust, healthy man, he had somehow managed to avoid the military service he had been threatened with three days previously when rebuked with his colleagues.

Stürtz saw neither simple soldiers, Volkssturm men nor civilians before he climbed into the co-driver's seat of a tracked vehicle, waved at those remaining behind and vanished into the darkness. Crouching in one of the vehicles in the convoy were the inhabitants of the town's old folks' home, who had been deserted by most of their carers and had hardly dared move outdoors since. When the vehicles arrived in Seelow, no one knew what to do with these old people. The latest fighting around the Soviet bridgehead at Reitwein had thrown the little town into confusion, especially as the population had received orders to evacuate that same day. Even in the offices, suitcases and rucksacks stood next to the desks ready for flight. The evacuees had to wait until morning in unheated pubs or even on the streets for transport to take them on, but Stürtz had only to get into his staff car to get away.[15]

By 28 February a month had already passed since the first Soviet tank appeared in the town on a frosty Wednesday. The 'Gateway to

Berlin' was being held, even though the walls on either side had started to crumble. Küstrin was the leading point of a narrow wedge between the two bridgeheads, between the 5th Shock Army in the north and the 8th Guards Army in the south, that the XIth SS-Panzer Corps under SS-Gruppenführer Mathias Kleinheisterkamp was still able to contain. It required no general staff education to appreciate that the Soviets must overcome this obstacle before they could start another campaign. Only the date and the possible tactical variations remained in question: a direct attack on the fortress, or its complete encirclement.

All the observers said that the enemy in the extensive woods northeast of the Neustadt were ready to attack. From there it was only 3 kilometres to the Warthe bridges, and even less from the flanks near Drewitz and Warnick. The field positions on the town perimeter were being systematically extended. Volkssturm men, for example, were working on an anti-tank ditch opposite Warnick in front of the Engineer Barracks. The barracks themselves had been developed into a strongpoint, the surrounding wall reinforced with sandbag barricades and barbed wire. Camouflage nets hung over the entrance and there were notices warning of enemy observation and snipers. Until recently it had not been necessary to have the greater part of the armed forces available in the front line. The 'unreliable' Hungarians and the so-called Eastern Peoples' Volunteers were now building anti-tank barriers in the streets of the inner town.

It will be recalled that the Neustadt sector commandant was Feldgendarmerie Colonel Franz Walter, who had been personally selected by Reinefarth for this position, presumably because they knew each other from the past, and despite severe criticism from the Corps staff. Walter was now in a difficult position. Should Soviet tanks penetrate the town, the newly built anti-tank barriers were only capable of holding them at bay for a few hours at best. Saving some of the troops and the most valuable parts of their equipment would only be possible under cover of darkness. However, that entailed – should the storm begin in the morning as expected – at least ten hours' resistance, or an hour's street-fighting for every 300 metres, an hour of blood-letting for the average distance between two bus-stops, should there be anything left to save.

Should the enemy have the nerve to cross the Warthe, which was only the width of a canal in places, they would come up against the nucleus of the fortress at its most vulnerable point. The Warthe frontage of the mighty rectangle of bastions that once enclosed the Altstadt had been reduced to almost nothing in the early 1930s, the demolished and levelled terrain having been built on only sparsely. There were few support positions for the defence, and the high water table near the bank severely limited the construction of earthworks. All the streets and alleys leading from this side to the centre of the Altstadt had barricades that could be quickly closed in an emergency. Even the side doors to these streets were blocked. Thus in one still-used building the only way to the cellar was barred and it could only be reached from the back yard. The engineers, who did not value its use too highly, let themselves be persuaded by the occupants to provide them with access by means of a set of stable steps to the adjoining property.

An especially zealous unit commander spoilt his men's off-duty time that evening by making them listen to Goebbels's speech on the current situation over the communal radio. 'The war is like a marathon,' said the Propaganda Minister. 'Every runner experiences a weak moment on the way and only he who overcomes it reaches the goal as winner. Since the time of Frederick the Great . . .' and so on. Every reluctant listener comforted himself with the fact that every sermon has to end sometime. Finally the day brought something to celebrate: the first post arrived, if only for a few lucky ones. Meanwhile the whole garrison had been allocated the number 18 203, with different letters signifying individual units.[16]

In late February and early March the commandant ordered all the members of the Hitler Youth to leave the fortress. The boys had volunteered to assist with the defence of their home town but belonged to no military unit and were unarmed. They had served as runners, helped to carry the wounded and assisted in the evacuation of people and animals, as well as carrying food and supplies from the Neustadt to the Altstadt, or the hinterland. They were officially evacuated because they were under 16, but also to spare them the possibility of capture by the Russians. The remaining men were members of the Volkssturm, the fire brigade or the police, doctors and nursing staff, duty personnel of important services and establishments, such as the water works, gas works, sewage farm, electricity supply and cemeteries, and an emergency administration as well as a small NSDAP county staff.[17]

In a letter written to his wife at about this time, Major Werner Falckenberg wrote:

The focus of attention is on the Bienenhof. An officer commanding there considers Monte Cassino, where he was from the beginning until it was abandoned, as child's play in comparison to what our men at the Bienenhof have to put up with! Perhaps a bit overstated, but it is certainly violent.

From Russian field post letters taken by us from them, it seems that the Russians have had enough of the war. Further, they have become anxious, for they write that they have come against an especially strong position that they cannot do anything about. They can be hit by a bullet at any moment!

Things are still all right for us now that I know where you are! The rations are very good. We also have water now, only the power has given up. Of course it does not come from main grid any more, but from one of the big plants. Yesterday a few cables were hit but are now working again.[18]

The new month of March arrived unkindly. Stiff winds whipped rain showers through the damaged streets. Bunker stoves emitted smoke and sparks. The Neustadt and Kietz lay under heavy shellfire from early in the morning, as did the Warthe bridges. Then ground-attack aircraft appeared and, after a long time, a couple of German fighters. The front line remained relatively quiet.

In Küstrin the Party officials were hoping to track down the last civilians with orders to report in. They tempted and threatened in order to achieve their aim. They tempted with the production of a unique identity card and threatened defaulters with punishment by the Standing Court. This was the third action of its kind within a few weeks, owing to the lack of an effective population census or labour force registration system.

The numbers appearing at the reporting centre were meagre, but the original purpose of giving these people a shock was essentially achieved on the evening of 1 March. About 150 people found themselves on the convoy, including also the last large emergency accommodation group that had been sheltering in a Neustadt brewery cellar until then. While they waited thickly wrapped for the night journey in the entrance to the Boys' Middle School and in the hallways of neighbouring buildings, the roar of two mighty explosions thundered over the town. No fires indicated the direction and no one knew what had caused them.[19]

These mysterious explosions, the blast from which had broken

windows in various places, gave rise to numerous avenues of speculation on 2 March. As no one had really reliable information, all
kinds of suspicions arose. One idea was that frogmen had blown
the Soviet underwater bridge north of Küstrin. That such an
attempt had been made was possible, but could not explain the
proximity of the explosions to the town. And any success would
surely have been mentioned in the local newspaper, successes
being so rare that such an opportunity would not have been
missed.

In one of the rare exchanges of fire of these days, a young Polish
girl was killed by a shell splinter. She left behind a baby only a few
months old that she had kept in the seclusion of her place of work,
a market garden in Neu Bleyen. With the death of her mother, the
child now became an outlaw according to the establishment. She was
handed over by soldiers to the police and so became an official case.
The local Gestapo chief ordered the 'thing' to be shot, but his subor-
dinates did not want to dirty their hands at this last minute. They
knew that word would soon leak out, and thus a 'silent execution'
would not be possible. Soon concern about the planned murder was
raised in the adjacent Party offices. In view of this, the Gestapo chief
withdrew his order without expressly rescinding it. The officials
could breathe again, having been spared the decision between
committing a crime and open disobedience, but someone had to be
responsible for the child. The hundred-odd foreign forced labourers
that had been retained in Küstrin to work on the fortifications were
due to be moved later that evening under SD escort, so the child was
given to a Polish woman. What would happen when she appeared at
the next camp with a child that was not entered on her papers,
nobody bothered about. They had done their 'best' and someone had
even surreptitiously slipped a 100-Mark note under the pram
blanket.[20]

The leading article in the *Feste Küstrin* on 3 March read:

> Anyone who deserts now will not be saving his life . . . We must
> free ourselves from all peacetime ideas to pursue this war. We
> have done everything to raise the soldier from the mass of the
> people as a warrior. We have simplified his life. He gets even
> more to eat than has to be worked hard for at home. We have
> made separation from their families back home easier with
> generous welfare measures. Now is the time for soldiers to show

themselves worthy of their homeland . . . If we don't do it, it will be all over for us.

This rallying call broke like a thunderstorm on the nerves of an already anxious garrison. The local situation report read: 'Some heavy weapons . . . damaged the Soviet bridge at Kalenzig.' The same day the news-sheet reported a Luftwaffe attack on the Oder–Warthe bend: 'Despite an unusually heavy flak concentration in this area, and permanent defensive flights by Bolshevik fighter aircraft, two almost completed bridges over the Oder were destroyed by bombs. This success is significant, for the Soviets possess no complete bridges in this sector.'

In a letter to his wife that day Major Falckenberg said that in the evening he had made a reconnaissance of the Gorin (the northern tip of the peninsula on which the Altstadt stood) and that he had been fired on by Soviet machine-gunners already installed there.[21]

'Today we realise that all that has happened until now was just a prelude. Our main task lies ahead of us': so one read in the article 'A month of Fortress Küstrin', contained in the Sunday issue of the newspaper on 4 March. It went on:

> The heavy weight of the encirclement around the fortress has moved during the course of this month from the daily and nightly skirmishing with enemy infantry and armoured forces to the battle with the heavy weapons, as shown during the course of today. [The garrison's measurable value in weaponry had virtually been eliminated, as the latest information in the last official statistics published showed only one tank and three aircraft destroyed in eleven days.] Meanwhile the Soviets have carried out a vast planned deployment of their artillery and engaged important targets in the fortress. On separate days they have increased their fire capacity quite considerably without revealing special objectives or using their whole firepower together.

Both bridges over the Vorflut Canal between the Altstadt and Kietz were among the more prominent targets of late. A direct hit on the road bridge tore it up and made it impassable. Since then traffic had been diverted over the railway bridge, which had been given a wooden decking. The trucks, particularly the nightly convoys, drove from the Oder dyke/Berlin railway crossing point and reached the road again from the Altstadt railway station by means of a provisional ramp. Communication between the individual sectors of the fortress, whose outermost points in an east–west direction were 6 kilometres apart, was thus assured. Nevertheless, artillery and low-flying aircraft caused even more interruptions to traffic, particularly on the Warthe bridges, which were wide open to enemy observation, so most deliveries were conducted during the evenings and at night.

In the daytime only those areas occupied by the headquarters and troop accommodation came to life. Civilians were rarely seen. The evacuation had practically come to an end and whole streets were blocked with debris. Individual small groups of civilians scattered among the protected ground floors and cellars kept going on their own (or ownerless) winter stocks of potatoes, coarse vegetables and preserves. Up to two or three bakeries were still working, but irregularly, providing no normal opening times, so it was of little importance when it was announced that the current ration period had been extended to 10 March, which meant that the already meagre rations must last another week. New ration cards would be issued in the forthcoming weeks but only on production of an NSDAP district office registration card.

The troops' food supply system functioned well. Apart from some particularly exposed positions, warm rations were delivered regularly from the kitchens of the three big barracks, even in the main front line. The food stores had been well stocked up at the end of January, enabling resupply from outside to be limited to fresh meat and similar perishable items. Nevertheless it should be noted that there were enough supplies in the depots for several tens of thousands of men for several months.

The hope of feeding the Volkssturm rather better and with greater variety from the packets and parcels in the Neustadt post office proved over-optimistic. After more than a week's work by at least five men, only a fraction of the contents had been examined, but none of it was suitable for augmenting the rations. The only exceptions were some Red Cross parcels containing tinned meat, fat, rice, currants and cigarettes, destined for a long-since-departed officers' prisoner-of-war camp near Woldenberg. Food and sweets were only found in small quantities and had suffered from the long storage. The search revealed tobacco, cameras and watches, material, underwear, even fashion-model clothing, mixed with bits of uniform and even a pistol. The majority of edible items found were cakes in various forms, from primitive potato cakes to the finest confectioneries. As it was impossible to sort out these diverse items separately, they were put in half a dozen mailbags. The Volkssturm men were annoyed about this pig-food mix of at least six-week-old confectionery. The only usable items went to the main dressing station, medicines and surgical instruments having been found in surprising quantities. Individual items addressed to soldiers formerly stationed in the town could also be delivered.[22]

Chapter Eight

Assault on the Neustadt

'Drumfire' was the title of a two-part article in the fortress newspaper of 5 March. The purpose was unmistakable, with its references to the First World War: 'Even after the most cruel bombardment . . . the men in field grey got up from the craters, tattered, hollow-cheeked, bleary-eyed, encrusted with dirt, stood up and fought' and 'remained unconquered in the field'.

Printing of the newspaper was still not complete when Soviet artillery and mortars abruptly opened fire early in the morning, particularly targeting the flanks of the Neustadt at Warnick and the Cellulose Factory, as well as Kietz. In Kietz alone 3,000 hits were recorded, including several of the heaviest calibres. The predominantly village-like buildings of this suburb collapsed in rows or burst into flames. The firing suddenly stopped at 0700 hours, but morning activity in the quarters and supply installations behind the front line and inside the town were soon to be interrupted again. The air sentries posted on roofs and other high places and armed with binoculars and whistles had just enough time to warn their immediate neighbourhoods as fighters, ground-attack aircraft and bombers approached. Seldom higher than 2,000 metres, the Soviet aircraft followed a wide curve over the Neustadt and delivered their loads virtually unopposed. The first wave had already turned away before any effective defensive fire opened up. Further groups of Soviet aircraft followed at irregular intervals until dusk.

The heavy flak weapons were deployed with their fields of fire, ammunition and positions almost exclusively in the ground role, while the light and medium batteries, mainly concentrated in the Altstadt, proved ineffective in defending the main target area. They picked off a few individual machines and prevented them from attacking specific targets, but the Neustadt was badly hit. All the important military installations withstood the bombing, although a thick cloud of smoke rose from the town centre, where nearly all the buildings had been destroyed by the double salvoes of a month ago. A roofing-felt factory caught fire and the engineer barracks were hit several times, setting the stores on fire. Everywhere big craters gaped or unexploded shells blocked the way. The obnoxious smell from broken drains gave rise to the rumour that gas bombs had been dropped. By late evening most of the fires had been contained and the main roads made passable once more, but the red glow from the smouldering ruins in the Neustadt lasted until morning. Of particular significance to the defence, the morning situation report revealed that the Vorflut Canal bridge had been destroyed 'by eight direct hits'.[1]

By 6 March the Soviet 32nd Rifle Corps had closed up to the Neustadt and completed its preparations for attack. The plan already prepared by the commander, General Sherebin, on 18 February would conduct its main thrust from the Alt Drewitz area towards the Warthe bridges. Assault teams had been formed in all the four regiments, each team having two heavy IS tanks, two medium T-34 tanks and two 76mm guns in support.

Artillery fire and air attacks commenced at almost the same time as on the previous day, once more mainly hitting the Neustadt, but also taking in other parts of the fortress. Even where there were no salvoes from rocket-launchers, such as in Kietz, a density of shelling was attained that made all that had gone before seem like mild skirmishing. Severe damage and heavy casualties were reported everywhere. The biggest fires raged in the Potato Meal Factory and in the neighbouring wood store of a waterproofing factory. From there the flames reached out towards the centre of the Neustadt. The firemen were virtually powerless to control the situation, but had some success when they emerged as soon as the firing lifted towards evening.

Even more significant than the bombardment was the lively Soviet reconnaissance activity indicating that the attack was imminent and would be aimed at the Neustadt, possibly simultaneously also at Kietz, where a thrust from the north-west had been driven back, as reported in the daily situation report: 'About 1300 hours enemy attacked Kietz from both sides of railway line supported by three tanks. The enemy penetrated the south-western part of Kietz and was only checked by throwing in the last of the reserves. Own counter-attack from Kietz slowly gained some ground against fierce enemy resistance.'

The crews of the tracked vehicles returned to Seelow at speed that evening. Just two vehicles sufficed for the civilians who had been chased out of their cellar quarters by the smoke and heat and had been able to get through to the assembly point at the Boys' Middle School in time.

The Wehrmacht Report the next day maintained that the Soviet activity was aimed at finding 'launching points for further operations on the west bank [of the Oder] and to knock out the Küstrin fortress from our front'.[2] The worst damage to trenches, bunkers and barricades on the curve of the front line around the Neustadt was hastily repaired during the night, but extinguishing and supervising fires, as well as clearing rubble, took more time, even in the 'quiet' parts of the garrison. From dusk onwards ambulances shuttled to and fro between the casualty collecting points and the main dressing station, but only a small number of the worst cases made it to the Seelow convoys.

In the early hours of the morning of 7 March, while it was still dark, a dozen boats with 60 men of the Soviet 1042nd Rifle Regiment approached the engineers' water training area on the Warthe, and a fierce fight broke out on the sparsely built-up area on the south-eastern edge of the town near the gas works and less than 1,000 metres from the bridges. The landing party withdrew again after about an hour, having been betrayed by unexpected moonlight and suffering heavy casualties. The success of the defence was wildly and undeservedly overestimated in the report to Army, then Army Group, being finally written up in the Wehrmacht Diary: 'A surprise night attack on Küstrin was repelled.'

The units on the far side of the Warthe – about three-fifths of the garrison were in the Neustadt – could not expect to be either replaced or reinforced. The Soviets assessed these forces as consisting of six combat teams, two sapper, two Volkssturm and two pioneer battalions supported by six artillery battalions and a mortar battalion, a total of about 7,000 officers and men with 280 machine guns, 50 mortars, 90 guns of 77mm calibre and over, 10 six-barrelled Nebelwerfer mortars, 7 rocket launchers and 25 self-propelled guns. Should the Neustadt fall, the Altstadt Warthe bank would become the main front line. Until then it had been held only by poorly armed Volkssturm and light flak units unaccustomed to ground warfare. Perhaps the troops in the Neustadt could be withdrawn at the last minute to take over this smaller position and so avoid certain destruction, but any such hopes vanished with the dawn. Again ground-attack aircraft dived down dropping bombs and firing machine guns on all worthwhile targets. The starting positions for the reconnaissance and assault teams in the forthcoming battle had hardly changed since the beginning of the siege over a month before. The tactical advantages and disadvantages governed by the terrain were varied. East of the Zorndorfer Chaussee the defence had a favourable view over open ground that extended to the Warthe on either side of the Engineer Barracks. On the left wing, however, the front line first ran through a wedge of woodland reaching to the edge of a housing estate, then over flat ground on which Soviets emerging from the cover of Drewitz could operate.

The assault on the Neustadt began at 0920 hours on 7 March with a 40-minute artillery preparation. Two regiments of the 295th Rifle Division in the first echelon headed for the railway bridges across the Warthe from Alt Drewitz, concealed from the German artillery by a massive smokescreen, while another two regiments of the 416th Rifle Division were held back in the second echelon to develop the attack in due course. By 1600 hours progress amounted to an advance of about a kilometre on the right flank and 500 metres on the left, and at this point General Sherebin decided to commit his second echelon, which went into action at 1830 hours. The fighting continued all night, but the Soviets failed to achieve any significant progress.

Towards noon an attack of estimated regimental strength led to the first breach of the town perimeter. Kietz, which had already lost its south-western part the day before, was attacked by three regiments of the 8th Guards Army and a battalion of Seydlitz-Troops with a view to cutting off the fortress, but the attack failed to reach the vital bridges across the Vorflut Canal.

Artillery fire and air attacks on the town centre intensified, the Soviets attacking with 65 PE-2, 64 IL-2 and 12 IL-3 bombers flying in groups of six to nine aircraft and supported by 85 fighters. Most of the telephone lines were cut. The regular army units were equipped with radios, but the combat teams that had been formed from various organisations such as the police and Volkssturm had none, so were left hanging in the air. Lightly wounded soldiers and troops of the rear services fleeing over the bridges under heavy fire suffered more casualties, then had to seek shelter in the next best trenches and cellars of the Altstadt. The Soviet aircraft were almost able to do what they liked. Even in the inner quarters of the Altstadt where many offices and staff quarters had begun the day behind glass windows on the ground floors, they now had to hang curtains and blackout materials over the shattered window frames.

A conference about the establishment of community kitchens was convened that morning in the town hall cellars, into which the remains of the administration had moved. The number of persons still fending for themselves was estimated at about 200. The provisions available to them in the cellars were running out, and the heavy bombardments of the last few days had rendered unusable many of their cooking facilities, electric devices having been out of action for some time through lack of power. Water was still available but flowed only thinly from low-lying taps. Those summoned to the meeting who did not live in the immediate neighbourhood of the market took hours to get through to the town hall, dodging from cover to cover. Once they were all assembled the bad news from the Neustadt and the ceaselessly detonating explosions close by made it obvious that there was nothing more for them to administer or decide upon. They broke up; the administration had ceased to exist.

Even the *Feste Küstrin* was finished. The 23rd issue had been printed but could not be distributed. The two Volkssturm men assigned to the Oder-Blatt printing house sabotaged the presses by scattering sand over them and then they tipped all the letters out before being reassigned to a combat team. One joined the flight to the Altstadt, the other was declared missing.[3]

Teenager Hans Dalbkermeyer remembered these difficult days:

On 7 March the Russians opened their long-awaited offensive on our position. Heavy artillery fire opened the attack. We could hardly see out of our cover. There were bangs and explosions everywhere. Along the road from the north-west came tanks and infantry towards us, almost moving into their own fire. From this point on I cannot remember what happened during the rest of that day. Apparently we quit the position in fear and fled in panic to south of the Warthe. I can still see a Russian who saw me around the corner of a building and, like me, pulled back in shock.

My memory returns that evening as we entered an industrial complex in the dark. It was the Cellulose Factory, already enclosed on three sides by the Russians that evening. Only the west side, the Warthe bank, was still clear and offered possible salvation. Nevertheless, we would have to swim across the Warthe.

Although we were still delighted to be defending the Fatherland and believed in final victory, none of us was looking for a hero's death. The possibility of imprisonment hardly occurred to us, as we had often heard from people in the front line how the Russians killed prisoners. There only remained the high risk and unpleasantness connected with crossing the Warthe. Various possibilities were discussed among the stragglers and those thrown together. Above all, the crossing of the Warthe could only be done under cover of darkness, as the sector concerned was under enemy observation and fire in daylight. Even in the darkness there was the danger of being seen through the light of fires and flares.

Together with my classmates Blauberg and Chmilewski, I decided to swim across the Warthe. Salvation before our eyes and the danger behind us gave us unusual strength to overcome the cold and wet. Staying together so as to be able to help one another if necessary, we reached the bank of the Altstadt peninsula. Two others from our school, Roeder and Specht, must also have swum across, for we met up with them again in the Altstadt in our next job. How the last two got across I have no idea, nor do I know what happened to our officer-cadet comrades. I don't remember what clothing we wore to swim across. I only know that we reached the far bank and walked on a few steps. Then my strength must have deserted me. I awoke in a cellar of the Boys' Senior School in front of the Oder bridge in the Altstadt. I was lying on a double-decker bunk under several water pipes and had no idea where I was for quite a long time.[4]

Officer Cadet Alfred Kraus also recalled the violence of the Soviet assault:

On 7 March the long-expected offensive from Alt Drewitz began. The Russians broke through to the southern end of Drewitzer Strasse and reached the railway embankment. On the morning of the 8th, Lieutenant Schellenberg took two sections from the north-western position and made a front facing southeast with them and the headquarters troop. As we in the Cellulose Factory did not know the reasons for this, we first thought the company commander wanted to go this way over the nearest railway bridge across the Warthe into the Altstadt. From the factory premises we established that the Russians were pressing from the three landward sides and only the fourth side bordering the Warthe was free.

Surrounded by the Russians, Lieutenant Schellenberg surrendered with both sections and the company headquarters troop. As all the others put their hands up, my barrack room comrade, Heinrich von Kölichen, wearing his steel helmet and overcoat, jumped into the Warthe. The Russians shot at him and hit him in the head. When he went under we all thought he was dead. But I met him about eight years later in Münich and worked with him in his business until his death 30 years later.[5]

Luftwaffe Gunner Josef Stefanski recalled:

From mid-February we were in the Neustadt Schützenstrasse with our two guns. At about the beginning of March, I was assigned to an infantry role in my battery. An anti-tank ditch was dug right across Schützenstrasse at about the level of the Apollo Cinema. Russian tanks breaking through were supposed to be stopped there.

When the Russians attacked the Neustadt they came from an unexpected direction and we had to withdraw. I was able to get over the Warthe railway bridge to the Altstadt. The swinging part of the bridge had already been pulled aside. We laid a wooden plank across to the swinging part to get across. As the plank was not very secure, some comrades slipped and fell into the water. No one could pull them out under the enemy fire. I crept across on all fours.

We were immediately sent into the trenches on the Gorin at the Böhmerwald Restaurant to prevent possible Russian attempts to cross.[6]

And Sergeant Horst Wewetzer had to take charge of his section:

Meanwhile my troop leader had been killed and I had to take over the role of observer myself. That was not the worst part. The artillery chief of staff had let it be known that the heavy weapons would be firing at a gap-free system of target areas, and thus not from the map. The whole thing had the air of a desk-bound illusion. It was hard to believe that two light infantry guns and a heavy mortar would be able to shoot on these lines, which took no account of their slow rate of fire, and depended upon numerous guns being available, which was not the case. Apart from that, we had not only one but several target areas to cover. The impossibility was clear to me as a mere NCO laden with a false responsibility.

In fact my superior, Second-Lieutenant Pfeiffer, had to take over the observation post. I asked him to come to the observation post, in order to see him at least once, as there was only an NCO on duty. He came. It was 7 March 1945. We climbed up the air raid observation tower, but when the second lieutenant saw the big hole in the roof made by the Russian anti-tank gun, the blood on the floor and the splintered map board of the artillery observer who had been killed here, he took a quick look at the landscape and we climbed back down into the cellar, where I was accommodated with my signalmen and had prepared a little breakfast with the motto: Always hopeful!

We had hardly taken our first bite when the dreadful din of the Russian barrage broke over us. It was proper drumfire – perhaps like the First World War in Flanders. I do not know how long it lasted. Who was watching the clock? We all knew that Ivan was attacking. It was also obvious that no one could survive the drumfire on the front line. Through the cellar window we could see big chunks of the upper storeys of the field hospital falling. The hospital doctors' quarters and the housing estate houses through which the front line ran were being smashed to the ground. I stood at the cellar gable exit and waited for the fire to ease off. When it did so, I could hear the tanks moving and the firing of sub-machine guns. The attack was under way.

When the firing of tank guns and handguns had about reached the level of the field hospital, the second lieutenant, his sergeant and I ran out of the cellar and behind the building. The signalmen and most of the infantry remained in the cellars. The first barrage had destroyed our communications. It was hoped that some of those remaining in the buildings would get out, but those that remained were all lost.

During the first day of the attack the Russians had taken half of the Neustadt as I saw it. Of the leadership on our side in the Neustadt nothing can be said, they had all gone.[7]

Officer Cadet Corporal Hans Dahlmanns found himself a witness to some horrors:

There were some quiet and warm days at the beginning of March that we enjoyed in front of the casemate on our sheltered peninsula. We had three or four hens, whose eggs were shared among the men. Things changed when the Soviet troops reached the east bank of the Warthe and attacked over the river.

My company commander was extremely concerned when the ordered demolition of the damaged road bridge for which he was responsible failed to work at first, as he imagined himself being put in front of a court martial. The delay, however, was advantageous, for several people were able to get back safely before the bridge finally blew up.

Four or five members of my company were captured by the Russians at the engineers' water training place on the east bank of the Warthe. One of them, whose mother tongue was Polish, was able to understand the Soviet soldiers. They argued as to who should take the prisoners back and then, as no one wanted to, they switched their sub-machine guns to single shots and shot them one after the other. Only the witness was able to save himself as, thanks to his knowledge of the language, he realised early enough what was going to happen. Knowing the area well from his training time, he threw himself desperately into the water and swam across the Oder to us. He told us everything.

There was a problem with the swing bridge. It had been swung open and so stood crossways, but this was not secure enough. A sergeant carrying a demolition charge crept out at night in his stockinged feet to the middle of the stream, prepared the bridge for demolition and ignited the charge. The required aim was achieved as the western part of the bridge flew into the air. This bridge had carried a single-track railway line from Kietzerbusch station in an almost northerly direction to Küstrin main station. Following the damage to the road bridge, it had been made usable for motor vehicles by laying railway sleepers on it. The traffic was controlled by allowing movement in one direction for half an hour at a time.

One day we received orders to erect a gallows on this road, as a sergeant was to be hanged for 'organising' bedclothes with his girlfriend. The penalty for looting was death. In accordance with our orders, we built a gallows on the substitute road, but the SS team responsible for carrying out the execution preferred to use an A-shaped telephone pole at the spot where the traffic waited for its turn to cross. It took the SS team 20 minutes to hang the man there where the substitute road began and the rails crossed the road leading across the Warthe to the Neustadt. Consequently we were spared having to watch the execution itself. The sergeant was stripped of his insignia and had a notice on his breast reading 'I am hanging here because I looted'. He was right in front of our position.

Two soldiers of my own company were executed in February or March. One had 'organised' a typewriter from a private house, which counted as plundering. The other, in deadly fear, had shot himself in the arm in an effort to get into the relative safety of a hospital, but such self-mutilation also merited the death sentence. The doctor bandaged the wound, which possibly saved his life, and then reported in accordance with orders that he had found traces of powder in the wound. This report cost the man his life. He was not even eighteen years old.[8]

The Neustadt enjoyed no peace, even during the night. By the morning of 8 March the front lines were so close that both sides reacted nervously to the slightest movement. Where the Berlin railway line crossed Plantagenstrasse leading into the town centre, panic firing had broken out whenever Soviet uniforms were thought to have been seen through the smoke of the burning buildings between the flames and bursting shells. The wreck of a Sherman tank shot up on 31 January was mistaken for a tank attack. It took considerable time before it was established that one group had fired at another while it was redeploying and was unfamiliar with the lie of the front line and the general situation. Fortunately there were no casualties.

The 32nd Rifle Corps resumed its attack on the Neustadt at 0900 hours, supporting the infantry with heavy tanks and flame-throwers.

Renewed Soviet air attacks kept the battered flak forces busy. The flak units tried to improve their effectiveness by coordinating the fire of those of their weapons that were still intact, but the communications could either not be repaired fast enough or fell victim yet again to the first bombs. Coordinated fire was now out of the question. The individual positions, even the individual guns, were now firing independently 'on sight'.

Bombs followed the shells and then early in the afternoon came the infantry attack. Unexpectedly, it developed first on the eastern edge of the Neustadt on either side of the railway line to Landsberg, where the ground was favourable to the defence. In fighting that lasted more than two hours the Soviet troops advanced as far as the loading ramp south of the main track to the Lagardes Mühlen housing estate, but were stopped there under fire from the strongpoint developed out of the Engineer Barracks. Further north on the approaches to the goods station and water works the front line remained practically unchanged and the garrison was able to hold the line of the town boundary.

The attack by the main forces had yet to come. A battalion-sized counterattack to clear the wedge forwards from Alt Drewitz failed, and when the real storm broke at midday from the woods on either side of the Stettin railway line, the German forward lines were overrun within a couple of hours. On the whole the resistance stiffened when bitter fighting started in the densely built-up area. The axis Infantry Barracks–Neues Werke bounding the breach to the east was not attacked energetically, but the Soviet forces pushing forward from Alt Drewitz quickly overran the approaches to the partly burning industrial complex along the Warthe. The prominent installations of the Cellulose Factory, Potato Meal Factory and Rütges Werke, although already in ruins, offered good cover possibilities and screened the direct approaches to the town and the bridges. The 1900 hours report to Corps said that the Cellulose Factory was still holding out, but shortly afterwards that installation fell.

Most of the cellars in the middle of the town had survived destruction. They were now interconnected by breaches in the cellar walls, and those who reached them could feel relatively secure. Some ended their senseless flight here, falling on a primitive air raid shelter bed and staying there, while others moved on after a short rest. No one bothered about them any more. SS patrols and the Feldgendarmerie dared not go so far forwards in this underground labyrinth any more. The fortress commandant had already let slip his control and influence over the course of events and Colonel Walter, the sector commander, appears to have lost control that evening. He could not prevent his main forces in the north-eastern part of the town from reaching the bridges any longer. Reinefarth wanted, far too late, to abandon the little bridgeheads around the crossings and save at least some of the troops now threatened with destruction, but Corps forbade him this step, in the useless hope that the 6,000 men in the Neustadt could, even in a tighter position, simply continue to withstand the Soviet pressure. The contested positions were overrun by the attackers late that evening and the Germans were obliged to blow the bridges across the Warthe, leaving the helpless survivors of the Neustadt garrison isolated.[9]

Officer Cadet Karl-Heinz Peters was a witness to these events:

> On the evening of 8 March I was sentry on the middle Warthe bridge. Its centre section was swung aside. Russians suddenly appeared in the darkness on the part of the bridge opposite. The glowing face of a soldier lit by the moon appeared in my carbine sights. But I could not shoot him, firing a warning shot instead. Shortly afterwards I was posted with a railway sapper directly on the Warthe road bridge. The sapper was withdrawn that same night and I was left completely alone with our machine-gun team exactly 100 metres behind me. It also had to cover the flooded land up to the Sonnenburger Chaussee and could not keep observation on the bridge.
>
> All night of 8/9 March I held on to a German bridgehead in front of the road bridge. Then it was abandoned and the bridge blown. From the other bank I could hear busy vehicle movement and also tank engines.[10]

SS-Grenadier Oscar Jessen was one of the lucky few that escaped over the bridge:

> The main enemy attack began at the beginning of March with a strong artillery preparation. When it quietened down again, we got up and moved our gun to a new position, which I believe was already in the Neustadt. At night the 'Sewing Machines' flew over and threw their bombs at us. We now lay with comrades of another unit, who had survived the bombardment together. We could hear sounds of battle coming from the Cellulose Factory.

There was another heavy bombardment next day. It was terrible. We received orders to render the gun unserviceable and to withdraw taking the machine guns with us. Chaos reigned. There were many dead and wounded crying for help. Of my gun crew only one other survived, a comrade from the Siebenbürgen who was carrying the machine gun, and myself with the ammunition box. The din was hellish. Suddenly a T-34 appeared in front of us. Dead scared we dived into a bomb crater in which live and dead German soldiers were lying. The tank swung its turret round with its gun barrel pointing towards us, but could not reach us because of the dead angle. As it turned away we could hear the 'Urrah!' of Soviet infantry. We left the machine gun and ammunition box behind in the crater and joined the others running away. The Russians pressed hard behind us. Suddenly it was back to the Warthe and over the railway bridge to the Altstadt. We crossed a park where, to our horror, snipers sitting in the trees fired at us. Many comrades fell dead or were left behind wounded.

We were unable to get across the bridge, for it was under heavy fire, apart from which several wagons on our side hindered the approaches. Further back behind us was a church in whose tower there must have been an enemy observer concealed and directing fire on us while firing himself. We found shelter in a trench. Many German soldiers were lying wounded outside the trench. Some kept calling: 'Help me, comrades!' Others were crying out aloud. More than a few of us wanted to help them, but those who dared to leave the shelter of the trench received deadly head shots from the Russians. Those comrades who risked their lives to help others are owed deep respect. It was horrible lying there as a little group listening to the ever weakening whimpering of the dying.

The way to the bridge from the trench had meanwhile been blocked by Soviet tanks that fired at anyone trying to get out of it. Several comrades tried to dispose of the tanks in the dark with hollow charges or Panzerfausts. They succeeded but it cost them their lives. Some of us, including myself, finally managed to crawl under the wagons. We were lucky and got across the bridge but were almost shot by the German sentries. They asked for the password, but of course we did not know it. Our appearance was hardly encouraging: filthy, bloody and unwashed.

Finally they believed us and took us to their headquarters, which was in a building near the town hall.

Apart from myself, I found two comrades from my unit that came from Kiel, Karsten Christiansen and Paul-Werner Schwark. Karsten had fought alongside his twin brother, but he must have been either killed or taken prisoner. (Both the boys from Kiel were released after one year's imprisonment and died in 1997 and 1998.)[11]

Hitler Youth Hans Dalbkermeyer also recalled the Soviet assault:

We five Birnbaumers had crossed the Warthe without catching colds or other health problems and were given a new task. We had to keep the road bridge under observation from the highest point of Bastion König on the east bank of the Oder. We had to keep an eye out for drifting mines, boats carrying explosives or any other forms of attack. We no longer had an enemy directly in front of us because of the proximity of the bridge, but they were often over us. During the frequent air attacks the firing of the Russian aircraft flying close over our heads towards Kietz was always fascinating. We could watch the show from the zigzag trenches when we wanted.

We were accommodated in the casemates below. I can still remember a room there filled with Red Cross packages for now unreachable Western Allied prisoners. We only took these packages for things we coveted and thanks to these supplementary supplies we were well fed.

Artillery fire and air attacks were intense throughout the day. From our high position on Bastion König, where the Russian memorial obelisk and anti-tank gun stand today, we had a unique view over the badly damaged and severely marked town. A short excursion into the Altstadt during a pause in the firing and our duties confirmed this impression. We found no building undamaged, the streets stacked high with rubble, and in one ruined building we saw a thick dud shell, altogether a sad sight.

In a wholly destroyed shoe shop, which may have been in Berliner Strasse, a pair of spikes attracted my attention. I took them, seeing myself having an advantage in future races.

My best friends and classmates, Blauberg and Chmilewski, lost their young lives in an air attack. A bomb crushed them in a foxhole in front of a building immediately in front of the north-eastern approach to the road bridge over the Oder. Attempts to dig them out after the attack and save them were unsuccessful.

Until now I had regarded my involvement in the war as a unique adventure, but now the full tragedy, cruelty and sorrow of this war gradually became apparent. Hidden in my own corner of the casemate, I cried, trying to get a grip of and understand my situation. The desire to get out of this witches' cauldron that arose from this was soon to be fulfilled.[12]

Sergeant Horst Wewetzer also had a lucky escape:

Once more there were no infantry to secure our guns, and so it happened that during the morning of 8 March the Russians were suddenly in among them. The gun crews, who were in a nearby cellar, were able to keep the attackers at bay with hand grenades until it was possible to flee into the maze of ruins. We reached the road bridge over the Warthe through piles of debris and completely destroyed streets escorted by artillery fire and ground-attack aircraft.

I lay under fire from the ground-attack aircraft, three of them constantly flying around in a circle, and firing at the bridge as they flew at it. As soon as each aircraft started firing, I ran behind the hits as fast as my feet would carry me. As bursts of fire from the next aircraft hit the road surface behind me I jumped into a doorway, thus reaching the Altstadt.[13]

Officer Cadet Alfred Kraus was injured during the assault:

On the evening of 8 March I was sitting with Second-Lieutenant Thom in the bunker. It was getting dark. It was obvious to us that our end as a German strongpoint was imminent. As Berliners we chatted about pubs and the bands on the Kurfürstendamm. Suddenly Private Koch came in and reported: 'Sir, the Russians are in the trench!' Second-Lieutenant Thom ordered the position to be cleared and a withdrawal to the factory. We left. At the end of the factory road we tried to make floats on the embankment to cross over the Warthe. The biplanes dropped parachute flares and watched us.

Remarkably, the Russians did not shoot, although they had closed in around us. At about midnight came the order to launch the floats. The current drew them into the fire of the Russian machine guns. We could hear the men on the floats shouting: 'Keep back!'

My attempt to cross failed from the very beginning. The float tilted through overloading and I was up to my stomach in the water. I met other stragglers on the riverbank. As I was still carrying my pack, I was ordered by Second-Lieutenant Metz to establish radio contact. It failed to work. The second lieutenant then ordered: 'Everyone to the air raid shelter!' Before we could cross the factory road a Soviet tank fired a shell into the factory wall in front of us. A splinter hit Second-Lieutenant Metz in the right breast, came out of his back and hit me in the lower jaw, splitting my lip and ripping out three teeth by the roots. We carried Second-Lieutenant Metz to the air-raid shelter, where he was given our individual tetanus injections. He was very brave.

Meanwhile Second-Lieutenant Thom had reappeared. As I was very wet, I was allowed to take dry underwear, socks, riding socks and boots from his suitcase. My nose was full of blood too, but I drank some orange liquor out of a jar and jammed some canned meat past my wound into my mouth. Second-Lieutenant Thom went on without me. (I later saw him at the entrance to the prisoner-of-war camp at Landsberg-an-der-Warthe wearing a postman's uniform.)

During the night I suggested we lay our weapons outside the bunker door and stick up a white flag. Second-Lieutenant Metz agreed. On the bunker steps sat four young German-Brazilians, who had come by a neutral ship via Portugal, Spain and southern France and reached Küstrin in December 1944. They were very proud and said that they would not go into Soviet captivity but would shoot themselves. Although I could only speak with difficulty, I tried to get them to change their minds: 'The Russians can shoot us, but perhaps we will survive.' It did not help. As we were leaving the bunker, they shot themselves.

Meanwhile I was wearing a blood-soaked bandage over my mouth. One of my Berlin comrades said: 'Half your mouth is gone.' On the morning of 9 March the first Russian came down the bunker steps and said: 'All comrades out!' and aimed his sub-machine gun going backwards. As I was sitting next to the steps, I went first.[14]

On 9 March the barricades on the streets leading to the centre of the Altstadt were manned. Some were already closed, others only passable through a narrow gap. All were waiting for the enemy to cross the Warthe. For the first time in days there were no swarms of bombers overhead, but instead ground-attack aircraft filled the skies. Smoke and fire made exact observation of the approaches in the parts of the Neustadt near the riverbank impossible. The only certain thing was that fighting was still going on in the factory area. Most of the radio links had been broken, many sets presumably destroyed in the heavy fighting or lost. Occasional contacts gave no overall picture.

'It cracks and thunders without pause. The walls of the courthouse shake, our candles flicker uneasily and a badly-burning carbide lamp goes out more than once from the blast of explosions', noted a Volkssturm member of the quartermaster unit stationed in the Altstadt. 'Just about everyone is thinking about their end when an officer pulls open the door: "The Russians are coming in rubber boats over the Warthe. The trenches behind the building are now the front line. Occupy them immediately!" We hesitate. What can we do outside without weapons? He goes off making threats but does not come back.'

There was in fact no effective attempt to make a landing. The Soviet regiments were putting everything into the destruction of the Neustadt garrison, which had been split during the course of the day into three groups. The backbone of the largest and most strongly defended sector comprised the massive defence installations of the Infantry and Engineer Barracks, together with the Neues Werke bastion. Also in the sector were the goods station, the big rations stores and the Water Works. The two knots of resistance in the west were in essence focused around the Potato Meal Factory and the Rütgers Werke. The third sector consisted mainly of the now-ruined shopping centre between the Neumarkt, Stern and Moltkeplatz that was linked to the river by gardens and meadowland. Lacking any substantial buildings, this area was now only just defendable. The terrain was already more of a place for flight rather than fighting for those soldiers who had lost their units. There was no coordinated fighting command any more, and it seemed no one had the strength or the initiative to combine the forces available, in order for the survivors to withdraw in a controlled way to the more solid sector to the north-east.

Already on the previous day it had been noticed that some units of the Soviet artillery that were originally directed against the Neustadt had changed their target to the Altstadt. In the close-quarters street-fighting in progress, with its frequently changing points of main effort and the close engagement of friend and foe, the most useful weapons were self-propelled guns, tanks and mortars. The dwellings built shortly before the war on the demolished walls and ditches on the Warthe side of the Altstadt island offered no worthwhile resistance to the shells. A few hits soon knocked down the thin walls from roof to cellar. These mainly free-standing buildings and new housing blocks had only shallow cellars, so no troops had taken cover there and therefore no one had bothered to risk their lives putting out fires there. Elsewhere in the inner town, where cellar after cellar lay under the massive buildings, the loss of quarters could be compensated with equally good accommodation. A row of quartermaster trucks with empty petrol tanks long since parked here and of no further use were left to burn. Even after dark Soviet planes flew over Küstrin and the town hall was badly damaged by a bomb after being previously damaged by shellfire, like all the other buildings on the market place.

The situation in Kietz also worsened. Following a heavy artillery preparation, during the course of the day Soviet tanks reached almost as far as the Vorflut Canal bridges. Once again the link to the last way out to the hinterland was under acute threat. Consequently the supply convoys ceased operating, taking with them (presumably) the last civilians from the place. They had to wait, as did a small group the previous evening, before room could be found for them among the densely packed wounded. There was no longer a reception camp waiting for the civilians. It was up to them how they got to Seelow to beg onward transport to Berlin the next day.

As the fighting continued in the Neustadt, staff at Headquarters XIth SS-Panzer Corps hastened to formulate some justification for the collapse there in a secret report entitled 'Over the Fighting in Küstrin Fortress'. Well aware that higher command would demand some reason for the disaster, or at least the name of the person responsible, they pointed the finger at Reinefarth. They blamed him for Colonel Walter's failure to hold the Neustadt sector, remarking that Reinefarth had brushed aside criticism of his choice as Sector commander, declaring Walter 'suitable'. They made it quite clear who was to blame, writing that: 'Colonel Walter was personally selected by the fortress commandant for this task.' Their criticism went much further than this apparently faulty decision. 'The failure of the staff involved to provide tactically responsible command assistance made command more difficult', they wrote, and 'the whole communications system of the fortress must be considered completely inadequate'. To cover their own backs, the staff report concluded: 'The Corps has taken into account the use of overlaying communications (telephone, teleprinter and radio) as well as the daily despatch of liaison officers.'[15]

Corporal Hans Arlt recounted his experiences:

We were relieved on 9 March and had two days in the von Stülpnagel Barracks to sleep it off, clean ourselves up and change our underwear. Although this was necessary, we found little peace as the situation became worse and we were surrounded.[16]

Sapper Karl-Heinz Peters concluded his account:

All hell broke loose at daybreak on 9 March. Ceaseless drum-fire of all calibres covered our sector. Machine guns were also firing. Suddenly I saw how the Russians were launching long thin boats on the opposite embankment. I began firing at them, causing them to give up their attempt to cross, but they resumed after a while. Again I was able to prevent them. Excitedly, I fired without interruption. Meanwhile my carbine became hot. I was standing in a well-camouflaged position in the embankment immediately off the western end of the bridge. Suddenly two machine guns were firing at me. The enemy had found me.

Then a belt of machine-gun fire caught me. I felt a hard blow on my left shoulder and could not lift my arm any more. Blood was running out of my sleeve. I thought I had been shot in the lungs, for I started breathing hard, but this could later be attributed to fear and overstress. In panic I ran back to our machine-gun position. At last I reached the end of this short stretch. It was without cover and the dam in front looked as if it had been ploughed up, but thank God my comrades were still alive. I reported the situation at the Warthe and took myself to the company command post. The machine-gun team was immediately sent to the road bridge. From the bursts of fire from their MG 42 that I could hear, I gathered that they were dealing with the rest of the enemy boats.

Once more I crossed the fully exposed Vorflut bridge. Again I ran for my life with bullets whistling past my ears, and rolled down the embankment. A sergeant was lying there with a frightfully shot-through foot, who had bandaged himself. We gathered up the shreds together and stumbled off with him on my back through the enemy fire to the command post. There the cellar windows were covered with iron plating so I had to bang hard until we were let in. Once inside both of us lost consciousness.

Later I was sent to a dressing station. Here, to my great surprise, there was warm barley soup, of which I gulped down two ladlefuls. Here I was shown that I must have had a guardian angel, for there were two holes in my steel helmet. One bullet had, without wounding me, gone twice over the top of my forehead, and I had not noticed it. The medical orderly thought my arm would have to be amputated, as a result of which I was given a wound chit to leave the fortress and was taken by night in a supply convoy to the hinterland.

Following a doctor's intermediary check, I landed next morning in a little field hospital in Strausberg, where I fell into a two-day sleep. When two young nurses woke me up, I thought they were angels and that I was in heaven. The glaring contrast between the hell of Küstrin and the peace in the field hospital had given my fantasy wings. Next day I was transferred to a big Strausberg school overfilled with wounded. Freshly wounded were being constantly brought in and the dead taken out. Here one could see what victims the Oder Front was demanding.[17]

SS-Grenadier Oscar Jessen witnessed the second Soviet assault on Küstrin:

As we no longer had a gun, I became a runner and saw how the destruction of Küstrin Altstadt continued daily. From my time as a runner, I recall the Alt Bleyen manor farm, a view of the enemy-occupied paper mill, and the Russians moving across the flooded land between the Oder and Warthe.

Next came action in the casemates opposite Kietz at the far end of the bridge [Lunette D]. If I remember correctly, there was an old cannon standing on the left-hand side. There was a field dressing station there where the wounded were given first aid. There were many dead in a little wooden hut in the inner court-yard. There was talk of a remote-controlled Goliath having been used in Kietz, and I believe I saw one.

Then we experienced the second main Soviet attack on Küstrin. After a strong artillery preparation, the Soviets attacked again somewhere. In the end we were down to one Panzerfaust. We reached the Altstadt by the railway bridge under enemy fire and over dead comrades. The church north of the Schloss and the buildings on the market place were on fire, with dead lying around.

I became a runner to Fortress Commandant Reinefarth, whose command post was in the Schloss behind the gate in the forward left corner. The thick walls of the Schloss had been breached to allow access to the communication trenches. A field hospital for badly wounded had been set up in the cellars. If I remember correctly, all the wounded lay on plank beds, only one of the worst injured was on a camp bed under a gauze tent. A doctor and a Red Cross nurse did what they could, but I believe there was a shortage of medical supplies.

The runners' route led me to a weapon that I had never seen before. It stood on the north-east edge of the Altstadt outside the casemate. At first I thought it was a V1 rocket until someone told me it was a 'Stuka zu Fuss' – a large projectile in a wooden case that also served as its launcher.[18]

On 10 March, two days after the fighting in the Neustadt had started, the OKW mentioned 'the reduced Küstrin bridgehead' in its official daily announcement. Despite the frequent mentions of the place in the Wehrmacht Reports, Reinefarth had so far waited in vain for an honourable mention of his name. Other commandants in similar situations had usually obtained recognition with an award or promotion, but of course Reinefarth knew nothing about the report from his headquarters staff.

At first glance the situation in the Neustadt had not basically changed despite continued bitter fighting. Outbreaks of fighting of varying intensity, in which the defenders lost ever more ground, marked the day, until the resistance in the ruined centre was down to a few small groups.[19]

Among them was Officer Cadet Corporal Hans Dahlmanns:

About 10 March I was ordered to take up quarters in the court-house. I could find nobody there, but found a cellar filled with camp beds and lit by a petroleum lamp, and had a long chat with a young second lieutenant. I believe his name was Schröter and he was about two years older than me. His idealism influenced me greatly. His brother had fallen for Germany and he too would give his life for his country. There was no such thing as a meaningful death for a young man. The second lieutenant said this without any fanaticism and completely calmly. And his simplicity impressed me immensely, although I knew that I would never think this way myself.[20]

On 11 March the pressure on individual sections of the Neustadt garrison appeared to have eased overall, but on this fourth day of the fighting it was noticeable that the Soviet troops were pressing for a conclusion. The still partly burning factory quarter had to be given up bit by bit. Individuals were able to reach the shrunken perimeter in the town centre over a field of rubble between collapsed sheds, broken pipelines and giant stacks of burnt railway sleepers, through the cellars of ruined buildings and shattered backyards. However, the organised resistance here soon collapsed. Isolated soldiers could find hiding places at first in the wrecked former business streets, still skir-mishing here and there with their opponents, but most soon gave up, either giving in to the overwhelming Soviet force or waiting to be captured in the air-raid shelters that still existed under piles of rubble. Only a few reached the deserted allotment and meadow area and found cover in concealed earth bunkers, still hoping to get over the Warthe. None of them succeeded.

By evening only the Neues Werke, the Army Supply Depot on the Heerstrasse and the Infantry Barracks were still in German hands as the core of resistance. The Soviet corps commander ordered a bombardment of the fort with its metre-thick red brick walls and deep moat for the next morning as the signal to start the final assault. Corporal Hans Arlt recalled:

Then came 11 March. In the early morning we moved to our last position in the Wald Cemetery. It was a Sunday and also Heroes' Memorial Day. The red sunrise reminded me of the words of the song 'Morgenroth, Morgenroth, leuchest mir sum frühen Tod' ['Red dawn, red dawn, light me to an early death']. In view of the ever-decreasing encirclement of the von Stülpnagel Barracks, this thought was not without significance in my state of mind.

After several air attacks and especially after their mortar fire, the Russian pressure from the west and north became ever stronger. Somewhere in the cemetery complex I lost my way. Somehow I became separated from my platoon and suddenly found myself opposite two Soviet soldiers in a trench; they had sub-machine guns in their hands but not aimed at me. Like lightning I threw aside the two hand grenades stuck in my belt and ran off to find my comrades, who had noticed my mistake and called me back. At first they thought that I was deserting, as I had not heard them shouting over the din of battle.

An SS man was calling from outside the cemetery fence: 'Comrades, I am wounded and from the SS! Shoot me!' His voice became more appealing, then weaker and soon could not be heard any longer.

In the late afternoon we withdrew to the von Stülpnagel Barracks. Some white flags could be seen hanging from one of the barrack blocks alongside the street. Bullets from Soviet sub-machine guns hunted us as we darted across the chaussee. Some officers with drawn pistols met us close to the barrack gate, south of the ranges.

With a shot-through bread bag and scarred water bottle, but without any damage to my body, I found shelter with other comrades in the cellars of the barracks.

About 25 to 30 men had managed to leave the cemetery. No one could or would say who had fallen there or had been wounded and left behind. The company strength had been about 70 men that morning. In this situation, and with the knowledge that in the end we were trapped in Küstrin Fortress, it was all the same to us. Latrine rumours began to circulate.

Further it was said that the enemy had already penetrated the northernmost of the second row of barrack blocks from the chaussee. Covered pathways connected all the buildings in this row. As our building was immediately next to it, I crouched in one corner of the cellar and imagined a flame-thrower directed at me.

A Soviet tank had driven on to the parade ground. The T-34 kept a safe distance from attacks by German soldiers armed with Panzerfausts.

Finally the order was given to pick up ammunition. Were we going to defend ourselves and fight back? Although I obeyed the order unwillingly, I collected 120 carbine rounds, then we were each given a loaf of bread and a tin of sausage meat.

Thoughts of various kinds, depression and the hope of staying alive, changed in this situation for many of us. Even the thought of eating until one's stomach was full once more before dying was understandable with our hunger rations.

We assembled to break out on the night of 11/12 March. Noisy items such as gasmasks and water bottles were set aside and our helmets were exchanged for forage caps so as to confuse the Red Army soldiers for at least a short time.[21]

Retired Major Werner Falckenberg, serving on the staff of the Volkssturm battalion in the Altstadt, wrote to his wife on 11 March:

Today is Sunday, and this morning I received your letter of 6 March with great delight. Fantastic! A courier brought it. He had spent a good two hours in the town looking for our quarters.

I am pleased and happy that you are relatively all right and that you have not had any bomb damage. According to yesterday's Wehrmacht Report the situation where you are seems a bit better. Let us hope it improves or at least remains that way. My concern for you, you can understand. Now I am feeling a bit better. I now have seven letters from you. I keep reading them. That is my comfort and my support.

The situation is not exactly rosy here. The Russians are creeping forward doggedly and unwaveringly closer. We have not been able to stop them. They have plenty of artillery and in good weather the bombers come too in rolling waves. Naturally there are fires burning all over the place. There are also no longer any buildings that have not been hit, but ours has got off lightly so far. We have not been able to get out for eight days now, but that does not matter. We on the staff were on maximum alert throughout the night, but nothing happened. The Russians have pulled back from our positions again.

The day before yesterday was our and my worst day. Continual shells and bombs so that often one could not communicate. But the Russian attack stalled and they cleared out during the night.

Of course the Russians keep on firing even now, but our 'Stukas zu Fuss' – 'bellowing cows' or 'Hitler's donkeys' as the Russians call them – are roaring over us comfortingly.

The rations continue to be good. Now we are getting additionally American canned food, raisins, Vitamin C and cigarettes, from which I am sending you the second packet of Camels in a separate envelope. (I will not put the letter in with it so that at least it arrives, while the cigarettes could be stolen.)

I am fine again after a bout of bronchitis eight days ago with 38.7 degrees of fever that I did not mention to you. But this was corrected perfectly by Dr Kordelle, who gave me Elcudron and Siran with three days of bed rest, so that the day before yesterday I was able to stay many hours in the trenches commanding my unit.[22]

It was still completely dark on 12 March when the Soviet gunners prepared their guns for firing on the Neues Werke, but even before they opened fire, a surprise attack was made from the von Stülpnagel Infantry Barracks, where the German combat teams had concentrated in the northern part of their encirclement. Their commanders apparently thought that an action directed away from the Oder would be completely unexpected by the besiegers. Both sides seemed to have overestimated their strength. As the costly fighting along the Stettin railway line broke out, keeping the troops together soon became impossible. The majority fled back to the Infantry Barracks and Neues Werke, after losing their nerve. A few hundred were able to make a breakout in the general direction of Zorndorf, only to be captured during the course of the day. Thus ended this short outbreak of fighting before the weapons around the barracks and fort fell silent. The battle for the Neustadt was over. One of the two Soviet divisions reported the capture of 76 officers and 2,698 men. The number of dead was estimated at 3,000.

General Berzarin's 5th Shock Army Headquarters reported the storming of the 'town and fortress' of Küstrin to Front Headquarters. This was then relayed at face value to Moscow and duly celebrated with a victory salvo from the city's guns. It was the 300th of its kind, and no one dared advise Stalin of the error.[23]

Panzergrenadier Johannes Diebe was among those caught in the Neustadt:

> During the night of 11/12 March a breakout attempt was made from the encircled Neues Werke/Infantry Barracks. Those driven back to the Infantry Barracks surrendered next morning. We were taken to a large square and relieved of all our things: watches, briefcases, bread bags, eating utensils, washing, shaving and tooth-cleaning items, family photos and handkerchiefs, everything was taken. Finally the vultures had us remove the swastika badges from our uniforms.
>
> We had to parade on the street. A German soldier with a white armband translated the Russian orders: '5 by 20 men!' I finally counted twenty marching blocks, in other words 2,000 men, and wondered how it came to be so many.
>
> We passed German civilians on the road, all refugees. On 15 March we reached a large reception camp in Landsberg. For four days we were given neither food nor drink. We sucked our aluminium identity disks to relieve our thirst. Some prisoners went crazy and were shot. Our numbers were then made up with civilians, either old men or 16-year-old boys.[24]

Corporal Hans Arlt was also part of the breakout attempt:

> We left the barracks in a southerly direction at about midnight in rows, bent over, as quietly as possible and alert to all sides. Then we turned to the east and left the Army Supply Depot behind us on our right, where some buildings were burning in the southern part. Shortly afterwards we came under rifle fire from there. We went on in complete darkness, following the man in front, across open ground and through a small depression. We could see burning houses in the background.
>
> Suddenly we came under fire from close by and an attack with 'Hurrah' cries that we countered with fire and 'Urray' cries. Chaos reigned. What had happened? Germans breaking out from the von Stülpnagel Barracks had clashed with German sappers breaking out from the Engineer Barracks, where they had been trapped since the beginning of the enemy attack,

without recognising each other. This was because we had tried to disguise ourselves as Russians and were unaware that further German troops were breaking out towards us from the south. The sappers recognised us but too late because of the shouting. We had lost the element of surprise and alerted the Russians.

An uncanny silence surrounded me. Hardly anything was recognisable. Any sound raised the question: friend or foe? Suddenly I bumped into three sappers and stayed with them. Later I discovered that one was a sergeant with Eastern Front experience and some knowledge of the Russian language, one a corporal and one a private. The sergeant immediately took command. Without local knowledge or a map, and only armed with a compass, he had to keep going east for safety. We marched until dawn and then hid in a little wood. Once during the day an enemy column passed within 100 metres of us but did not discover us.

But 300 metres further to the west of our hiding place the Russians successfully searched a wood for German soldiers, and the cries that we heard I have never forgotten.

While two men remained on watch, the other two slept. With nightfall we set off north towards Stettin, hoping to reach the front line and German troops within six days, wanting to avoid Soviet captivity at all costs. We checked the provisions we were carrying and divided them up to cover this period.

During the following nights we sought to avoid inhabited areas, roads, tracks, bridges and enemy movement, although it did not always work. Sentries challenging us were answered by our sergeant with a well-known Russian swearword, as our hands grasped our carbines in wary reaction.

Our second worst enemy was the countryside, the Neumark. It continually forced us to make diversions and wade through knee-deep water channels. Whenever the situation allowed, we hid ourselves in daylight in barns and haystacks, where we were able to dry off our clothing a bit.

In one wooded area we found ourselves in an expansive Russian bunker system. Too late we recognised the freshly laid path in the sand as a noise reducer. The sentries must have heard something. We could hear their voices and some shots. We lay still between the rows of bunkers. We erected a small screen out of the undergrowth with our bare hands and had to remain there until dark. A cold day lay ahead of us, only the fear of being discovered keeping us warm.

The strain up to now had weakened me and now hunger was bringing on brief signs of exhaustion. Once the bread and sausage had been consumed, coffee beans that the sappers had brought with them were shared out. About half a handful of chewed coffee beans had to serve as a stimulant. Water for rinsing them down and for thirst there was ample. Only its drinkability was open to doubt from the animal bodies found in the streams.

On the sixth day we stumbled unexpectedly on wide, flowing water that could only be the Oder. We reached a bridge under construction that was about 2 metres high. It was unguarded and we went along it until coming to an abrupt end that obliged us to turn back. Upon leaving the bridge, we suddenly found ourselves standing in front of a T-34 beside a shell store. We could not stay here, and as we could find no boat, we looked for a convenient hiding place near the river.

The building site came to life at daybreak. German farm carts and Russian panje wagons delivered tree trunks. This work continued for about 15 hours. My engineer comrades considered the construction of a raft and we started to work on one in the dark. Careful hammering was done some distance from the unguarded bridge and a raft was constructed out of tree trunks and planks. Despite the noise, we remained undisturbed. When we then poled ourselves off from the east bank, we were only able to avoid capsizing by constant balancing. This journey was to last two nights.

After the first night's journey we first had to check the raft, which was driving a bit downriver. We punted for hours until a pontoon bridge offered a place to halt, as it was supported by a tree trunk rammed upright between two pontoons. After a careful landing and reconnaissance, we discovered a sentry sleeping in a large metal drum. We did not disturb his sleep, but noted that there was a boat fastened to the bridge that we could use the following night.

This time we sought accommodation in a barn. Here we were not alone, for from time to time one could hear Morse code-like sounds. This did not disturb us, but increased our alertness.

Next night we took possession of the boat, despite the

sleeping sentry, and were able to move faster on the Oder. Our attempt to go over to the left bank immediately failed, as sentries were posted at regular intervals, who fortunately revealed themselves with the lighting or glow of cigarettes. Actually we wanted to go north as far as possible to reach the front line, which showed itself even more clearly before dawn with flares and the noise of fighting.

At this juncture we approached a bridge that was still under construction in the middle of the stream. It was higher, presumably to take greater weights, and partly lit. [This was the 60-ton capacity bridge at Zellin.] The alert sentries opened fire on us at long range. In order to get out of enemy sight we had to turn around and thus reached the west bank. There was little cover on the flanks and it could not be far from the front line.

The decisive moment now lay before us. With our last strength and an inner surge we had to break through to our lines. The coming daylight drove us on. Haystacks, barns or woods for hiding in were not to be seen.

From a geographical point of view, we were in the Oderbruch. Our way on land led us directly past an enemy mortar position. Our sergeant said to the Russian sentry: 'Come with us to Berlin!' We breathed out as we were allowed past. Next we crossed an unoccupied communication trench, but in the next, the foremost in the Soviet system, were two shaven-headed soldiers occupied in trench construction, who recognised us as Germans, hurried for their weapons and immediately fired at us.

The distance between the Soviet and German trenches was about 500 metres. We raced in zigzags like hares, crossed another water ditch, running bent over and stumbling forwards. The ground was as flat as a plate, and the last running sapper was caught by the Russian bullets. We others dropped as soon as the fire behind us stopped.

In front of the German trenches, the sergeant noticed that we were lying in a minefield, and shots were coming from the trenches. Then came abuse: 'Traitors!' 'Pigs' 'Seydlitz-Troops!' A machine gun was brought up and aimed at us. At the same time rifle bullets whistled close to us. Then we were ordered one by one and with raised hands and well apart to approach the German trenches. We stood up with our carbines slung and carefully watched every step on the earth in front of us.

Pistols were aimed at our breasts. We were taken to be members of the 'Free Germany' National Committee, which we later discovered was active here. This dangerous situation first altered when a corporal in the group occupying the trench identified me. We had qualified together at the NCO School in Arnswalde. An odyssey of over nine days and nights ended at about 0700 hours on 21 March 1945.

We had not eaten for days, only chewed coffee beans. The bread offered us was too hard and so we held it in our hands on the way to the platoon command post, during which we came under close bombardment from enemy mortar salvoes, after which the tightly-held bread of a bluish-grey colour tasted better than cake.

After our first interview we were taken under guard to the company command post. The same again, but now more thorough. With our physical condition, our appearance and the description of our experiences and observations, all doubts were put aside. After our first food and warm drinks we were able to climb into bed in the company command post. Although completely exhausted, I could not sleep. My feet hurt under the covers and my stomach rebelled.

On the afternoon of the day we broke through, German sentries saw the punishment of two Russian soldiers at gun-point, presumably the two that three of us had escaped from that morning.

Wearing only socks on my feet, next morning I was sent to the main dressing station at Wriezen with badly swollen feet and a skin infection. From there I went to the field hospital for lightly wounded at Tiefensee, near Strausberg, and thus became separated from my sapper comrades.[25]

Chapter Nine

Assault on the Altstadt

The fall of the Neustadt now led to the fate of the Altstadt and the Küstrin Fortress being decided on the flat, soggy plain of the Oderbruch.

On 13 March Marshal Zhukov issued fresh orders for the reduction of the Küstrin Fortress and the unification of his bridgeheads, just as the 32nd Rifle Corps of General Berzarin's 5th Shock Army was attacking the Küstrin-Altstadt garrison in conjunction with another attack by the 4th Guards Rifle Corps of General Chuikov's 8th Guards Army from Kietz. Neither of these attacks succeeded, and the plans for this operation had to be reviewed once more. The urgency of Zhukov's orders showed that he was not too involved with the East Pomeranian operation or with the operational control of his main forces to look ahead to the earliest resumption of the main operation on Berlin.

The 5th Shock Army was now ordered to use two reinforced rifle divisions in a main attack on Golzow, with a subsidiary attack from the Alt Bleyen area on Gorgast. The stated aim was to break through the German defences in the Genschmar/Alt Bleyen sector, take the area Genschmar/Golzow and Kuhbrücken-Vorstadt, seize the 16.3 and 10.3 elevations, but not Golzow itself, and then go over to the defensive.

The 8th Guards Army, also using two reinforced rifle divisions, was ordered to break through the defences in a north-westerly direction, complete the taking of Kietz, and then go over to the defensive in the area Golzow/Alt Tucheband/Hathenow. The main attack was to be conducted towards Golzow with a subsidiary attack on Kietz as far as the Vorflut Canal.

The operation thus planned involved these two armies using only part of their resources, while their main forces had the task of defending the existing bridgeheads and of tying down the German

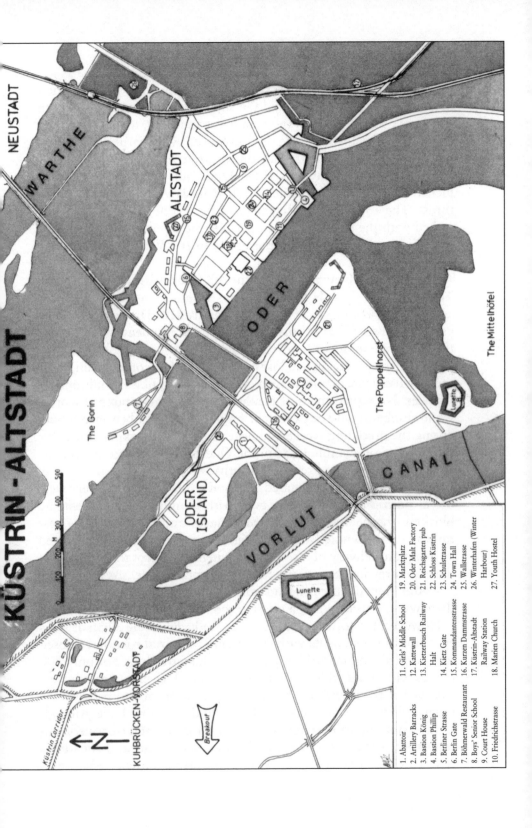

KÜSTRIN - ALTSTADT

NEUSTADT

WARTHE

ALTSTADT

ODER

The Pappelhorst

The Mittelhöfel

The Gorin

ODER ISLAND

CANAL

VORLUT

Lunette D

Küstrin Corridor

KUHBRÜCKEN-VORSTADT

Breakout

N

0 100 200 300 400 500
         M

1. Abattoir
2. Artillery Barracks
3. Bastion König
4. Bastion Phillip
5. Berliner Strasse
6. Berlin Gate
7. Bohmerwald Restaurant
8. Boys' Senior School
9. Court House
10. Friedrichstrasse

11. Girls' Middle School
12. Kattewall
13. Kietzerbusch Railway Halt
14. Kietz Gate
15. Kommandantenstrasse
16. Kurzen Dammstrasse
17. Küstrin-Altstadt Railway Station
18. Marien Church

19. Marktplatz
20. Oder Malt Factory
21. Reichsgarten pub
22. Schloss Küstrin
23. Schulstrasse
24. Town Hall
25. Wallstrasse
26. Winterhafen (Winter Harbour)
27. Youth Hostel

Lunette R

troops with diversionary attacks by small groups. Close coordination between these two armies, and the supporting elements of the 16th Air Army, was essential if the plan was to succeed, for it was appreciated that the fortress was well favoured with natural obstacles, which would make it extremely difficult to overcome.

The 5th Shock Army picked the 32nd Rifle Corps, which in turn picked the 60th Guards and 295th Rifle Divisions, for the main thrust. The 1373rd Rifle Regiment of the 416th Rifle Division was tasked with the subsidiary thrust, while the other two regiments of that division were to secure the banks of the Warthe opposite the fortress.

The 8th Guards Army detailed the 4th Guards Rifle Corps, whose 47th and 57th Guards Rifle Divisions would be used for the main assault. Two regiments of the 35th Guards Rifle Division would be used for the subsidiary thrust, while its third regiment would secure the Oder embankment.[1]

The Küstrin garrison had lost more than half its complement, most of its artillery pieces and an incalculable amount of ammunition and supplies. No replacement of personnel or heavy weapons in worthwhile numbers could be expected. Supplies had already been minimal during the preceding weeks and never balanced the expenditure, for the forming of a stable front in the Oderbruch opposite the threatening bridgeheads had received priority.

In Küstrin itself a decimated garrison could still hold a relatively useful position on the Oder, even with its modest equipment, by blocking the nearest river crossing places and the only east–west railway on the whole front. The nightly supply convoys guaranteed an adequate delivery of life-sustaining items and kept the numbers in the main dressing station down to an acceptable level. As long as the 'corridor' remained open and convoys could continue to operate there was no need to fear a crisis in food and ammunition supplies.

However, the fortress area was now reduced to the Altstadt in its encompassing peninsula with the remains of the old bastion-enclosed town centre – a piece of land about 2 kilometres long but only 800 metres wide at its widest point between the Oder and Warthe rivers – as well as the Island of similar size to the west formed between the Oder and the Vorflut Canal. The Island contained the Altstadt railway station, the Artillery Barracks, an abattoir and a brewery, but relatively few houses. Deeply flooded scrubland and meadows covered wide expanses of the Altstadt peninsula known as the Gorin in the north and the Island in the south. This was a difficult area for the garrison, for only two or three spades down one struck ground-water and so no effective trenches or foxholes could be dug, but the attacker was equally disadvantaged from lack of cover. Consequently no serious attempts had been made to cross here until now.

The front around the fortress had now consolidated on this new line. A German attack on Kietz from the north in regimental strength achieved little. Enemy reconnaissance and assault troops kept the squeezed-in garrison busy every day. One night some Soviet scouts in rubber dinghies came down the Oder and were first spotted opposite the Altstadt walls, coming under fire from both banks.

Tied down, the garrison was being subjected to wearing artillery bombardments. The intensity and frequency of air attacks depended upon the weather and varying target priorities along the whole middle Oder front, but even individual aircraft almost always found a target within the narrow fortress territory. Everywhere shells of German origin were being fired, the large number found in the fortress leading to the depressing realisation that they could not have come from a German long-range battery on the Seelow Heights, but had been fired from Soviet guns. In fact the 8th Guards Army had collected up all the guns and ammunition captured on the way from Posen to the Oder and some 65,000 captured German shells of 105mm and 150mm calibre were used in the fighting for the bridge-head south of Küstrin.

When the bombardment lifted in the evenings or occasionally died away, men climbed up into the open by the dim glimmer of shaded pocket torches to stand in line at the water pumps or to gather sand-bags from burnt-out or collapsed buildings to reinforce the entrances and windows of their own bunkers. In some places, such as at the town hall, the cellar doors were barricaded with squashed clarified butter cartons taken from destroyed stores, as they had proved good at stopping bullets and shrapnel.

Stores not required by the garrison were taken to Seelow by the nightly convoys. Even some goods that had been stored by Neustadt firms in the supposedly bombproof Altstadt and subsequently damaged were taken away by the halftracks. Off-duty Volkssturm men stuffed boxes full of shoes, clothing, suits, coats, etc. into sacks for this purpose.

However, the most important task for the convoy's journeys was the removal of the wounded. Losses and damage had made the lack of beds, medical equipment and medicines even worse. Some of the forward dressing stations had already fallen. A former Luftwaffe medical depot in the Neustadt that the fortress had taken over went up in flames. Consequently, with a daily increasing proportion of casualties, the seriously wounded had a lesser chance of being evacuated, and with this in mind, in the middle of the month the combat units of the Volkssturm and the Hitler Youth were moved out of the railway offices on the Marktplatz to make room for them.

The seriously wounded could not always be brought back to the middle of the town from some of the exposed front line before dark. Too often help came too late, but even a proper burial site was lacking, the town cemeteries lying outside the defended area. A provisional cemetery in the yard of a housing block near the main dressing station was soon overfilled, and consequently many of the dead were being buried indiscriminately wherever there was a patch of workable earth. Not all the dead were treated in this manner, for some were smothered under collapsing buildings or blown apart by direct hits. At least among the combat teams, even if the men had only been together for a short while, their names could be recorded, and there were some so-called grave registry officers keeping the lists of the dead of some units somewhere among the ruins. There were also many reported missing in the fighting. A list published by the German Red Cross in 1958 gave a total of 1,400 names of soldiers, Waffen-SS, Volkssturm and policemen aged between 17 and 61 years missing in Küstrin at the war's end.

Some of the severely wounded were buried in the collapsed beer cellar of a restaurant on the Marktplatz opposite the town hall. Shells and low-flying aircraft made transportation to the main dressing station impossible, so some were taken into the crypt of the nearby church, which was soon destroyed. That evening several shells hit the roof and flames immediately engulfed the straw-dry timberwork. The heat caused the bells to ring before the nave and bell cage collapsed, burying everything under them. The wounded could not be saved, and even their names remained unknown.

While the church was alight, soldiers on the equally shot-up roof of the nearby Schloss prevented the clouds of sparks from setting fire to Reinefarth's quarters. There was no longer any organised fire-fighting. The firemen and air raid wardens had suffered casualties proportionate to the front-line troops, while their vehicles had become victims of the bombardment and could hardly be used in the rubble-strewn streets. A few portable, petrol-driven pumps provided an inadequate replacement. Sappers used the demolition of individual buildings and ruins to prevent the spread of fire, turning them into natural anti-tank barriers. Furniture, doors and floorboards – as far as they were available – were ripped up by the Hungarian troops no longer in the front line. Wood for reinforcement work had meanwhile become as rare as fuel for the stoves in the cold, wet earth bunkers, cellars and fortress casemates. Nevertheless, day after day the flames continued to consume.

Eventually there was only one motor pump left intact, which was used in the Marktplatz to draw water from a deep well. In a surprise air attack most of the men fighting the ensuing fire fled into the hallway of a partially ruined building, but a bomb ripped its walls apart and the few firemen that were left waited in vain for their comrades to reappear.[2]

Officer Cadet Corporal Hans Dahlmanns recalled:

When the Soviet troops reached the east bank of the Warthe, the situation on the peninsula became very dangerous. The way in, following the railway line, led in full enemy sight over an about 50-metre-long railway bridge spanning across the flooded land to our peninsula. Anyone moving on it could expect heavy machine-gun and mortar fire.

One of the two officer cadets that had come with me to the peninsula lay in a small dugout just a few paces from the bridge. He was wounded by a mortar bomb splinter in the upper thigh and had to wait until darkness before he could be extracted. He was in great pain, which he bore bravely. Presumably he got away from Küstrin as the fortress was not completely surrounded at this stage. The other officer cadet died from a mortar splinter to the head while delivering a message.

The route to the peninsula was little liked, but had to be managed every day, not least because of the water level report, which had to be read at the risk of one's life at the foot of the swing bridge and reported to the company command post. Since the Russians had arrived on the Warthe, this had been located in a cellar of the first house on the edge of the Altstadt. If we did not receive the water level report, I had to do the job, something I particularly disliked.

My main task at this point was maintaining contact between

the company commander and the individual platoons deployed near the bridge. Apart from this I had to deliver the Warthe water level report daily to the fortress commandant in the Schloss. This message carrying became increasingly dangerous as the fortress area diminished, as firing could come from all sides and there were big stretches offering little cover. More and more often I saw the bodies of soldiers lying on the streets and squares that had been hit by sudden barrages far behind the front line. The Red Army had plenty of ammunition and used it industriously.

On my messenger rounds I regularly came past the Oder Potato Meal Factory, where I could call on my father. From mid-February until the end of March I saw him practically every day.[3]

Teenager Hans Dalbkermeyer concluded his account:

It must have been between 15 and 18 March that a Führer-Order demanded all the youths be evacuated from Küstrin. Some 40 to 50 youths assembled in a casemate room one evening. We were told that we would leave the town with the nightly supply convoy. We were briefed about the route and the way the convoy operated between the almost completely surrounded town and through the Russian lines. We could put our packs on the tracked vehicles, but would have to walk behind. Meanwhile I had acquired a pack again with some laundry and utensils. All weapons were to be left behind, but I took a small 6.35 pistol and ammunition with me despite the prohibition. As well as our packs, the tracked vehicles took the wounded to the hinterland.

Long thick ropes were attached to the rear of one of the vehicles to enable us to walk behind without losing contact. The convoy set off, left the town over the Oder and Vorflut Canal bridges, and set off into the night as quietly as possible, without any noise and without lights. We three remaining Birnbaumers kept together with others behind an armoured personnel carrier, and during the dangerous section were protected by being in the middle of the tracked vehicles. Hardly ever on proper roads, mainly on tracks and fields, we went stumbling on, but never letting go of the life-saving rope, towards safety and freedom.

We reached Seelow in the early morning, recovered our packs and felt saved and at peace.

After a break in a Wehrmacht shelter on the Marktplatz, 30 to 40 of us were ordered to go on by rail to a retraining camp. The train left Seelow at midday. The orders to go to the retraining camp did not apply to us, so when the train stopped at Eberswalde we secretly got off. There was a local train on the track alongside going to Berlin-Bernau, so we stepped straight across from one carriage to the other without using the platform. As both trains set off in opposite directions, we separated from that closed and supervised group.

We knew that the main administration of our Heim Schools was based in Berlin-Spandau, so we reported back there. After three days in Berlin with nightly bombing attacks and the exchange of our fantasy uniforms for civilian clothing, my war service came to an end. With some difficulty we went by train from Berlin to Thuringia at the end of March. In Haubinda, near Hildburghausen, we found our Birnbaum school encamped, and with them my younger brother.[4]

Officer Cadet Corporal Fritz Kohlase arrived at Alt Bleyen with the 303rd Fusilier Battalion on the night of 19/20 March to relieve elements of the 25th Panzergrenadier Division, which was being pulled out of the line for a short rest:

We relieved units of the 25th Panzergrenadier Division and took up positions in the area around Alt Bleyen manor farm, the battalion headquarters and dressing station being set up in the farm. The 2nd Company's command post was set up in the cellar of one of the few farm labourers' cottages. The company itself occupied the prepared trenches directly in front of the farm, with a field of fire covering the Schäferei [sheep farm] and Alt Bleyen. The dugouts, however, only provided protection from splinters and light shells. Immediately south-west of the farm were two infantry guns, and two machine guns were positioned about 100 metres south-west from them. From there they could cover the whole western and southern sides with their fire. Another 100 metres further on towards Gorgast was an 88mm flak gun dug in for ground fighting. A communications trench connected these firing points and ended in the trenches we were occupying. The flat terrain started in front of our positions, extending to the Schäferei and Gorgast to the south-west. Far off to the south, towards the railway, a line of trees obstructed our view. The land was completely flat and easy to observe. Behind the labourers' cottages were three self-propelled guns. The supply route between the hinterland and fortress ran past near the farm. Every night German tracked vehicles went along to the Altstadt and back again.

We obtained our ammunition and food supplies at night, as our supply column was located well behind the main front line. The noise of fighting came from Küstrin and the Gorgast direction all day long. At night fires reddened the sky over the fortress. For us at the Alt Bleyen manor farm Tuesday and Wednesday passed peacefully. We just had to be careful, for the Russian snipers reacted to every movement.[5]

The whole area was now facing four days of aerial bombardment preparatory to the ground attack by the 8th Guards and 5th Shock Armies, as witnessed by Officer Cadet Corporal Fritz Kohlase:

On Wednesday afternoon [21 March] two to three hundred twin-engined Soviet bombers in close formation dropped two bomb carpets on the boundary line near Gorgast. Although the bombing area was 3 kilometres from us, the earth around us shook. This and an otherwise suspicious silence indicated that the next enemy offensive was imminent.[6]

Officer Cadet Corporal Hans Dahlmanns continued his account:

On 20 March my company command post moved into the cellars of the Court House. It was no longer possible to check the Warthe water level and report it to fortress headquarters, but nobody asked for it. I made my rounds as a messenger under fire, visiting my father every day, on the last occasion just a few hours before his death. I believe this was on 24 March.

I remember that I returned to the Court House at dusk and was given the job of mending a shot-though cable providing power from a generator in the town to the courthouse cellar to enable us to hear the news on the radio. It had become dark, but nevertheless I still had to take cover from the 'Sewing Machines' flying overhead and dropping flares and incendiary and explosive bombs on anything that moved. Once the aircraft had flown off, I resumed looking for the break in the cable and was suddenly shocked by a tremendous explosion that must have occurred close by. But I had heard no bomb falling, which shocked me, as it was completely unusual. Soon afterwards I found the fault in the cable, repaired it and turned back for the Court House cellar. Then I heard on the radio the news that Allied troops had crossed the Rhine and were fighting around Dinslaken, my home town.

A little later, an NCO of my company came in and told me that my father's command post at the Oder Potato Meal Factory had been hit by an incendiary bomb that had ignited a stack of shells. After a while the fire had reached the hand grenades stored there, setting off a violent explosion that had destroyed the north-west side of the factory. Second-Lieutenant Schröter had been left hanging head down in the beams, still conscious, but he died soon afterwards. Nothing had happened to my father, however. So I had another quiet night.

The next morning I went to my company commander asking to go to the Oder Potato Meal Factory to see what had happened. The whole way I thought what the worst could be. The previous evening the NCO had said that my father had not been seen. I found the factory mainly destroyed, above all glowing as hot as an oven so that it was impossible to go in. I then went to the nearby Artillery Barracks to ask Captain Fischer about it. On my way I passed a soldier named Müller in a trench who was in my father's company and asked about him: 'I cannot say', he replied and turned away, and at that moment I knew that my father was dead.

I remember the feeling that suddenly overcame me and blanketed out everything else. I felt no sadness or despair, rather a frightful emptiness before a background that was filled with anxiety, an increasing depression and returning anxiety. A strange rigidity gripped me. If I had recognised it, it was as if I had slipped out of myself.

It was in this state that I met Captain Fischer, who officially informed me that my father was dead and expressed his sympathy. My father had personally led the team trying to extinguish the burning ammunition with water from the Oder and wet sacks. The explosion caused the building to partially collapse, burying the firefighters under the debris. They experienced a mercifully swift death, while those who had survived the collapse in the hollow space beyond were behind a wall of fire that no one could penetrate. Their cries for help could be heard but no one could get through and they were burned alive. Between ten and twenty men of my father's company died with him.

I went back to the command post in the Court House, but cannot remember what I did or felt.[7]

The 25th Panzergrenadier Division, whose fighting strength had been reduced to 5,196 men by 17 March, had been withdrawn to rest and refit near the village of Friedersdorf on the Seelow Heights. Hitler had come up with the unrealistic idea of using this and three other experienced divisions to attack northwards from Frankfurt, where the Germans still had a bridgehead on the east bank, in order to cut off the Soviet Reitwein-Lebus bridgehead and eventually relieve Küstrin. This operation, which depended upon getting four divisions across the only bridge, was to be achieved within three days commencing on 24 March. On the first day of the operation there was to be a big surprise attack that would methodically destroy the enemy bridges between Frankfurt and Küstrin. However, the Soviets forestalled this plan by attacking on 22 March before it could be implemented, and the 25th Panzergrenadiers had to be thrust back into line in considerable haste.[8]

That same day Colonel General Gotthardt Heinrici, until then commander of the 1st Panzer Army, reported in Zossen to the Chief of the General Staff, Colonel General Heinz Guderian, who had surprised him in Upper Silesia with a telephone call announcing that he was Heinrich Himmler's successor as commander-in-chief of Army Group 'Weichsel'. Guderian briefed him on his area of responsibility, which extended from the Baltic to the mouth of the Neisse river, and his forces, which consisted of the 3rd Panzer Army in the north and the 9th Army in the south. Guderian especially stressed the critical situation at Küstrin.

That evening Heinrici arrived at the Army Group Headquarters near Prenzlau, where Himmler received him in front of a portrait of Frederick the Great, saying that his relief was due to some important tasks that Hitler had given him. He then gave a widely rambling account of his leadership since January. Then came an important telephone call. The commander-in-chief of the 9th Army reported that a Soviet attack to combine the two bridgeheads, cutting off Küstrin, had occurred. Himmler handed the telephone to Heinrici saying: 'You now command the army group.'

In detail, the Soviet attack by about four rifle divisions from the

Closing the Corridor
22-23 Mar 45

south and two from the north was launched at 0715 hours, and the leading elements of both Soviet armies met at the Förster Bridge over the Alte Oder north-west of Gorgast that afternoon. Successful as the operation had been, it had only been achieved at considerable cost. Captain Horst Zobel's 1st Battalion of the 'Müncheberg' Panzer Regiment claimed the destruction of 59 Soviet tanks that day, not counting damaged or immobilised ones, and the 9th Army's overall claim was 116 Soviet tanks.

The 25th Panzergrenadier Division moved off eastwards from Werbig at about 1800 hours to launch a counterattack along both sides of Reichsstrasse 1 and the Berlin–Küstrin railway line with the 'Müncheberg' Panzer Division on its left flank. By dusk the Alt Tuchenow–Golzow railway line had been reached and Golzow railway station retaken. The German formations, now supported by Army Flak Battalion 292, went over to the defence.

Meanwhile the inner sweep of the Soviet attack had successfully bottled up the 'corridor' defenders with those of the fortress garrison west of the Vorflut Canal. The 'corridor' elements included the 303rd Fusilier Battalion, a mixed armoured company of self-propelled guns and Mark IV tanks of Captain Zobel's battalion that had become cut off in the fighting for Gorgast, and the 2nd Battalion of the 1st 'Müncheberg' Panzergrenadier Regiment.[9]

Officer Cadet Corporal Fritz Kohlase recalled how it began:

The second Russian offensive on Küstrin began with an artillery preparation on the morning of Thursday, 22 March 1945. The whole front line as far as our horizon, the southern and north-western parts of the corridor position lay under heavy artillery fire, but no shells fell on us. We had orders to hold our fire. The central part of the corridor was to remain as quiet as possible, but barely 2 kilometres from us was a frightful wall of fire, steel and earth.

As passive spectators, we had to look on as the barrage began to move. Then came the Soviet infantry and, behind the storm troops, enormous columns, including panje wagons.

The self-propelled gun commander sought me out to complain strongly about our battalion commander. Despite orders to the contrary, he had begged Major Quetz for permission to open fire, and having been refused, he said: 'We will never have the Russians so concentrated in front of us. What losses we could inflict upon them now! All those that we don't put out of action today we will have to defend ourselves against tomorrow under worse conditions of increased superiority. Apart from that, we would be supporting our comrades on the main front line!'

The sounds of heavy infantry and cannon fire came from Gorgast and the Schäferei that seemed to move a little and then increase into a strong cannonade. Towards noon it changed to short, raging infantry fire, then became weaker and finally ended with a dull explosion.

Since the assault that had gone past us that morning we had seen no one, either Russian or German. At dusk a wounded SS man came towards us unimpeded across the open fields. He belonged to the Leibstandarte 'Adolf Hitler' and reported the destruction of his battalion. He now wanted to join the other Leibstandarte battalion that should be somewhere near Berlin. When he realised that he was in an encirclement and had also been heading east, he asked for some bread and water and went back the way he had come.

Later that evening the battalion was redeployed to cover the farm from the south-west. One section took up position every 100 to 150 metres. I had to dig in with my men about 75 metres from the 88mm gun with no communications trench to the rear. The company commander personally gave me my orders: 'This position is to be held to the last man. Evacuation only on orders!'

Towards midnight Sergeant Hoffmann and I made a reconnaissance towards the railway line. We went forward about a kilometre without seeing or hearing anyone on this dark night. Only from Küstrin was there occasional artillery fire and burning fires.[10]

Officer Cadet Corporal Hans Dahlmanns takes up the story in Küstrin:

It must have been one or two days later [after 20 March] that ground-assault aircraft attacked the Court House with heavy bombs. I was about to leave on my messenger rounds, but stayed in the cellar with my back to some steel air-raid shelter doors as both neighbouring cellars had been partly destroyed by direct hits. The company command post was in one of them. When the clouds of dust subsided, the steel doors were completely buckled and two men pulled the company commander out into the open.

The company command post was then established in an earth-covered bunker that was about in line with the Court House, but further north-west near the railway line in quite thick under-growth. That afternoon or the next day, I was given the task of reconnoitring the area and trenches to the south-east. These stretched from behind the Court House, parallel to the Warthe, to the road leading to the Neustadt, where Soviet troops were expected soon. In an earth bunker I found a Russian soldier who had been wounded in the foot. I ordered him to come with me, but finally I had to put his arm around my neck and support him.

I took him to the wooden bunker and we tried to carry him between four of us to the field hospital, but this did not work, as the Friedrichstrasse that we had to cross was under heavy shellfire and we had to turn back. When we returned to the bunker, the order to retreat arrived together with the news that the railway and road bridges would be blown up behind us.

An NCO saw the wounded man and said: 'In a fortnight he will be fighting against us again.' He handed me his pistol and went on: 'Take him outside and shoot him!' I refused, as did the others, until the company cook took the pistol, led the wounded man outside and shot him. The whole scene took place in the presence of the company commander, Lieutenant Schröder, who said nothing, as if he was not in charge. I have long thought that I should have left the young Russian soldier in his hole. He would have been in safety next day, and I am convinced that his foot would have taken the rest of the war to heal.[11]

Sapper Ernst Müller remembered:

On 22 March we moved our battalion command post from the Law Courts to the Oder Malt Factory, which was not far from the Artillery Barracks on the west bank of the Oder. As I knew the town well, I had to go back over the Oder bridges into the Altstadt. The road bridge had already suffered considerable damage in the meantime. It was often difficult taking messages to the Altstadt.

Once I had to find out at night in complete darkness whether the Warthe bridges had been completely destroyed. This was not the case with the road bridge. For this task I had an escort of several men, one of whom was lost. Upon our return to the command post I had to take some bitter words from his friend.

It must have been on 22 March that Soviet bombs hit the casemate in the Friedrichstrasse. The event was devastating for us. Among those platoon commanders gathered there for a conference were Lieutenant Hagen, Second-Lieutenant Behr, Battalion Sergeant Major Gleiche, and Staff Sergeants Tewes and Kukei.

On or about 20 March the fortress commandant, SS-Gruppenführer and Lieutenant-General of the Waffen-SS Reinefarth, moved his command post out of the Altstadt to the Artillery Barracks. About five days later he gave over command of the fortress to Captain Fischer, who mockingly said: 'So a little captain will now take over the fortress.' This fact has not been noted in any book to appear so far. However, I had this from the mouth of Captain Fischer himself![12]

The Wehrmacht Report of 23 March pulled a veil over the fatal development at Küstrin with the fable that a Soviet attack on the flanks of the bridgehead had been checked by 'the effective defensive fire of our Oder defences after a minimal initial success'.

The Soviets resumed their attack to the west with new forces. The XXXIXth Panzer Corps commanded by General Karl Decker, with the 'Döberitz' Infantry Division on the right, the 25th Panzergrenadiers in the centre and 'Müncheberg' Panzer Division on the left, had to withstand the heaviest pressure all day long, the focal point being in the centre astride Reichsstrasse 1, but they were able to hold all their important positions or regain them by counterattack.

In the now fully encircled fortress, the worsening of the now critical situation became noticeable. A new line of defence had to be drawn straight across the 'corridor' near Bleyen, and the forces thrown back in this encirclement were now having to fight facing west.

Ground-attack aircraft attacked the Kommandantenstrasse leading from the Marktplatz to the fire brigade depot, where a group of armoured personnel carriers was standing. Within minutes these vehicles, condemned to immobility by the rubble-strewn streets, were in flames under a hail of bombs and explosive shells. A platoon of Volkssturm just released from the front line was surprised by this attack, only a few of the men being able to reach cover in time.

For the first time there were no night convoys, but food reserves gave no reason for concern and there was enough ammunition left for several days, as hardly any of the heavy weapons were still service-able. But the closure would have a disastrous effect on the main dressing station as now no serious cases could be evacuated to the hinterland and the number of casualties was mounting by the hour.[13]

Officer-Cadet Corporal Fritz Kohlase described the Soviet advance:

> The Russians attacked us on Friday afternoon without any preliminary reconnaissance, artillery or armoured support. They came from the direction of the Gorgast–Kietz railway line in line abreast, widely spaced out and several metres apart, holding rifles or sub-machine guns in their hands. The first row was followed by a second, this by a third, then the fourth, fifth and sixth. Despite orders to the contrary, the two machine guns behind us opened fire at 800 metres and all the other weapons joined in. The Soviet infantry then advanced in bounds as our artillery in the Seelow area joined in the battle. They merely dug themselves in before us as they came under direct fire from the 88mm gun. This position was the turning point of the Russian attack. West of us the attackers stormed further northwards, thus thrusting eastwards and digging in 100 to 200 metres from the heavy machine guns and the rifle trenches west of the farm. This attack was a difficult but precisely executed manoeuvre, assisted by the inaccuracy of the German defensive fire.[14]

Shortly after midnight on 23 March the 25th Panzergrenadier Division attacked along the Golzow–Gorgast road to reach the Alte Oder. By daybreak it had penetrated Gorgast, where bitter fighting broke out, but later overwhelming Soviet forces forced a withdrawal to the starting point.

Both sides were preparing for big operations to decide the Küstrin situation. The 9th Army was planning a relief attack for Küstrin that would include the 'Führer' Grenadier Division under Major General Otto-Ernst Remer. The 8th Guards Army was preparing to attack the

Altstadt fortress. Meanwhile the commander-in-chief of the 1st Byelorussian Front, Marshal Zhukov, had been summoned to Moscow for consultations about the forthcoming Berlin Operation. Before leaving, recalling the false report of 12 March on the taking of the fortress, he asked the commander of the 8th Guards Army when he thought he could take it. Chuikov riposted that it lay in the attack path of Berzarin's 5th Shock Army, which had already claimed to have taken it. Zhukov said that when mistakes occurred they had to be corrected. Chuikov promised to take Küstrin before Zhukov met Stalin. The attack was fixed for 29 March and would be led by divisions on both banks of the Oder. Heavy batteries were dug into the dykes to provide direct fire on the bastions. Soviet units had already worked their way forward into the corner between the Oder and Warthe rivers at the Kietzerbusch railway halt and skirmishing no longer died down at night.[15]

Officer-Cadet Corporal Fritz Kohlase again:

During the night leading to Saturday [24 March] more fires flamed in Küstrin. In the south-west German troops sought to break out of the encirclement. They forced the Soviet front back with strong artillery fire and started fighting for Gorgast in the depths of the night. However, they were brought to a halt and shortly afterwards were driven back to the west by the Red Army.

For my comrades and me this failure was a great disappointment. With my section I had marked the south-westerly point of the Küstrin encirclement and seen the fire of our relieving troops about 3 kilometres away.

The noise of combat came from Küstrin all day long. At night, when it was quiet, fires lit up the town. The Russians also shot a building within the farm area into flames practically every night, making the delivery of ammunition and food difficult. Sometimes it took more than two hours for the few hundred metres to be covered, and once it succeeded only at the second attempt. Every night the 'Orderly Sergeant', an armoured Soviet biplane, appeared and would switch off its engine near its target then glide over it dropping small shrapnel bombs. During the day several German aircraft flew over Küstrin and dropped supply containers by parachute.

The Russians penetrated a gap in the positions between us and the 3rd Company, and occupied an isolated farm. From there a gun brought us under such uncomfortably direct fire that the battalion's assault platoon received orders to regain the farm. The badly led attack in the dark, without the support of heavy weapons, failed.

One evening I had a stupid altercation with the 88mm battery commander. He inspected the flak position and then came to my section under cover of darkness. A steel helmet protected the head of this officer. After I had made my report, he told me off for wearing a field cap in the front line. When I told him that we only wore steel helmets under certain conditions, and that my company commander also wore a field cap, the altercation became louder until in the end I had to give way, if only for a few minutes, until he had disappeared in the direction of the manor farm.

The battalion lay under heavy fire on the Saturday and Sunday from infantry weapons, Stalin-Organs and guns. The worst were the often hour-long attacks by ground-attack aircraft, which concentrated on the infantry guns but failed to put them out of action. The battalion's losses increased, but my section was lucky so far.[16]

The Küstrin garrison's fighting capacity rapidly diminished. All movement by day outside the foxholes, bunkers and casemates was unthinkable. The Soviet artillery observers had virtually every bit of the remaining fortress within view of their binoculars, even in the Altstadt, whether over heaps of rubble or through the skeletons of burnt-out buildings, and even their infantry weapons could reach almost everywhere. Ground-attack aircraft tackled systematically every street that showed signs of life. The police station on the Marktplatz collapsed under their bombs. Those units not deployed in the front line kept within the hollow spaces of the old fortifications. Numerous stable cellars had been destroyed in the previous days, shattered or burnt out.

Officer-Cadet Corporal Fritz Kohlase recalled:

On Saturday [24 March] the 3rd Company on our left was thrown out of its positions. Their counterattack on Sunday failed because of the company commander having a nervous breakdown. The immediate enemy response thrust into the company's departure line, occupied it and closed up to the south-eastern corner of the manor farm complex.[17]

Officer Cadet Corporal Hans Kirchhof was wounded at about this time:

In March I received orders to build and occupy a new position, also on the Oder dyke, but about 100 metres from the infantry bunker. This put us about 500 metres from the Bienenhof, lying on a mound where once a pub had stood. From here I could fire towards the Sonnenburger Chaussee. Far off to the south-west, south and south-east we could sometimes see enemy vehicles, but did not fire at them. Sometimes when we had permission to open fire, we fired at targets on the west bank of the Oder.

In the course of the offensive on the Altstadt we too came under strong artillery fire. The dugout in which I was received two direct hits, causing the entrance to collapse and making a hole in one of the walls. At least the latter served me well, for I was able to crawl out through the hole. The cause of this was a Soviet anti-tank gun on the west bank of the Oder.

My right eye had been hit and was falling out. In addition one nostril had been pierced through and a large wooden splinter was stuck in my upper lip. One of my men suffered a bruised groin from the same shell-burst. There were no other casualties as at the beginning of the barrage the men had spread out so that a direct hit would only get one man. I said good-bye to my men and went back to the Altstadt alone. There were no communication trenches from our position to the rear, only individual foxholes. My route was along the foot of the dyke across the Oder levels, followed for a long time by bursts of enemy machine-gun fire, fortunately too high or too far away.

Because of my sudden reduction to one eye, my progress was uncertain and not very fast. To avoid the enemy fire, I crossed the dyke and went on along the Chaussee. Here, however, the Russian rifle positions were closer, so I crossed back to the Oder levels, where I soon reached the dead angle.

Our company command post was in a casemate near the Kietz Gate, right on the road and a bit north of the big road junction. There was also an infantry command post here, a room for the Panther turret crew and the replacement crew for my gun.

I sought out the latter first and was bandaged for the first time. The infantry company commander had me brief him on the events at the Bienenhof. I was able to stop Wolfgang Paul from going forward with his men for the moment, as it made no sense to do so, and also avoided unnecessary injuries.

As the Altstadt was under strong artillery fire, I remained in the casemate. Only at nightfall did the firing reduce to harassing fire. When comrades took me to the Schloss the streets were still burning right and left. The field hospital was in a cellar with the rooms for patients laid out with mattresses. I did not receive the attention of a doctor until the following day, because, in my opinion, the only doctor was expecting many acute cases of badly wounded soldiers. When I asked the doctor about the condition of my eye, he replied that I would have to get used to it for a long time.

How long I was in the field hospital in the Schloss cellars, I do not know. The weak lighting was the same day and night. There was plenty of coming and going, but I lost all sense of time. I lay on my mattress and dozed.[18]

Luftwaffe Gunner Josef Stefanski also came under heavy fire:

Later I was sent to a flak battery located on the west bank of the Oder near the Reichsgarten pub. There were two guns in the position, and from there we were able to shoot up two Soviet tanks coming up the Sonnenburger Chaussee. Several German dead were buried behind the Artillery Barracks at the Reichsgarten pub.

When we had run out of ammunition for our guns, or the guns had been hit by enemy fire, I was assigned as an infantryman in the Altstadt. We were accommodated in the Girls' Middle School on Schulstrasse, which received a direct hit one day that buried twenty-eight of our comrades. We could only dig out seven men alive, and the remaining twenty-one could well still be buried under the rubble.[19]

Meanwhile there were conflicting opinions over the conduct of operations between Headquarters 9th Army and Army Group 'Weichsel' on one side, and the Army General Staff (OKH) and the Armed Forces General Staff (OKW) on the other. The former

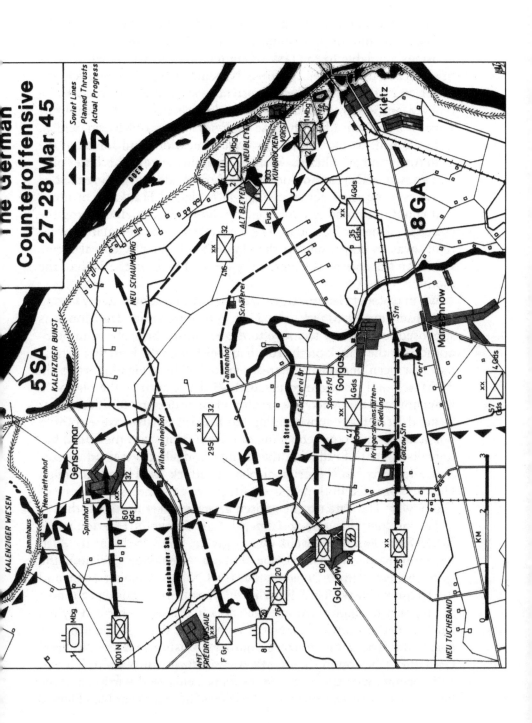

The German
Counteroffensive
27-28 Mar 45

Soviet Lines
Planned Thrusts
Actual Progress

5 SA

KALENZIGER BUNST

KALENZIGER WIESEN

Dammhaus

Henriettenhof

Genschmar

Spinnhof

ODER

NEU SCHAUMBURG

Wilhelminenhof

Gonschmarer See

100 N

Mbg

60
Gds

32

32
295

Der Strom

Tannenhof

Schäferei

NEUBLEYEN

ALT BLEYEN

Fus

303

Mbg

KUHBRÜCKEN-
VORST

Lietze Gr

Mbg

Kietz

8 GA

4 Gds

35
Gds

Sports Fd

Försterei Br

Golgast

4 Gds

47
Gds

Kriegersheims-Gärten-
Siedlung

Golzow Stn

Stn

Fort

Manschnow

57
Gds

4 Gds

AMT
FREDRICHSAUE

F Gr

8

76

20

Golzow

90

50

25

NEU TÜCHEBAND

0
KM
2
3

wanted, with a new but limited attack, to facilitate a breakout by the garrison, to hold the line established on 23 March, and to put all the divisions available to the task of eliminating the 5th Shock Army's bridgeheads in the Kienitz–Gross Neuendorf sector. However, the OKH and OKW, at Hitler's insistence, wanted the fortress to be relieved and ordered an attack to be launched from the Frankfurt Fortress's bridgehead on the east bank north-west of Küstrin, which, it was hoped, would shatter the communications and forces of the 69th Army and 8th Guards Army holding this sector. This latter plan was known as Operation Boomerang. It depended on getting the five divisions concerned across the single bridge at Frankfurt, a move that could not possibly have gone unobserved, thus eliminating the essential element of surprise. The controversy over this matter eventually was to contribute to the causes for Colonel General Heinz Guderian's dismissal as Chief of the General Staff on the 28th of the month.[20]

When Colonel General Gotthardt Heinrici took over Army Group 'Weichsel' on 22 March, the 25th Panzergrenadier Division was supposed to be about to move to the Frankfurt bridgehead in preparation for the attack on the east bank, although the Küstrin Fortress had just been encircled. Heinrici visited Führer Headquarters on 25 March and managed to persuade Hitler to change the plan to a reopening of the Küstrin corridor. The orders to SS-Lieutenant General Reinefarth commanding the Küstrin Fortress were to hold out at all costs, so the reopening of the corridor (with the added but unrealistic goal of reducing the Kienitz bridgehead) was an acceptable alternative to the original plan of attack for Hitler, although Heinrici regarded both proposed attacks as an unnecessary waste of manpower. The date for the revised attack was set for the 27th.[21]

To conduct this attack General Karl Decker's Headquarters XXXIXth Panzer Corps was given the 25th and 20th Panzergrenadier Divisions, the 'Führer' Grenadier Division, the 'Müncheberg' Panzer Division, the '1001 Nights' Combat Team and the 502nd SS Heavy Tank Battalion.[22] These formations had the task of breaking through the Soviet defences in the sector formed by the Küstrin–Berlin railway line as far as the Oder dyke on the Kalenzig meadows. The 20th Panzergrenadier Division and the 'Führer' Grenadier Division in the middle were to thrust through to Küstrin and, together with the forces on the flanks, enlarge the strip up to the line of the Küstrin–Berlin railway/ as far as the Oder near Neu Bleyen/

the Oder dyke at the Kalenziger Bunst/the Kalenziger Wiesen (meadows).[23]

Officer-Cadet Corporal Fritz Kohlase recalled:

On the night leading to Monday [26 March] we lost our left flank protection about 150 metres away. The leader of the three-man section there was wounded. A warrant officer, who was a bit simple but also very brave, sorted out the men. As the enemy situation was not clear to him as a result of the changed circumstances, he simply crept over alone and orientated himself. All went well while he traced the enemy position, but he was spotted on the way back and shot through the thigh by one of his own men. While his comrades were taking him back to the dressing station, the Russians established themselves in the abandoned trench and took us under uncomfortable fire from the flank.

The infantry guns, the heavy machine guns, the Hoffmann section, the 88mm flak gun and my section still formed a long, narrow finger into the enemy, from which we were connected to the manor farm only by a trench from the flak position. Our battalion position in the manor farm area was itself only a part of a wedge reaching from Kuhbrücken to the north-west.

Night after night the Soviet units moved in closer, spending the day in quickly dug out scoops ready to take another jump forward the following night. With our 42 machine guns and the necessary supply of ammunition we were able to slow down their rate of advance. Nevertheless we were not able to sleep any more. Only during the day, crouched in our foxholes, could we take a short nap or sink into a light half-sleep in which any change in the position would immediately awaken us.

My section received no more cold rations on the last night, only a few canteens of drinking water. The Russians had worked their way forward to less than 100 metres from us and dug foxholes all around us. The night was as disturbed as if daylight had driven off the darkness.[24]

The first serious plans for a breakout were developed in the fortress on 26 March, when even some of the SS officers close to the commandant began to feel uncomfortable with their situation. It was thought that a breakout had some chance of success while the encirclement at the junction of the two Soviet armies had still not been fully consolidated and the units there remained unfamiliar with the terrain. The increasing pressure on the small German-occupied strip along the west bank of the Oder, which was the only possible starting point for a breakout, called for haste.

At the time of the first brief closing off of the town at the beginning of February, any mention of breakout plans would have led to a court martial. Now, with the indication that the relief attack had been repelled, or at least had been unsuccessful, the situation had changed dramatically.

Reinefarth had reasons enough for delaying making a decision. The penalty for disobeying Hitler's orders was quite clear, and while there was still a chance of the fortress being relieved, he could not claim to have been under pressure. Apart from this, should the 'corridor' reopen, even briefly, he could not guarantee reaching the German lines safely, even if he used a tank. The landing strip prepared weeks before for just such an emergency was still in reasonably good order, but could only have been used in daylight by a very skilful pilot and almost every metre of it was now under Soviet observation and even within range of light infantry weapons.[25]

Officer Cadet Corporal Fritz Kohlase continued his account:

This Monday morning the Red Army units made a concentrated attack on the Alt Bleyen manor farm. Katyuschas opened fire, and were joined by guns and mortars. The opening blow was so strong that we could not see the flak position 75 metres away.

Because of the proximity of the enemy and his overwhelming superiority in numbers, we had no choice but to keep firing during the fire preparation so that he could not get up to attack. Within a short time four of our six machine guns were out of action with ripped barrels from lacquered ammunition. Our lives depended upon these machine guns. Replacements were needed. To get through the barrage only Fischer, Krell and I were available. The machine-gunners could not leave, so I had to go. I jumped out of the trench and dived into the wall of fire. Suddenly I received a blow, was lifted up and lost consciousness. When I came to, I carefully moved my arms and legs and felt my head and body. Nothing. My steel helmet lay several metres away. Now I crawled on until I reached the flak position, where a sentry pulled me into the trench. I sought out my platoon commander and the gun commander. Together we controlled the gun. It was ready to fire. The crew had so far had only a few wounded. The flak machine gun also began to fire. I took two of its four replacement barrels. Then the gun commander pushed me up out of the trench. This time I was scared and crawled back.

Then the storm began on the manor farm. First a Soviet storm troop broke into the trenches of our 1st Platoon, rolled it up and approached the company command post, threatening to split the battalion in two. The company headquarters troop was able to clear this breach in an immediate counterattack using submachine guns, hand grenades and Panzerfausts. The troops attacking the flak position were gunned down by the 88mm gun at point-blank range.

The battalion commander also sent the three self-propelled guns to our support. They drove right up to the Soviet rifle pits and turned, squashing all who lay there. Immediately the Soviet fire concentrated on our self-propelled guns. When one of them received a direct hit, the others turned back.

The firing slowly died down. The noise of combat could only be heard from the dyke road to Kuhbrücken. Here, between the parallel dyke roads to the southern hamlet of Alt Bleyen, a panzergrenadier battalion of the 'Müncheberg' Panzer Division was defending itself, together with an officer-cadet company and another dug-in 88mm flak gun, against the tank-supported enemy attack from the north. That afternoon the attackers were able to break through to the southern edge of Neu Bleyen. By evening nine destroyed enemy tanks stood in the area, the officer cadets were down to only a few men and the 88mm gun had been rendered unserviceable. The Russians had reached the dyke road between the manor farm and Kuhbrücken.

On this beautiful sunny Monday morning the Soviet artillery resumed firing at us, slowly increasing in intensity. This lasted several hours. Then the ground-assault aircraft appeared flying sometimes in threes, sometimes in sevens. They crossed over our battalion's positions always in the same order: orientation, dropping bombs, firing with machine guns or rockets. Once one group was finished, another would follow. When the aircraft tipped over to attack, one could only pull one's head in and trust

to luck. The infantry guns were attacked the most. In the afternoon even phosphorus was dropped on them.

I was afraid that the Russians would overrun us when the
ground-attack aircraft forced us to take cover. But, despite their
superiority, the Soviet infantry did not dare to do so. Apparently
they had not recovered from their bloody repulse that morning.

One had to be unbelievably cautious. My field cap was shot
through several times when raised to see what would happen.

That afternoon, as the relentless fire from Soviet artillery and
ground-attack aircraft continued and it became simply a matter
of luck whether my foxhole would suffer a direct hit, I lost my
last belief in a higher Being connected with human history. My
belief no longer existed, driven out by the fearful development
of air attacks on the civilian population and the knowledge that
the Christian priests on our side prayed to the same God as the
Allies for the success of their weapons.

The enemy attack had cost us a lot of ammunition. I had only
two Very light cartridges for the coming night. For supplies we
had half an iron ration and half a canteen of water per man.
That afternoon supply containers were dropped on Küstrin
again.

With darkness a runner from the company appeared. Because
of the losses the division into platoons was cancelled and the
number of sections reduced. Half an hour later I was shot in
the chest during a short exchange of fire. I reported to my
platoon commander, whom I found in the flak position, and
went on through the trenches of the Hoffmann section over the
dead bodies left from that morning. The Russians were dug in
here close to our positions.

It was half dark in the dressing station in the cellars of
the manor house. In the flickering of the Hindenburg Lights, the
doctor told me: 'That is not a shot in the lungs. You have been
lucky. If you can walk, then get away. Alt Bleyen is about to be
evacuated. Take the lead with the sergeant over there of all the
walking wounded.'

It was pitch dark. We went slowly past the pond to the dyke
road and then along the foot of the dyke, even more cautiously,
our weapons ready for action in our hands. For a distance of
several hundred metres the Russians were on one side of the
dyke and on the other side were our men at long intervals. About

100 to 150 metres from the dyke there was a shallow, weakly occupied trench on the other side of the 'corridor' connecting the manor farm with Küstrin. This is where I saw out the rest of the evening. We expected hand grenades to come over the dyke at any moment, but everything remained quiet.

The survivors of Fusilier Battalion 303 were able to withdraw to Kuhbrücken during the night, but only by leaving behind the heavy weapons, including the three self-propelled guns. Together with the remains of other units, they took up new positions here as Combat Team 'Quetz'.

When we reached the spider's web of tracks in Kuhbrücken that night, we met Volkssturm men in the cottages there who believed the Alt Bleyen manor farm to be surrounded. Together with others they had been ordered to fight open the way back to the farm complex and get us out. They were mightily relieved not to have to clear the complex.

We went over the Kietz railway bridge to the main dressing station that had been set up in the cellars of the Artillery Barracks on the Island. The doctors could hardly keep their eyes open from sheer exhaustion. One instructed me to take the next wounded transport back to hospital, but when I told him where I came from he fell silent.

Then we were sent on into the Altstadt. We passed a large burning building, apparently stacked full of tins of preserves judging from the constant dull explosions emerging, crossed the Oder Bridge and finally reached the auxiliary hospital in the cellars of the Boys' Middle School. I was allocated the lower bunk of a two-storey air-raid bed and immediately fell asleep.[26]

Sapper Ernst Müller told a similar tale:

In the evening darkness of 26 March I noticed in leaving the cellar of the Potato Meal Factory that cartridges were on fire in front of the building between heaps of stick grenades. The culprit was apparently a 'Sewing Machine', an enemy aircraft dropping bombs. When I reported this, Captain Fischer ordered the fire to be extinguished using sacks soaked in the Oder. Later I was ordered to fetch some firemen. On my return I had just reached the Artillery Barracks when the stack of munitions blew up. The cellar of the Potato Meal Factory was on fire. A wall of fire prevented every attempt to reach those trapped in and behind the rubble. Several of them were burnt alive. Between twenty and thirty men lay buried in the rubble, among them Captain Dahlmanns, Second-Lieutenant Schröter and Corporal Grosch. Second-Lieutenant Schröter should not actually have been in Küstrin. He had been given the job of taking us to the front, and then should have returned to Armoured Engineer Replacement Battalion 19 in Holzminden, as his wound was not yet fully cured. The already mentioned Corporal Hans Dahlmanns thus lost his father, whom I knew as a good man, who had treated me in a fatherly manner. I was also present when Captain Fischer expressed his condolences to Corporal Dahlmanns upon the death of his father.[27]

The German counterattack began at 0400 hours on 27 March and after a few hours got halfway to Gorgast and as far as the Wilhelminenhof farm and Genschmar before the German divisions were driven back to their start points with heavy losses. According to the 9th Army's situation report of 27 March, 5 commanding officers, 68 officers and 1,219 men had been lost. The reasons given included minefields, heavy mortar and anti-tank fire with accompanying artillery fire, well-constructed strongpoints in the individual barns and lack of ground cover. In fact the Germans had given the Soviets far too much time in which to consolidate their positions in a greatly enlarged bridgehead.[28]

On the northern flank, with flanking protection from the 1st Battalion of the 'Müncheberg' Panzer Regiment, the '1001 Nights' Combat Team started the attack with three infantry companies and a total strength of 390 men and 49 Hetzers; by the end of the attack it was reduced to only 40 men per infantry company, having lost 51 killed, 336 wounded and 32 missing, and having had 25 Hetzers destroyed. According to Captain Zobel, the Hetzers were late getting into their start position, having first to negotiate a railway underpass, by which time the Soviet artillery had been fully alerted. One infantry company of this elite battle group reached as far as the western edge of Genschmar, but at daybreak came under such heavy artillery, tank and anti-tank fire from the Henriettenhof farm, Genschmar village, the southern edge of the Genschmarer See and the Wilhelminenhof farm (the latter having fallen to the Soviets in the meantime) that it was forced to withdraw.[29]

Despite the XXXIXth Panzer Corps' initial lack of success, on the same day at 1730 hours the 'Führer' Grenadier Division and part of the 'Müncheberg' Panzer Division made a fresh attack on the Wilhelminenhof strongpoint and the wood 700 metres north-west of it, making some progress before having to go over to the defensive.[30]

In the fortress they waited hour by hour for a sign of salvation. The disappointment increased, as did the fire from the Soviet artillery, reaching at times as much as 1,000 shells per hour. Air attacks concentrated more and more on those structures still holding out, the old bastions. The Bastion Christian Ludwig containing the youth hostel was destroyed by three heavy bombs, the casemate used as a front-line cinema being partly destroyed, leaving buried under the rubble numerous soldiers who had sought shelter there. The already badly damaged town hall took another direct hit, the cellar collapsing and burying Volkssturm men lying there in an underground room with some of the lightly wounded. Only a few shattered men were saved by chance hours later.[31] The fate of Johannes and Otto Dawidowski was described by a survivor:

On the morning of 27 March we were told to go from our accommodation in Wallstrasse to the company command post for new orders for the next day. One group of four Volkssturm men set off. We had hardly gone 100 metres when a sudden bombardment took us by surprise. The Russians were firing with heavy calibre weapons on the area we were in. At the same time aircraft were dropping bombs. We sought shelter under a high and thick wall where the Zorn firm stored its coal.

The Dawidowski brothers and another comrade from Drewitz sought cover under the third arch of the wall, while the fourth one of our group and other comrades went under another arch and in a somewhat deeper situated building. The coal-yard wall was under particularly heavy fire, and was swaying to and fro from the hits. Suddenly there was a tremendous explosion and a flash of fire. It was a direct hit on the third arch in the wall, exactly where the Dawidowski brothers and the other comrade were standing. This part of the wall collapsed. The men standing under it were buried under the falling masonry and were certainly killed instantly.

The shooting increased. It was no longer possible to get through to the company command post. Although the way back to the platoon accommodation was only about 100 metres, I did not get back until evening. There was no chance of looking for the dead and burying them, as next day the Altstadt was to be evacuated following the Russians coming in through the Kietz Gate. So the dead still lie today under this wall.[32]

Chapter Ten

Breakout

On 28 March, almost at the same time as the first groups in the Altstadt were preparing to leave, an angry exchange between Hitler and Guderian took place at the Reichs Chancellery. The original reason for their meeting, Küstrin, was quickly forgotten. Hitler accused the generals of losing the war. Guderian equally bitterly rejected this accusation. The exchange ended with Guderian being sent on leave.

Meanwhile Küstrin lay under the heaviest fire and bombing. The withdrawal to the Oder Island took longer than expected, as some of the designated units were unable to leave their positions because of hefty fighting, air attacks and heavy artillery fire. The Volkssturm, now reduced from the original 900 men to only 135 still capable of combat, were meant to remain behind as a rearguard with other units, and to hand over their automatic weapons to any combat teams crossing over the railway bridge, the road bridge having already been impassable for some time.

Surprisingly, the Volkssturm personnel were belatedly assigned to the withdrawal that evening, presumably as replacements for units that were originally intended to leave but either had not received the orders or had been eliminated in the meantime. Reinefarth needed every available rifle in his new position if he was to hold out for at least another 24 hours, as it was too late for a breakout that day. At 1455 hours he received a Führer-Order to fight on to the last man – presumably the outcome of Hitler's argument with Guderian. Soviet assault troops were in the course of establishing themselves at either end of the Island and slowly but steadily were pushing forward. But the order cancelling the original orders for the Volkssturm to hold on came too late, the bridge being blown before the eyes of the first group heading back. Only a few managed to cross in inflatable dinghies and fishing canoes. After a last commanders' conference of those units left behind in the Altstadt held towards midnight in a bunker near the Böhmerwald restaurant, the unit commanders were given a free hand to do as they wished. The Volkssturm commander, Captain Tamm, suggested to his men that they surrender.[1]

Sergeant Horst Wewetzer was part of the grim defences of the fortress:

Soviet troops from Kietzerbusch penetrated the Altstadt on 28 March 1945. By this time the Altstadt was just one heap of rubble. During the last two weeks the Russians had been attacking two or three times a day with twin-engined dive-bombers. Hardly any of our heavy weapons were serviceable, so there was no longer any air defence, artillery or anti-tank artillery. On this last day in the Altstadt the only heavy weapons available were one 150mm heavy infantry gun with six shells, and two 75mm light infantry guns with about 30 shells left. We all knew that the end in Küstrin would come quickly, but we wanted to fight on as long as possible.

Our three guns were deployed right on the northern edge of the Altstadt. Fire directing was not possible in the Altstadt, as our observation post was in Lunette Dora, west of the Oder-Vorflut Canal, so we could only fire in front of Lunette Dora or at the edge of Kietz. If we remained on the edge of the Altstadt with our guns, there was a danger that the Russians would crush us without our being able to aim a last blast at them. I therefore sought permission to bring my gun – the heavy infantry gun – over the railway bridge to the west bank of the Oder and re-deploy it at the abattoir.

By about 1800 hours on 28 March 1945 the Soviet infantry had penetrated about as far as the Schloss in the Altstadt. With the permission of the second lieutenant in charge of the gun's firing position, I went across to Lunette Dora to get Captain Wüstenhagen's permission to redeploy. The captain told me that he was not authorised to do so, but agreed that I should take my request to the fortress artillery chief of staff. I went straight back to the firing position and told the second lieu-tenant before going on to the Schloss, where the staff were still located. On my way I passed through a casemate in which I met Captain Langenhahn coming towards me clad in a steel helmet, camouflage jacket and carrying a sub-machine gun, all brand new. With him were two or three gentlemen of his department, all similarly newly equipped, and a quite deranged prisoner.

Captain Langenhahn gave the impression of being in a very excited state as I made my report. His decision was that Second-Lieutenant Schmitz should fire off the remaining ammunition, blow up the gun and then deploy with his men in a certain Altstadt street. He then disappeared in great haste. The order made no sense: it was too dark for aimed fire and there were no explosives to destroy the gun with. I later understood why the captain had been in such a hurry. Apparently the Oder bridge was about to be blown and he wanted to get across in time.

I turned back again and begged our second lieutenant, who had no front-line experience and had been combed out of Norway, to ignore Captain Langenhahn's order and carry out the change of position on his own initiative, but he did not feel himself competent to do so. So I went back to Captain Wüstenhagen again to get him to take a personal interest in the matter and give the orders, but he refused. Even if everything fell apart, strict obedience to superior orders applied.

It was at about 2100 or 2200 hours – in any case it was fully dark – when I set off to return to my battery in the Altstadt again. I was just about level with the abattoir where we had another gun in position, although damaged and no longer operational, and approaching the railway bridge to cross the Oder, when I was ordered to take cover as the bridge was about to be blown. As my gun team was still over there, I asked if all the soldiers in the Altstadt had come across, but received no answer and was once more ordered to take cover, so I went back to the cellars in the nearby abattoir.

Once the bridge had been blown, I went to Lunette Dora again to tell the captain that he was now without any guns, but when I returned to the abattoir I met all of my gun team except for one man. Staff-Corporal Macknow had long before, and without informing anyone, acquired a large rubber dinghy from the engineer stores and hidden it on the Oder river bank. Once the line of retreat over the bridge had been cut, he led his comrades to the dinghy, inflated it and crossed the river. Only Corporal Block had refused to come. He could not swim and was afraid of drowning should something happen to the dinghy.[2]

Officer-Cadet Corporal Fritz Kohlase recalled:

I remained two days in the Middle School. Here were wounded
for whom no immediate operation was necessary. Early in the
morning and in the evening we were given a thick slice of bread
with canned meat and a large glass of cognac. Two of the field
hospital personnel stood out on account of their goodness,
peacefulness and personalities, one a woman wearing the golden
Nazi Party badge on her jacket, and the head of the hospital,
a fat lieutenant whom I only saw wearing his steel helmet in the
cellar.

There was the constant sound of explosions coming from
outside. The building shook, sometimes more, sometimes less.
Only at night was it quiet, except for a little artillery fire. I found
nobody I knew. News was hard to come by, only rumours. The
radio merely gave the Wehrmacht Reports, commenting among
other things on the increased attacks on Küstrin and the advance
of the Americans on the Lower Main River.

In a small neighbouring room there was a pile of books on the
floor. I sought out *Apis und Este* and *Das war das Ende* by
Bruno Behm, but I could not read. I now realised that I had
become nervous and that my hands were trembling a little.

On Wednesday the sounds of battle increased considerably.
The Altstadt lay under constant attack from Soviet bombers and
ground-attack aircraft and artillery fire. The constant howling,
roaring, explosions and crackling broke through the regular
discharge of our 'Stukas zu Fuss' that must have been stationed
in the immediate vicinity of the Middle School. The noise and
shuddering was so strong that we failed to notice when a heavy
bomb hit the school; fortunately it was a dud that stuck in the
ground floor.

A room in the cellars accommodated signallers, and another
two engineer platoons guarding the nearby, still intact Oder
Bridge. Those guards were happy when they returned to the
sheltering cellars without having suffered any losses.

Volkssturm men carried wounded into the Middle School.
Their platoon leader needed to use a lot of persuasion to get the
men back out into the inferno.

The latest Wehrmacht Report contained nothing good:
constant attacks on Küstrin, street-fighting in Gotenhafen and

Danzig, further advance by the Americans in the Wetzlar area.

Towards noon and through the afternoon the situation reports worsened. 'The Schloss is on fire!' then 'The Russians are in front of the Law Courts!' And that was in a wing of the Schloss. The engineers too were restless. They had to keep the Oder Bridge ready for immediate demolition and the enemy were getting closer and closer.

At last came pleasant news. The enemy had been stopped and thrown back. But hardly an hour later darkness had fallen, the noise of fighting had died down, when came: 'The Altstadt is to be evacuated!' All the walking wounded were sent back to their units.

The Fusilier Battalion was supposed to be in Kuhbrücken. I set off together with Hans Schmidt, the sergeant from 3rd Company. Half an hour later the Oder and Dammvorstadt were behind us, we had already crossed the railway bridge to Kietz when a mighty explosion sounded behind us. Our engineers had blown the last bridge over the Oder.

First we tried to find accommodation in the lunette, but unsuccessfully. The wounded were lying on the floor there practically on top of each other.

We separated in Kuhbrücken, each seeking his own company. I was directed to a cellar in which Sergeant Manninger lay with the remaining platoon of the 2nd Company and a number of wounded. I was greeted enthusiastically. There was much to relate. The worst news was the destruction of the Thomagk section. In order to keep the attackers away from the dyke road, the section leader had had to dig in with his section on the enemy-facing side of the dyke at night, and without connection to the rear. When the Russians discovered them next day they engaged every foxhole with an anti-tank gun at close range until it was eliminated. Only the section leader was left alive that evening, albeit with a broken jaw bone.[3]

SS-Grenadier Oscar Jessen was also in the thick of the fighting:

The last day in the Altstadt gradually became confused. The wounded in the Schloss cellars were given hand grenades with which to commit suicide should the Russians break through and start a bloodbath. With three other comrades I was attached to a squad and equipped with Panzerfausts and Panzerschrecks. We were deployed in a still-smouldering ruin on the right side of the Marktplatz, where we were supposed to stop a Russian attack from the Kietz Gate. All around us we could see only ruins. The Schloss was on fire.

Soviet storm troops attacked through the Kietz Gate and from the north-west and took the Marktplatz as far as the Court House that afternoon. There was a desperate German counter-attack shortly after dusk that was supported by a Hetzer.

Following the heavy bombardment during the day there came a sudden pause. Some time later we left our position and went through the communication trenches to the Schloss. The fortress commandant and his staff had disappeared. No one was there except the wounded in the field hospital. An uncomfortable feeling crept over us. All we could hear were occasional machine-gun bursts, the cries of the wounded and the crackling of flames. We followed some soldiers who had also realised that we had been left in the lurch. Later I heard that Gruppenführer Reinefarth had left the Altstadt in a Königstiger with many soldiers and had the bridge over the Oder blown once he had crossed it, even though there were still German soldiers on it, who all lost their lives.

Our group, which had meanwhile grown to 28 men, tried to get across the blown bridge to reach the steep west bank of the Oder. We got through soaking wet but only as far as the last pier, where we stayed and waited to see what would happen next.[4]

Hans Kirchhof was lying semi-comatose in the Schloss hospital when:

Suddenly it was announced that all who could walk and wished to do so, should go over to the west side of the Oder. A breakout would be attempted. With the help of some comrades I went along too, having nothing wrong with my feet.

Later I met up with men of my company, including Wolfgang Paul. He had been the gun layer in the Panther turret at the road junction in front of the Kietz Gate. When the Russians attacked, in the exchange of fire he received a sudden blow, opened the hatch and saw a metre-long tear in the gun barrel. An enemy shell must have hit it, putting it out of action.

In fact I first met Wolfgang Paul when we gathered together for the breakthrough west of the Vorflut Canal on the dyke road. We lay down together until the order: 'All non-wounded to the north!' and were finally just a few men.

Suddenly there was a mighty barrage from mortars and light infantry weapons, so we went back towards the railway bridge. More Germans joined, both wounded and unwounded, including a sergeant. Under the circumstances, we wanted to wait. By chance we found some dugouts with plank beds. I found a tin of dripping and a can of sardines in oil in my satchel. We lay down on the beds and I fell asleep. My comrades fastened a white cloth to a stick and stuck it in the earth on the roof of our dugout.

In the morning we went into captivity between Soviet soldiers with their sub-machine guns slung. At first I held my arms up, but after passing the first Russians I let them drop again.[5]

Lieutenant Alfred Bölke:

When enemy fire put an end to my observation post on the Marien Church, I left the Schloss Barracks. Captain Langenhahn wanted me to stay with him, but I went to my men, about 20 to 30 of them, who were sleeping in the casemates. On the evening of 28 March, a Wednesday, when the Altstadt was abandoned, the last Oder bridge, the railway one, was blown, so my men and I crossed the blown road bridge over the Oder and reached the Island wet, exhausted and only partly clothed. I sent my men to the abattoir and then went to the Artillery Barracks, bathed my feet and had just had my jacket replaced by my men when a colonel unknown to me appeared and wanted to know why I had not reported immediately; he accused me of shirking, and did not want to know when and how I had got there or that I was shaking from the wet, cold and exhaustion. Just as the situation threatened to become dangerous for me, my superior Captain Langenhahn fortunately appeared and immediately engaged the colonel and described me as one of his most reliable and bravest officers. Nevertheless, the colonel took me with him to the blown road bridge over the Oder and left me there to guard it. But one or two hours later Captain Langenhahn had secured my release and brought me back to my men at the abattoir. Thank God, for with the crowd at the bridge it was every man for himself. My men had already constructed a float for us to leave Küstrin by the Oder.

But the situation changed that evening when I discovered from Second-Lieutenant Haug that he had destroyed the radio in the Artillery Barracks immediately after sending the last message from the Küstrin Fortress. We were about to break out.

It had been quiet since dusk. A German voice called from a Soviet loudspeaker: 'Soldiers, come over! Nothing will happen to you! Let the SS keep on fighting! Everything will end tomorrow anyway!'[6]

Luftwaffe Gunner Josef Stefanski barely escaped over the Oder:

On the night of 28/29 March I tried with other comrades to cross over the already blown Oder Bridge. It was an almost impossible undertaking. We climbed over the rubble of the bridge in the darkness. Part of the way we had to slide over the upper works of the bridge as the lower part was under water. The Oder was in flood and had a strong current. A comrade of mine slipped and drowned. I could only hold on with the last of my strength, but on the morning of 29 March I made it, I had crossed the Oder.[7]

Sapper Ernst Müller remembered:

The following night [28 March] I spent partly in the Artillery Barracks, partly in provisionally constructed positions behind the Altstadt railway station. The cellars of the barracks were packed with wounded.[8]

By Thursday, 29 March the Soviet attack could no longer be restrained. Again swarms of aircraft dived on the Altstadt and, after their last bombs had been dropped, the artillery fired for 40 minutes, including the three 203mm batteries dug in on both dykes only 400 metres from the fortress. The attack from the south began at 0830 hours. When the Volkssturm formally surrendered, together with the main dressing station in the Boys' Middle School, fighting was still going on in the ruins of the Altstadt and the Grossen Glacis, which was like a woodland park, but the last shots were fired at about midday. Á first Soviet count gave 1,760 prisoners, including presumably the wounded in the Boys' Middle School.

Meanwhile Reinefarth's group that had crossed the Oder to the Island during the night had to withstand some strong attacks, but held on to the area around the Artillery Barracks and the Altstadt railway station until the evening of the 29th, when Reinefarth convened an officers' conference to discuss the situation. The overwhelming opinion was that, in view of the heavy losses, lack of heavy weapons and ammunition, as well as the exhausted state of the troops, they would be unable to withstand a further Soviet attack. Reinefarth referred to the last Führer-Order forbidding him to abandon Küstrin, but admitted that further resistance was impossible and, although the breakout of the remains of the garrison was forbidden, he gave the commanders permission to decide matters for themselves, thus absolving himself of responsibility for the decision.

The timing of the breakout was agreed and unit preparations were made. Only hand and close-quarter weapons were to be carried, everything else being left behind. Non-walking wounded would also have to remain behind. Individuals ripped up their pay books and discarded their medals and decorations.

Reinefarth issued his last radio message: 'The enemy has reached the Artillery Barracks – Island no longer tenable – attacking west of the Oder.' He sent SS-Captain Siedke to inform District Party Leader and Mayor Körner and his team, who had meanwhile moved into Kuhbrücken as there was no room for them in the Artillery Barracks, and himself arrived shortly afterwards. Meanwhile the decimated combat groups withdrew over the Vorflut Canal, blew the bridges and gathered along the dyke between Kietz and Kuhbrücken. The cellars of the few houses in this area offered a semblance of shelter to a lucky few against the hail of mortar bombs. Apart from the occasional skirmish, the preparations were relatively undisturbed. The troops divided themselves into several columns, each of which would try independently to reach the German lines in front of the Seelow Heights about 7 kilometres away.[9]

Sapper Ernst Müller recalled:

It looked bad for us. The enemy occupied the last part of the Altstadt on the morning of 29 March. He had already landed on the Island between the Oder and the Vorflut Canal and was attacking the Artillery Barracks from the south. Our unit now only held a small bridgehead west of the Vorflut Canal. We no longer had any heavy weapons, only hand weapons, machine guns, hand grenades and Panzerfausts. Water for drinking could only be obtained at risk of one's life from the Oder or from a pump in full view of the enemy. I had not changed my clothes for three weeks.

On the evening of the 29th I escorted Captain Fischer to a conference with an artillery officer, where the breakout from the fortress was discussed: to the west, attacking the Russian positions in three ranks with the Fortress Engineer Battalion in the centre led by Sergeant-Major Schulz.[10]

Officer Cadet Corporal Hans Dahlmanns was also caught up in the chaos:

We left the bunker and moved parallel to the railway towards the Oder. We had two rubber dinghies, one large and one small, but had to leave the big one behind. We simply could not get it out of the undergrowth. The little one was extricated without trouble and quickly inflated. The company picked it up and launched it from the middle of the railway bridge. 'I'll come back for you!' called Lieutenant Schröder from the boat, waved and vanished. Many soldiers were in front of the railway bridge and on its intact part. The noise of combat came clearly from the middle of the Altstadt. Possibly some were able to crawl over the girders to the far bank, but they went so slowly there seemed to be no chance for all those waiting to get across.

Among the men on the east bank I thought I recognised Dr Feldmann in uniform, the former head doctor at Küstrin Hospital. I had once been entertained by him with my father while I was still a civilian. It was obvious that he had given up the attempt to cross to the opposite bank.

With several comrades I went along the road bridge to where two bits of it lay in the water. Now we had to hurry, for the darkness was slowly giving way to the dawn. I crawled along the left upper girder until it sank into the water and dived across with widely spread arms over the strong current to the other upper girder, which led back out of the water. I pulled across a comrade who could not swim with a rope from the other side, and we crawled along until this upper girder also went into the water.

This time the distance across the water was even greater. I took off my uniform jacket and asked my comrade, who had come behind me, to throw my bread sack and jacket – all that I owned – after me when I got across. I would then pull him across with the rope. But my attempt to reach the upper girder on the other side failed. A really strong current grabbed me, drove me away, and I came to the bank at the end of the Oder Potato Meal Factory, only a few metres from where my father lay under the rubble.

Meanwhile the day had begun to dawn. An NCO behind me had stripped himself naked in order to swim more easily. His pale body could be seen from the opposite side and there was some infantry fire, but, God be praised, he was not hit. I then tried to get to the western end of the bridge to help the others, but the first part of the bridge went straight down into the water. It had no handrail, making impossible any attempt to approach the place in the stream where some of the comrades were.

I hung up my clothes to dry in the Artillery Barracks and was given bits of clothing by several people. All I could find for my feet were some rubber boots. Outside it was full daylight. I came out of the cellars and thought over recent events. I knew from the Führer-Order that Küstrin was to be defended to the last man and the last bullet. Some German aircraft came – the first that I had seen for a long time – and I later heard that they had dropped ammunition.

For me this hour, in its short silence as the battle took its breath, was the hour of truth. All my experiences forced me to the certainty that the great majority of Germans, and above all German youth, had been frightfully mishandled by leaders who claimed power and used it ruthlessly to constantly overtax the people, while at the same time being totally cynical about all the consequences. Whoever died was a hero, whoever survived had failed. That was the logic of our damnation.

During the course of the afternoon I looked for the rest of my company and found them in the cellar of another block in the Artillery Barracks. As I wanted to get my dry clothes, for I had nothing else other than trousers and shoes on, and went to get them, the cellar was blocked by SS sentries who would not let anyone out. 'We are breaking out!' was the word. A sergeant gave me an assault rifle: 'Take it, I don't need it any more.'

Shortly afterwards we marched as quietly as possible over the railway bridge and then turned right on the narrow strip of land between the road and the canal that delineated the front line here. There was no cover apart from a narrow trench in the bank of the chaussee and that was much too small to take the several hundred men moving north-west between the water and the road. Mortar bombs would have caused terrible losses.

Finally the groups of men closed up as the leaders stopped and then we climbed down the bank in complete silence. Of course we were expecting enemy rifle fire to break out but despite our fears, it remained quiet and the men formed into three columns, which moved through the uncertainty of the dark night in single file.[11]

Sergeant Horst Wewetzer also recalled the events of that night:

On 29 March 1945 we still held the Artillery Barracks area, the Küstrin-Altstadt railway station and surroundings, the abattoir and the north-western corner of the Island, i.e. everything between the Oder and the Oder-Vorflut Canal. Further on we held Lunette Dora, the causeway from the Oder-Vorflut Canal bridges to Kuhbrücken-Vorstadt and the suburb itself. The enemy had pushed up close to our positions and was said to have advanced from the south to within about 50 metres, breaching distance, of the Artillery Barracks.

This everyone knew would be the last day of 'Fortress' Küstrin. My impression of an organised defence was over. Each unit, as far as such organisations still existed, was defending itself wherever it happened to be. Everyone sought an acceptable compromise between their duties as a soldier and self-preservation, for unfortunately, as everyone knew, the Fatherland could not now be saved.

On this last day I moved into Lunette Dora as I was determined not to become a prisoner of the Russians and wanted to get as far west as possible. That afternoon I performed an infantry role for several hours on the Vorflut Canal causeway, as the infantry previously deployed there had abandoned their foxholes, presumably because of the continuous Soviet mortar fire. It was in fact very unpleasant, but we held on until dark, when the Russians ceased fire.

Going back to Lunette Dora, I discovered that the fortress commandant, SS-General Reinefarth, had tried to obtain permission from Führer Headquarters to break out with the remainder of the garrison, but Berlin had refused, having the intention of 'sending us into the history books', as it was rather pathetically called when sending victims into last stands. The officers had then gone to the commandant to appeal to him to break out without permission, as it was tactically and strategically the same whether the fortress was abandoned that night or the next day.

That evening the officers returned at something between 1800 and 1900 hours and told us that a breakout would be made, despite the Führer-Order, but participation would be voluntary. This decision released me from my conflict of conscience whether to desert or not. Those wishing to take part got themselves ready. Anything that made a noise was discarded, faces were blackened, radios rendered unserviceable and thrown into the moat surrounding the Lunette. Not all the soldiers in the Lunette were taking part. While I oiled my assault rifle, others lay around sleeping.

We were told that the breakout would be made in four groups. Those from the Lunette and its vicinity would be in the southernmost. As Kietz had long since been in Soviet hands, no one would be breaking out between Kietz and ourselves. We assembled on the causeway and then moved about 200–300 metres north-west along it to reach our start point.[12]

At about 2300 hours the assembled troops thrust forward into the Oderbruch along a broad front of about 2 kilometres. A dark night with low-hanging clouds and rain showers favoured the enterprise. The progress of the main group containing Reinefarth and guided by Senior Corporal Friedrich Kruse, a local inhabitant, is described by District Leader Hermann Körner in some detail in Annex C.

The first Soviet line, where no German action from that direction was apparently expected, was relatively quickly overrun. But then came close-quarter fighting with rifle butts, knives and spades, and a furious exchange of shots that immediately alerted the whole sector, and the action dissolved into numerous individual fights. The next trenches could only be taken with high losses. One 30-man team pushed through almost a kilometre to the north to reach the Tannenhof sheep farm.

Fearing a Soviet night attack, and apparently unaware of the last radio message from Küstrin, the German artillery also started firing on the breakout area, and several groups ran straight into its salvoes. At dawn the survivors, soaked through from having crossed numerous ponds and irrigation ditches, and close to nervous and physical collapse, reached the 9th Army's positions at several places in the Oderbruch. Army Group Headquarters reported 32 officers and 965 NCOs and men of the Küstrin garrison having got through. However, they bore the stigma of not having fought to the last man, and an investigation of the commandant was ordered.[13]

Lieutenant Victor Hadamczik was the adjutant at the headquarters of the 20th Panzergrenadier Division, commanded by Colonel Scholze:

Shortly before the attack on Berlin began, elements of the Küstrin garrison broke out at night. Colonel Scholze (the divisional commander) ordered me to take two vehicles and two or three men to look for the Küstrin garrison men fleeing through our lines and take them to certain collecting points. He came up close and said: 'Should the commandant of the fortress, an SS officer, be among them, bring him to the divisional command post.'

During the course of the morning a vehicle carrying an SS-General approached and I informed him of my task. He told me: 'You surely have enough to do,' and had me show him on the map where the command post was. When I reported back to the command post late that afternoon, I was asked about the SS-General. He had not reported there and Scholze threatened me with court-martial for not fulfilling his orders.[14]

Lieutenant Erich Bölke was also part of the breakout:

As we paraded on the dyke of the Vorflut Canal near the railway bridge for the breakout on the night of 29/30 March, the word was passed: 'Second-Lieutenant Bölke and his men to lead!' We crossed the dyke road quite a distance further north. Some considerable time later we stumbled on some quiet Soviet tanks. Until then there had been no enemy activity. The quiet ended when a German soldier shot an enemy tanks in flames with a Panzerfaust. The Russians raised the alarm, manned their tanks and drove apart. Shortly afterwards there was the sound of a mighty explosion behind us coming from the direction of Küstrin, and I saw the flames of an explosion. From then on the devil was loose behind us.

We came across Russians in a trench. One of them threw a hand grenade. I was lucky and was only wounded by a splinter but lost my men through it. In front of the German lines I stumbled over a tripwire. The German artillery was firing a barrage at us! When I looked at my watch, it was 0345 hours.[15]

Officer Cadet Corporal Hans Dahlmanns also broke out of Küstrin that night:

It was a wonder that no shots were fired. Nevertheless, heavy infantry and mortar fire broke out behind us towards Küstrin. I was happy to be away from there, where it must be bad.

There was no sign of any Soviets when my column passed a few metres from an anti-tank gun. I do not know how long we marched silently through the night, but it must have been for some time. Finally an even darker line appeared through the dark night, a road running along a slightly raised embankment. A horse-drawn cart was moving from left to right. We could hear it but not see it. Suddenly the driver began to shout; the horse started galloping and we began running.

At the same time firing broke out from left, right and in front of us and we ran as quickly as we could across the weak ground, up to and across the road, and as we ran we sang: 'Deutschland, Deutschland, über alles, über alles . . .'.

It was so exhausting that I had no strength left to sing. We could not do anything but run through the night over the heavy ground through the continuing fire. But the firing was not always intended for us. One could get out of it with a bit of luck. My main thought was to keep going forward. They were not firing at individuals, and I found myself quite alone at one stage. I knelt down until I saw or heard the first man behind me. Then I looked for the lead again and jumped over a trench, seeing in the middle of my leap three or four Russians on my right who were beginning to shoot.

Then it was quiet for a short while, after which machine-gun fire opened up and mortar bombs started exploding. I was so exhausted that I could only run on when a machine gun turned on me. Someone fell close by who had been in the lead with me.

Again it became quieter. I jumped into a stream. The water ran into my rubber boots and cooled my feet and then became uncomfortable. I had to go round a large pond, passing some dead lying in the mud. I recognised the uniforms as Waffen-SS. I went round a shot-up tank with a German cross on it and was shocked when I saw and heard another tank a little later as it slowly moved across my line of march. I got out of the way, as I could not make out whether it was Soviet or German.

Then another dark strip appeared out of the darkness of the night. I thought: 'If it is another trench, then I will stop and lie down. I can't go on any more!' It was a railway embankment, hardly higher than a metre. I let myself fall on the slope. A steel helmet appeared a few metres away. 'German?' I asked and received in reply: 'Man, I nearly shot you!' Ever after I was grateful that I had come across a man who had inhibitions about killing. I crawled across and embraced him. He was, I believe, no older than myself and appeared very insecure. He told me that the company command post was in a farm behind him. I reached it a few minutes later. Some German soldiers came up to me and said: 'We have just stopped firing our mortars.'

Trucks arrived at first light, loaded us aboard and drove a while and then we climbed up to a railway line that took us, despite the proximity of the front line, to Fürstenwalde.[16]

Sergeant Horst Wewetzer again:

The breakout took place at about midnight. It was a purely infantry attack without any preparation or support from heavy weapons. In the darkness of the night there were no orders, no leadership and no general engagement. The whole crowd marched, at first closed-up, simply westwards. After about 300 metres we came to the Nork Ditch (a name I learnt later), which was full of water and too wide to jump across, so we had to wade through and became wet up to our stomachs.

The enemy was alerted as we climbed out of the ditch and the first shots fell about 20 metres from us. We immediately took cover and wanted to wait, but then I said to a captain next to me: 'If we take cover at the first shot, we will never get out of here!' That acted like a signal – or so at least I thought – for they all climbed out of the ditch firing blindly into the night and shouting 'Hurrah!', storming the first Soviet position.

For a short while I thought that was the main task complete, but it then appeared that this was only the outermost Soviet line that we had broken through. Because of the lack of manpower on our side, we had become accustomed to only having a thinly manned front line and I suspected that it was not very much different with the Soviets, but I was grossly mistaken and we had only overrun one of their forward positions.

After perhaps another 200 metres we came up to the real Soviet front line. They had naturally been alerted and fired flares, in the light of which I could make out our seemingly compact group of some two to three hundred soldiers at most. The Soviets now opened fire on us and we spread out as far as possible, only a few of us dropping to the ground. It was a repeat of the first line, fire and 'hurrah!'. I had already been wounded in the lower thigh during the attack on the first line, but it was only a flesh wound right through the leg, and I was still able to carry on.

During the course of the night we stormed one Soviet trench after another. No sooner had we crossed one than we came under fire from the next. As I remember it, we crossed six Soviet trenches, three facing Küstrin and three the west.

As the first weak morning light appeared, presumably at about 0500 hours, I saw the outline of several tanks, but could not make out whether they were German or Soviet, not that it made any difference, we had to keep going. The tanks did not fire at us, and today I think that they must have been German tanks that had been shot up or abandoned on 27 March during the attempt to relieve Küstrin.

In any case we also stormed the first German line, and when we reached the second German line we found a few apparently bewildered soldiers, who showed us the way to the first aid post. This was accommodated in a barn on the edge of a village and so far from the front line and so conveniently located that the ambulances could drive right up to it without being shot at. I was driven to Schlagenthin, seen to by a doctor, and then sent off from nearby Müncheberg station to a field hospital in

Naumberg on the Sale. My Staff-Corporal Macknow, who had also been wounded in the break-out, was in the bed next to me.[17]

Sapper Ernst Müller continued his account:

As far as I know, only the middle rank got through. I was one of those that Captain Fischer had told that when we reached the first Russian positions we should quickly cross the first line and run to the west so as not to be cut off by the enemy. Accordingly, I hurried forward, although hampered by rheumatism. I threw my Panzerfaust away after a while as I could not carry it any further. Loud sounds of heavy fighting had broken out behind us. It was a dark night. The only chance of finding one's way was when a flare went up, then I ran towards where I saw comrades.

After a long time I met a technician who gave me a compass that I still have 50 years later. The technician later trod on a mine and was killed. At that time we were only 20 metres apart as we were disputing which direction to take. From then on I kept to tank tracks, where presumably there were no mines. Finally I was alone.

At dawn I reached a railway embankment with a watery ditch in front of it. There were several dead near a shot-up tank. Here I met a Luftwaffe second lieutenant who had a slight wound in the heel. We discussed whether there could be German or Russian positions behind the embankment. We first quenched our thirst in the ditch, then the second lieutenant went ahead over the low embankment and called me after him. We had made it and reached the German lines.

I was at the end of my strength and could hardly move. I could not climb up on a truck without help. Many hundreds who had broken out of Küstrin were assembled in the Mars-la-Tour Barracks in Fürstenwalde. Among them were Captain Fischer and Corporal Dahlmanns. I was put in the sick bay suffering from severe rheumatism.[18]

Not all were so fortunate. Luftwaffe Gunner Josef Stefanski:

On 29 March I was once more deployed as an infantryman on the Island near the Reichsgarten pub, opposite the Kattewall.

On the same day came the order to withdraw from Küstrin. I was in the last group that left the positions around the Artillery Barracks late evening in darkness and crossed the Vorflut Canal by the railway bridge. Shortly afterwards the bridge was blown. We had not come very far when we came under heavy fire from all sides and had to flee to the lunette off the dyke leading to Kuhbrücken. As I had had no sleep over the past days, I was totally exhausted. I did not care. I only wanted to sleep. So I stayed the night in this lunette with about 30 comrades. There was also the crew of a Tiger tank that had run out of fuel.

Next morning the Russians appeared and took us prisoner.[19]

Officer Cadet Corporal Fritz Kohlase's attempt to break out was less successful:

On the morning of Maundy Thursday the Soviet firing resumed and lasted until late afternoon. Then followed the Russian attack that we had been waiting for for hours. The dyke road near the spider's web of tracks was crossed with jubilant cries of 'Urrah!' making a breach in the last German lines. But the resistance stiffened, growing more and more like the tension of a spring under frightful pressure. Beyond the dyke road there were only 300 metres to the Vorflut Canal and the Oder. It developed into close-quarter fighting, in which the members of the Küstrin Volkssturm and their District Leader joined in on the German side.

At this point the German ammunition was finished. One went into the cellars and pleaded for every cartridge and hand grenade from the wounded. The forward artillery observer in Kuhbrücken had our heavy 'fortress artillery' in the Seelow area firing on the grid, firing within 100 metres. The heavy shells bellowed down on us, but were all duds! A runner panted up from the battalion commander: 'Hold on until dark; then we will be saved!'

The jubilant 'Urrahs' of the Russians had lessened, mixed more and more with rifle and pistol shots and bursts from submachine guns, the explosions of hand grenades and Panzerfausts with the cries of the wounded and shouted commands, and above all with the shouts of 'Hurrah' from the defence that grew ever louder and finally replaced the others.

Yet again the determined German defence was stronger and threw the attackers back, partly even to the other side of the dyke. And then the sounds of fighting broke off as suddenly as they had begun.

Manninger came down the steps with his section and slumped completely exhausted into a corner. The wounded had their wounds dressed as well as was possible. Not much was said for it was clear to everyone that the next attack could not be repelled for lack of ammunition.

Somewhat later a second lieutenant appeared with a doctor. They took Manninger's section with them and every man that could hold a weapon. Then an SS officer came into the cellar with the same objective. I was one of those that remained in the cellar, together with Heinz Buder, another officer cadet from Wandern who had been wounded that day. Together we waited for nightfall.

Among those wounded that afternoon was my company commander, Lieutenant von Burgsdorf, who had been hit by three bullets. My machine-gunner had been killed. Fischer, the Alsatian, who had always said that he would not fall in this war and that he would not die, had been shot in the head.

Both sides were so exhausted from the close-quarter fighting that they now waited for darkness and did nothing although they were only the width of the dyke apart. At night came suddenly: 'All out for the breakout!' It was pitch black. We quickly destroyed all our papers, including our pay-books and removed our officer cadet flashes while others removed their rank insignia and decorations. Everything superfluous was left behind.

Before the still-mobile remains of the fortress garrison had finished assembling behind the Vorflut dyke our engineers blew the Kietz railway bridge and with the explosion we lost the element of surprise. The enemy immediately noticed that the Germans were forming up for a breakout on the dyke road and began a constant barrage, mainly with mortars. At the pond both Heinz Buder and myself were wounded again. Shell splinters hit his shoulder and the back of my left knee. There was no time to bandage them, so we tried forcibly to move shoulder and foot and they worked.

Our first attack had resulted in the Russians becoming aware of the breakout attempt and was beaten back. While the beaten spearheads wanted to go back, those coming from the Kietz bridge and from Kuhbrücken pushed forward. The narrow bank of the Vorflut Canal was limited by a minefield. Only a trench running along the dyke offered any cover for those in it. All the others remained exposed to the murderous fire. When the mortars fired, up to five men lay on top of each other in the trench. The individual units had tried to keep together when they assembled, but now everything was lost. The confusion increased when some of our own mines exploded. The call: 'Officers forward!' was answered by only a few.

When Heinz Buder and I reached the breakout assembly point, the second breakout attempt had already failed and increased the panicky confusion on our side. We realised that it was highly dangerous to remain in this leaderless mass. We therefore decided to hide ourselves in the ruins of the Dammvorstadt and to try to reach our main front line 24 hours later, by which time the inner enclosing ring would no longer exist.

We worked our way across the Kietz railway bridge. Several men had already sought shelter behind the bridge pillars. When even more bombs hit the dyke, a rough voice said in the darkness: 'So perishes the Third Reich with fire and the sword.' At this moment I too realised that everything was lost.

Once we had completed the necessary bandaging of each other, Heinz Buder and I climbed over the blown bridge to the Dammvorstadt. At the station we encountered the lightly wounded Klaus Kothe, who convinced us that hiding on the peninsula would be more promising than in the buildings. We crossed the mine belt with thumping hearts across the entrance to the peninsula. But it offered no cover. One could hide in the light undergrowth on the riverbank, but there was only enough room for two persons and we were one too many. Heinz Buder decided to return to the Dammvorstadt. We shook hands in parting for the last time.

Heinz Buder had reminded me beforehand that this was Good Friday, 30 March, and that we had now been soldiers for exactly one year.

Meanwhile further German attempts to break out had succeeded. The last one went well and we could hear the fighting some distance away.

Our hiding place was wretched. It was on a sandbank overgrown with bushes on the bank of the peninsula and consisted of a hollow of a man's length and about 30 centimetres deep. We could get in with our arms either stretched alongside our bodies or tucked under our chests. We dared not move, as the bushes were so meagre that they only offered scanty protection from enemy sight. Apart from this, the hollow was half full of water and we would have to lie in it.

We took our places when it became light. All was quiet for a long time. Only a rising lark sang. Then came the first loud guttural shouts, occasionally broken by a shot or burst of fire. The Red Army was taking over the last German positions in Küstrin, including the important railway and road bridges over the Oder, even if they had been destroyed. All the while the trilling of the larks could be heard.

Russian could be heard everywhere: from the Dammvorstadt, from the other bank of the Vorflut Canal and from Kuhbrücken.

Uninterrupted sounds of work could be heard coming from the Kietz railway bridge. The crossing was being restored and at about noon the first truck slowly crossed the bridge that had been blown the night before.

It was torture lying in that hollow. Only a few times during the day did we dare change the positions of our arms or move our heads from one side to the other. We dared not do more from fear of discovery. If we stayed still, then even if we were seen we would have been taken for dead.

Although we lay in water the whole day, we did not freeze. Our fear of falling into Russian hands, our determination to break through to the German lines and our conviction that within 24 hours at the most we would be lying in a German field hospital and able to rest gave us the strength to remain alert and not freeze. We even hardly felt hungry.

Red Army soldiers fired often at the trees on the peninsula. If we lay directly in the line of fire, the shots went closely over us or crossed over us as ricochets from the water, making us break out into a cold sweat, as everything hung on chance whether we were fired on as targets or were hit unintentionally. We had not counted on this when we selected our hiding place.

We went through an even bigger period of anxiety that afternoon. Shots and explosions went off around our sandbank, sometimes closer and sometimes further away. At first we thought that we had been discovered and were being fired at with light mortars. After some time we recognised the cause: the Russians were firing captured Panzerfausts at the trees behind us. Unfortunately we were lying directly in the line of fire and not far from the trees. Because of the mine belt the Russians did not dare come on to the peninsula. In the late afternoon, however, two of them landed from a rowing boat. They first wandered around on foot, then went around the peninsula and came close to our sandbank. We were lucky. They both rowed past within 5 metres of our hiding place and either did not see us or took us for dead.

At last the darkness came and we could sit up and move around, take some sodden biscuits from our pockets and eat them. But still we could not move off. As it became dark the Red Army soldiers set fire to a house on the railway embankment, illuminating the Vorflut Canal so that we dare not cross it. It took hours before the fire died out and the soldiers went to rest.

My wound was hurting throughout the long lying down and my left knee and right arm would not move properly. Consequently I had great difficulty swimming the canal. The strong current carried me several hundred metres and tore off my boots. Completely soaked through, barefoot and limited in my movement, but still armed with two pistols, two spare magazines and a hand grenade, we set off towards the main front line. We had neither map nor compass and orientated ourselves simply by the noise and lights from the distant front line. Oddly, this night appeared nevertheless quite quiet.

Again and again we had to cross water ditches and twice swam the Alte Oder. We gradually began to feel the effects of exhaustion. As the first signs of dawn were appearing on the horizon we reached the Soviet front line. Unnoticed, we stumbled into a mortar position in a bushy area where Russian soldiers were lying around in unexpected numbers. Further forward the land was flat and uncultivated. Even further on was a little wood from which shots and bursts of fire came from time to time. That was the German front line.

In view of the time and my condition, we decided to leave the breakthrough until the following night and looked for a new hiding place. We wanted to go back to the meadow thicket that we had passed on the way. Suddenly I was overcome with such exhaustion that nothing mattered any more. Instead of going around two cottages that stood about 100 metres apart, we simply walked through between the Soviet sentries. In the firing that followed I became separated from my comrade.

Once more I managed to escape. On the other side of the Alte Oder I reached some shot-up German positions with lots of dead lying around that had not yet started to decay. On one of them I found an open tin of meat that satisfied my great hunger. Then I found a Soviet leaflet calling upon us to surrender, which contained a pass written in several languages, crept into a foxhole, camouflaged myself a little and immediately fell asleep.

When I awoke I found myself looking at the muzzles of Russian rifles. Several men in earth-brown uniforms were standing in front of my hiding place and signalling for me to come out. Once I was out, the rifles were still aimed at me and someone said, 'Stoj, Gemane!' I slowly raised my hands over my head. It was Easter Saturday and the sun stood high in the sky. I did not look like a hero. I was barefoot and wore only my underwear, uniform trousers and shirt, all torn. I was wearing blurred Wehrmacht spectacles, and my hair was completely dishevelled. I was also very dirty.[20]

SS-Grenadier Oscar Jessen was also taken prisoner:

The Russians appeared next morning, climbed on the blown bridge and examined its condition. They did not see us at first as we were below their line of sight, and they did not suspect our presence. I had previously removed my SS uniform jacket and thrown it into the water. Those comrades who did not do so were later to pay for it with their lives. Once we were discovered, we had to clamber back to the east bank of the Oder, where some female Soviet soldiers immediately searched us. About eleven men were either beaten to death or shot. I only had my teeth knocked out.

We survivors were next kept in a ruin near the church. Next day we had to throw all the dead into an anti-tank ditch on the right of the Schloss together with all their military equipment. This also included the dead from the field hospital in the Schloss, who had all committed suicide. The doctor had shot himself and the nurse had taken poison. Both were sitting at a table, where they had opened a photograph album. I will never forget the sight.

We then marched via Zielenzig and Landsberg on the long journey to Posen. The villages we passed through gave the impression of awful wretchedness. There were many dead along the road that had been crushed by tanks. At night came the cries of women being raped and calling for help. From Posen we went by train to Siberia for fully five years.[21]

Chapter Eleven

Consequences

The fall of Küstrin was acknowledged in the Wehrmacht Report a day later. The breakout battle had cost the lives of 637 soldiers, with a further 2,459 wounded and 6,994 reported missing. One of those killed near the Tannenhof in the breakout was Major Otto Wegner, the 55-year-old Altstadt Defence Sector commander. His remains were removed to the military cemetery at Gorgast on 3 December 1953, having been identified by his identity disc.[1]

After the Volkssturm surrender in the Altstadt, the few troops still holding out in the ruins and glacis outside that had not been party to the surrender were captured and shot. The 200 or so wounded in the Main Dressing Station were supposed to have been honourably treated by the Soviets in accordance with the terms of surrender negotiated by the Volkssturm commander, Captain Gustav Tamm, but it appears that some of those who could not walk were also shot.[2]

However, a few Volkssturm men already on the Kietz side of the Oder got through to the German lines in the breakout. They were given ten days' leave to help them recover from their wounds and had orders to report to Nedlitz in Potsdam on 21 April. They were then deployed in defence of Wannsee Island between the Jungfernsee and Weissensee, from where they took part in another breakout that got them as far as Stahnsdorf cemetery before they were captured.[3]

The 32 officers and 965 NCOs of the Wehrmacht who had survived the breakout from Küstrin were sent on by the narrow-gauge railway connecting the Oderbruch via Seelow with Fürstenwalde and accommodated in the Mars-la-Tour Barracks there on Good Friday, 30 March.[4]

Officer Cadet Corporal Hans Dahlmanns was one of the lucky ones:

As I recall, for three days we had special rations, even chocolate in round tins intended for airmen or U-boat crews. I was given new trousers, a summer field jacket, two handkerchiefs, and a set of underwear, a mess tin, a spoon and a knife, a gas mask in a canister and a canvas washing kit, but no boots, no overcoat, no cap, no steel helmet, no fork and no toothbrush. I was given a new pay book on 5 April, my 18th birthday, but without a photograph, which had to be dispensed with at this time. I was then given a few days to recover before I was sent to a company at Wriezen in which no one knew each other.[5]

Lieutenant Erich Bölke also survived the breakout, but his treatment at the hands of the Germans was hardly what he had expected:

With others that had broken through, I was taken to the Mars-la-Tour Barracks in Fürstenwalde. Next morning, Easter Saturday, we were issued with new clothing, and in the process I met Captain Langenhahn again and followed him into a room where I saw Captain Wüstenhagen. The Küstrin officers had had to give up their weapons and had been placed under guard. They were in a building with double sentries at the entrance. SS-Gruppenführer Reinefarth's quarters were somewhere else. When going for a walk he was always escorted by two other SS officers. I often talked with Captain Langenhahn and he said among other things that he would ask the Führer for his officers to be released.

That Easter Saturday, 31 March, we celebrated our reunion with beer and schnapps, as originally it had been said that I had been killed. Other officers took part, including Major Fenske and a captain decorated with the Knight's Cross. During our celebrations an ADC appeared and informed us that all officers from the former Küstrin fortress were to appear in the officers' mess next morning at 0900 hours.

If I remember correctly, there were 30 or so officers in the Officers' Mess on Easter Sunday. There the Führer-Order to continue the fight for the Küstrin fortress was read out to us. Then began the individual interrogations.

I was questioned two or three times. We were asked why we had not complied with the Führer-Order and had taken part in the breakout. When I said that in Küstrin basically we could only bring a few weapons against the Russians and in the end had hardly any ammunition left, the interrogating officer said:

'It would have been better if you had had an assault knife on your back to slit the throat of a Russian and now lay dead in Küstrin rather than sit here before me.' I then said that I had received an order to break out. I was not accused by him of other things at the further interrogations, but he upset me by saying that the Führer was disappointed with his officer corps. It went similarly with Captain Langenhahn.

After that we continued to remain under arrest while awaiting the decision of the Führer. Then it was at last said that we all had to serve afresh and should volunteer for front-line duty. Captain Langenhahn volunteered immediately and told me: 'Bölke, you are coming with me!' I obeyed his order. Captain Langenhahn had several times telephoned people he knew at a central location during the Fürstenwalde process and kept himself informed of what was going on. His idea was to be posted to the Werwolf in Thuringia, as he came from Friedrichroda, where his father was a priest. But that was not allowed and front-line engagement against the Russians was demanded. Captain Wüstenhagen and Major Fenske remained behind. The latter said to me that I should remain in Fürstenwalde and let Captain Langenhahn go ahead on his own, but I could not do that. Meanwhile several days had passed since our breakout from Küstrin.

We reported back to duty with the artillery in the Mars-la-Tour Barracks. We went to our allocated sector of the front between the Märkischer Schweiz and Wreizen via the Anhalter railway station in Berlin. The officer positions in the new unit were already taken, making us surplus to establishment.

When the Russians started their main offensive on 16 April, my last unit neared its end, in which I survived the following experience. I was supervising the change of position of the artillery train. Captain Langenhahn sent a sergeant as a dispatch rider back from the front that I could meantime send on a short journey. Then he was to report back to me and return immediately to Captain Langenhahn. I waited and waited for him. The sergeant turned up hours later. The Feldgendarmerie had arrested him and some others. Those not carrying weapons were shot in the presence of those carrying them. The latter were then sent into action and their previous orders declared invalid. The sergeant had used a suitable opportunity to escape with the motorcycle. Neither of us understood what was going on any more.

On 19 April 1945 I was captured in Reichenow, near Strausberg. We were surrounded and wanted to break out. Captain Langenhahn fell from a shot in the head during this action. His adjutant and I then occupied the servants' quarters of a manor. Later the adjutant shot himself.

I met Major Hassler in Soviet captivity in the Posen and Dorpat camps. He had been the flak commander in Küstrin. He had not taken part in the breakout but had been captured. He told me that when he was captured, the Russians had already known his name and rank and even his last appointment.[6]

Ad hoc units formed from demoralised survivors of the Küstrin garrison were later deployed in the defence of Seelow main railway station at the foot of the Seelow Heights and were involved in the Soviet assault of 16 April 1945, when they were overrun on the first evening.[7]

SS-Gruppenführer Reinefarth clearly had a lot of explaining to do. His somewhat shaky account of his actions is to be found in Annex B. Luckily for him, it does not appear to have come under Hitler's close scrutiny, presumably because the latter was engaged with more urgent matters by that time. The result was that Reinefarth got away with his failure to obey Hitler's orders. As Norman Davies wrote:

In the final reckoning, relatively few of the Nazi murder-mongers who had operated in Warsaw met with the retribution that they had earned. SS-Gruppenführer Reinefarth, for example, escaped scot-free. After leaving Warsaw, he was appointed commander of the fortress of Küstrin. But in the chaos of the German collapse in March 1945 he was arrested for leaving his post. This incident no doubt helped his later claim to have been an anti-Nazi Resistance fighter. All attempts to have him extradited to Poland were vetoed by the Americans to whom he had surrendered and for whom he acted as an adviser on Soviet military methods. So he was free to pursue a political career in West Germany. He never stood trial, and publicly denied that he had ever been a member of the SS.[8]

Yet in Warsaw: 'They concentrated on massacring every man, woman and child in sight. No one was spared – not even nuns, nurses, hospital patients, doctors, invalids, or babies. Estimates of the non-combatant victims in the suburbs of Ohota and Vola vary from 20,000 to 50,000.'[9] Worse still: 'Reinefarth complained about the shortage of ammunition. "We just can't kill them all," he grumbled. On 5 August alone an estimated 35,000 men, women and children were shot by the SS in cold blood.'[10]

Reinefarth was released from captivity in June 1948 and later became mayor of the bathing resort of Westerland on the island of Sylt, where he died on 7 May 1979.[11]

Hermann Körner was later cleared by a denazification court and was for a long time mayor of Reinbek, near Hamburg.[12]

In all it is estimated that the defence and attempted relief of the Küstrin fortress had cost the Germans about 5,000 killed, a further 9,000 wounded evacuated to their own lines, and another 6,000, mainly wounded, taken prisoner, while the Soviets lost about 5,000 killed and 15,000 wounded.[13] The Soviets now had a bridgehead about 50 kilometres wide and 7–10 kilometres deep, the vital nodal point at Küstrin had been secured, and preparations for the next phase of operations could proceed from a far stronger base. Soviet engineers could now get on with their extensive preparations for the forthcoming Berlin operation, including the rebuilding of the heavy capacity bridges at Küstrin. However, some of these bridges were so badly damaged that a new road route had to be introduced. An aerial photograph dated 7 April 1945 shows the old bridges under repair with a new bridge across the Warthe between the damaged road and rail swing bridges, and another new bridge extending at right-angles from the Schloss across to the Island next to the Artillery Barracks.

The Luftwaffe's Kamikaze pilots made thirty sorties against the Soviet bridges across the Oder with their Mistels and claimed to have destroyed 17 of them on 17 April, including one of the Küstrin railway bridges, for a loss of 22 pilots.[14] In fact they destroyed both the Küstrin railway bridges, as Lieutenant-General N.A. Antipenko, chief of Zhukov's Rear Services, later wrote:

> On the night of 17/18 April, just as the work on the railway bridges over the Oder and Warthe was finished, the enemy made a strong air attack and destroyed both bridges. Troops of the 29th Railway Brigade and Moskaliov's bridge-building unit

restored both bridges under continuous bombardment within a week, so that they were ready by 25 April. So the first train carrying heavy artillery was able to make its way to Berlin-Lichtenberg simultaneously with the entry of our troops into Berlin at 1800 hours on 25 April.[15]

Thus the Soviets were able to bring up the necessary supplies, ammunition and artillery, including captured German siege artillery from the Crimea firing shells weighing half a ton each, to deploy in the marshalling yards of the Schlesischer station (today's Ostbahnhof) and pound the city centre.[16]

A young Küstrin boy passed through the town on 21 June 1945:

I arrived at the goods station in an adventurous manner in the brake cab of a goods wagon. It was said that those caught at the Oder were put into a camp, but those that got across remained unmolested, and so it seemed to be the case. A wide wooden bridge had been erected next to the destroyed Warthe Bridge. It led from the crane on the Warthe quay across to the winter harbour quay. The railway crossing at the GAGFA buildings was guarded by a Soviet Army female soldier, who had made herself comfortable under a sunshade. There were still two allotment huts standing left of the railway. The nave of the Catholic church was only slightly damaged, but the tower had been destroyed. The block of flats opposite the church had been reduced to blackened walls. The Wendrichs' family home on the corner of Wallstrasse was almost undamaged. Voices coming from there led me to believe that someone was living there, but they might have been looters. I got away from there. All the buildings in Wallstrasse were shot-up or burnt out, the ruins partly collapsed. The law courts on the corner of Friedrichstrasse appeared, but were fully destroyed beyond the first floor, the surrounding walls of rough field stones shot through with several metres missing. The adjacent officers' block, as we called it, is now only a flattened heap of rubble, revealing only the iron central heating boiler. Scraps of paper waved at me, a page from a children's songbook. Only the yellow compound walls of the Senior School survived the chaos; the janitor's house and the gymnasium were destroyed, as well as the nearby petrol station with Pritzel's Garage. Three vast bombs had completely smashed the youth hostel area. The one-time public air raid shelter, later the Front Cinema, had taken a direct hit on its entrance. In an earthen bunker on the Wallkrone I found boxes with thousands of rounds of rifle ammunition – away from here! On the grass in front of the old prison, the area of the 'Hohen Kavalier', stood cars and even guns that had become unserviceable and been towed here during the fighting. Next to them was a double-decker Berlin bus that had brought the flak gun crews here in January and had been used as an anti-tank barrier on Kurzen Dammstrasse. There was no petrol for the return journey. Schulstrasse was a picture of horror. The burnt-out ruins had been ploughed through by bombs and shells, and there were the skeletons of vehicles that had been brought to this narrow street thinking that they would be safer here. The masses of debris from the buildings in Kurzen Dammstrasse had piled up into a hill. Bulldozers or other equipment had flattened it out a little so that the 'street' was usable again. The war memorial still stood in the middle of the Marktplatz, only lacking the eagle on top. Only a few metal scraps remained of the telephone box on the tram stop island. The words 'Town Department of Works' were still visible on the barely 2-metre-high wall of the Ration Office in the Danziger House. Of the town hall there was still a quite high section of the Kommandantenstrasse façade, otherwise only rubble. The skeletons of burnt-out German armoured personnel carriers stood in the street, distinguishable from the piles of rubble. The buildings here fell relatively early, well before the middle of March's bombs and shells. The ruined landscape was depressing. Bits of walls threatening to collapse warned me not to go any further. I returned to the Neustadt, where I met a woman who was afraid to go back alone to her former home in the Altstadt, so I escorted her. The building lay next to Pritzel's Garage, naturally only rubble, but the woman identified a few plates lying around as her property. Who knows who took this crockery out of the apartment before it collapsed. On the way back I stumbled upon a tin of jam and picked it up. My companion also found two cans – both without labels, a little eerie, but later the contents proved to be an expensive pea soup. The woman also found a frying pan, but now we could not stay any longer in this desert that was once our home.[17]

One day later the expulsion of the remaining Germans from this now Polish-administered area began, and Küstrin became Kostrzyn. The ruins of the Altstadt were stripped of suitable material to assist in the rebuilding of Warsaw and the site abandoned, but now there are plans for the possible reconstruction of the former Aldstadt in 2015.[18]

Annex A

Küstrin Garrison Units,
as at 22 February 1945

1. Fortress Commandant's Staff
2. Fortress Infantry Battalion 1450
3. Panzergrenadier Replacement Battalion 50
4. 1st Battalion Armoured Troops Regiment 346
5. 2nd Battalion Armoured Troops Regiment 346
6. 3rd Battalion Armoured Troops Regiment 344
7. Engineer Replacement & Training Battalion 68
8. Territorial Engineer Battalion 513
9. 1st Battalion, Fortress Artillery Regiment 3132 (4 Batteries)
10. Artillery Replacement Battalion 39
11. Flak Regiment 114
12. 5 x 75mm Tank Turrets (non-operational)
13. Fortress Communications Company 738
14. Stragglers, assembled in the von Stülpnagel Barracks (including elements of the Woldenburg Infantry Division)
15. Convalescent Company
16. Probationary Infantry Battalion 500
17. Hungarian Infantry Battalion IV
18. Turkomen Action Battalion (German)
19. Turkomen Action Battalion (Turkish)
20. North Caucasian Action Battalion (German)
21. North Caucasian Action Battalion (Caucasian)
22. Officers and officials from the Schloss Barracks
23. Volkssturm

Total Combatant Strength: 8,196 men
Source: Bundes-Militärisches Zwischenarchiv Potsdam, WF-03/5084 Sheets 966–7

Reinefarth's Report on the Fall
of Küstrin Fortress and the Breakout
of the Surviving Garrison

I. I took over the Küstrin Fortress as commandant on the 2nd
February 1945. For troops I found only soldiers of whole
Wehrmacht units that had fled, completely undisciplined
(one was rarely saluted in the street), lounging about and
without any unit organisation. Artillery, described in the
Fortress Regulations as the backbone of any fortress, was
there none. No trenches or fighting positions were to be seen
whatsoever. Here one should note that Russian tanks had
already broken into Küstrin on the 31st January 1945 and
some had been shot up. The suburb of Warnick and a part of
Alt Drewitz were in Russian hands, the front line to the north
had been pushed in and, in particular, Height 63, which gave
a view over the whole fortress, had been occupied by the
enemy. The town already lay under artillery and mortar fire
in the first days of February, and my office in the
Kommandatura Building received a direct hit.

My first concern was the rounding up and organisation of
the stragglers, as these alone would form the fortress's
combat teams, as well as construct the defences. The particular difficulty here was that a considerable number of them
were either gunners or flak gunners that would have to be
deployed as infantry. The fortress was divided into two
sectors, the Neustadt under Colonel of Gendarmerie Walter
and the Altstadt under Major Wegener. The construction of
the defences was undertaken with the help of the troops, the
civilian population, prisoners-of-war and foreign labour. In
the course of time it was established that the cellars in Küstrin

were not at all proof against artillery fire and that many had already collapsed when the sappers blew up the narrow passages to prevent fires from spreading. The casemates were crumbling away and had already been penetrated by medium calibre shells and collapsed.

II.   Regarding the fall of Küstrin-Neustadt, I refer to my attached report of 9.3.45. As I reported in the conclusion, the timely occupation of the inner defensive ring was missed by the sector commander. I cannot attribute personal blame to the sector commander for, as a Gendarmerie officer, he obviously lacked adequate training to deal with the situation. There was no other officer available to me as sector commander. I had given Captain Felk to Colonel of Gendarmerie Walter as tactical adviser, but he apparently did not oversee the situation adequately enough during the fighting. Captain Felk fell during the fighting in Küstrin.

III.   On the 28th March 1945, my command post was transferred to the cellars of the Artillery Barracks in that part of the town between the Oder and the Vorflut Canal after the enemy had destroyed all the trenches and casemates in the Altstadt and set the Schloss on fire. The enemy had come up to within about 30 metres from the Schloss. At the time the command post was moved, the enemy had occupied the parade ground right up to the Artillery Barracks' trenches. Several counter-attacks activated by me threw back the enemy, but the positions could not be held, as all of them had been flattened under artillery and mortar fire as well as bombing. The small bulwark off the parade ground south of the barracks was in enemy hands. The attempt to regain it on the night of 29th March 1945, using the last of the good troops, led to the momentary closing down of the work, but also to the destruction of the attacking troops.

The situation in this last part of the fortress deteriorated during the course of 29.3. The barracks were on fire and the fires could not be extinguished for want of equipment. The still unbuttressed cellars were full of wounded and soldiers who had retreated. I had the cellars constantly combed through by officers commanded by a captain to lead those men still capable of fighting to an assembly point in the cellars. From there they were led back to the defences by

officers in order to close the gaps caused by flight and casualties as best as possible. Even these trenches and positions
had been completely levelled meantime.

Gradually the ceaseless fire from enemy heavy weapons
clearly began to increase, together with dangerous signs of
breaking up among the troops. From fifty sought-out soldiers
the officers brought only about five to the positions, while the
remainder falsely pretended to be wounded or actually fell
wounded from enemy fire. As continuous artillery and
mortar fire fell over the whole area, control was made
extremely difficult. I gave strict orders that weapons should
be used against anyone wavering in their duty. Several
soldiers were thus shot by the officers, whereupon those
remaining declared that it was all the same to them whether
they were shot by German officers or Russians, they would
not go any further.

Meanwhile the officers in the defences were calling for
ammunition, giving rise to the idea that the ammunition had
not only been fired off or lost to enemy action, but had partly
been thrown away. Finally the regiment's last ammunition
was distributed. From then on there was neither a Panzerfaust
nor a hand grenade to be had.

From midday the reports piled up that the troops were
leaving their positions and going into the barrack cellars and
that soldiers were even hiding under the beds of the wounded.
Towards evening, the battalion commanders with other
officers and SS leaders came to my command post and in a
clear, dutiful manner reported that the troops had declared
that they would go over to the enemy that night. They had
still hoped that help would come from outside but now the
ammunition had run out and they felt themselves betrayed.
A large number of the soldiers emphasised this with the
words that they were now going over 'to the side of the
victors'. It was already known among the troops that two
officers and several men had gone over with white flags.

I summoned the battalion commanders as well as some
officers and SS leaders to an official conference and also
called in the sector commander and regimental commander,
Major Wegener. First I told them of the radio message
received by me at about 1630 hours from Headquarters 9th

Army with the Führer's order to continue to hold on to the fortress. Then I reminded the officers forcibly of their oath to the Führer, requiring unconditional obedience, even to death. I then described the tactical situation. The Russians were sitting on the burning barracks and on the Vorflut Canal road bridge that had been blown on my orders meanwhile. The most important strategic point was now the Vorflut Canal railway bridge that unequivocally had to be defended and must in no case fall intact into enemy hands.

The officers told me unanimously that they no longer had control over their men, and the experience of the past few days had shown that neither encouragement nor threatening with weapons would avail. They thus no longer had any possibility of influencing them in the general collapse, with the new units raised during the past two months breaking up yet again. Finally the darkness and the continuing fire by heavy weapons made any supervision impossible.

Again referring to the Führer-Order and the Soldiers' Oath, I told the individual officers and SS leaders that due to lack of ammunition and the soldiers' refusal to do their duty, holding on to a few square metres was no longer possible. Thus the Führer-Order to hold the fortress to the last bullet had been fulfilled.

There was now only the choice: **Either**, having lost every opportunity of defending themselves, to proffer the Führer and the German people the shame of 1,000 German soldiers going over to the Bolsheviks, **Or** to grasp the only opportunity of gripping the fully demoralised troops once more, give the order to attack, and so avoid a shameful outcome.

I decided, after a difficult inner conflict, to give the order to attack Kuhbrücken-Vorstadt, a small part of which was still in our hands, with the aim of re-establishing the old front line. I waved aside the repeated appeals from my officers to break through to our own lines. Nevertheless, I had to consider that the troops upon the first successful advance with practically no ammunition would not be held back from breaking through any longer. I took this possibility into consideration.

This undertaking, in the assessment that an attack from the west appeared unlikely, had the moral advantage that the troops at least would die a decent soldiers' death and be spared shame, and finally that the Russians would be prevented from acquiring over 1,000 labourers. Thus I was completely convinced I was dealing with the matter in the way the Führer would wish.

The attack, which then itself led to further breakthroughs, succeeded simply with 'Hurrahs!' without firing through the whole enemy lines. In so doing, two firing anti-tank guns and two heavy machine-gun crews were put out of action with rifle butts. Overall, how many of the remainder of the garrison got through, I have no overall view, but believe that it was a high percentage. Finally, I note that all the bridges, including the Vorflut railway bridge, were destroyed.

Kreisleiter Körner's Report

Potsdam, 5th April 1945
Reichsleiter Party Comrade Bormann
Wilhelmstrasse
Berlin

I have the following to report about the events of the last weeks in Küstrin Fortress. As all my notes, papers, etc. were destroyed without exception, I cannot give precise details and dates on individual events. I quote them only so far as my memory extends.

The Küstrin men and soldiers knew from the beginning of the battle that Küstrin had a great historical past and has a political and historical significance for the Greater German Reich. Their application to the fighting was thus particularly honourable. We were all imbued with the willpower to defend this old fortress town to the last round. This willpower alone, however, is only useful when the supply of manpower, weapons and ammunition is adequate. Unfortunately, during the ten weeks of siege we received no assistance from outside and no replacements for the tens of thousands of men either killed or wounded. To give a rough picture, I should mention that during the fighting the Wehrmacht was reduced from 11,000 to 1,200 men. The Volkssturm were reduced from 900 to about 118, the police from 65 to 14, the fire brigade from 80 to 20, and the Kreis administration from 30 to 12. Of these 12 only 4 Party members have reported surviving the breakout so far. These figures should bear witness to how heroically the battle was fought and with what meagre numbers a massively overwhelming enemy was held at bay for ten weeks. At a time when Küstrin was still relatively well equipped with heavy weapons, the artillery superiority of the Russians was calculated as 100:6, i.e. there were 100 Russian guns for every 6 German ones. During the last weeks, however, we had absolutely no heavy weapons

274

any more. The enemy could do with us as he wanted. His aircraft romped around in the sky over the fortress unhampered by either German fighters or flak. In my opinion, Küstrin would only have fulfilled its role if it had had an establishment of about 60,000 men with the corresponding weapons. This strength was anticipated on paper, as far as I know. The most important aspects for Küstrin fortress were that the fortress outworks and the heights at Reitwein, etc., were occupied by our troops. In fact the Russians occupied those heights and thus had an advantageous view and excellent target in the fortress. Words do not suffice to begin to describe the courage and achievements. One must call to mind that the Küstrin garrison was completely cut off from the outside world for ten long weeks. Gas, electricity, sewage and water were lacking right from the beginning of the fighting. Thus there was no chance of listening to the radio, and no newspapers arrived. But there was strong artillery fire day and night. One alert followed another as the Russian attacks started. The air space over Küstrin was almost constantly overflown by Russian aircraft, dropping bombs and shooting up everything they could see on the streets. German flak and fighter protection were completely lacking. The men were under immense psychological pressure as they felt themselves completely abandoned and saw and noticed absolutely nothing of German military forces. The only fact on their minds was that they were fighting in a trap.

When the whole of Küstrin-Neustadt was lost in an afternoon in mid-March, the psychological pressure reached its climax. The Russians had taken the Neustadt from Alt Drewitz with tanks and infantry after several hours of artillery preparation. Allegedly it was not possible to receive warning of this danger in time. Elements of the fire brigade, police and other civil services, including the local Party leader, remained in the Neustadt. Apart from this, about 4,000 troops remained in the Stülpnagel Barracks and Engineer Barracks. But there were also other major installations of exceptional importance in the support of the fortress garrison. I mean the Army Supply Depot, the big Army Bakery, armoury and ammunition stores. For example, in the Norddeutschen Kartoffel-Mehlfabrik were stored foodstuffs to the value of 3.5 million Reichsmarks. The German soldiers in the Neustadt were commanded by Police Colonel Walther.

What became of those 4,000 troops nobody knows as yet. It was astonishing that the military authorities did nothing to rescue these soldiers or regain their fighting capability. No radio contact was made. At least one pitiful attempt was made to get radio sets across, but it failed. I have not heard of any repetition of this attempt. It should have been possible to arrange combat communications with these troops in advance.

The Wehrmacht had a dove unit in Küstrin, but the 270 letter-carrying doves had been taken away to Berlin several days previously. In any case I did not get the impression that everything was done to release the surrounded troops. I must also doubt that the commitment of the Luftwaffe in this urgent matter was asked for. One has an overall impression that the senior military authorities did not take the situation in Küstrin to be as serious as it really was.

If one had always reported the true situation clearly and unequivocally without embellishment, I cannot imagine that effective assistance would not have come from the outside. The bridges between the Altstadt and the Neustadt were blown at the correct moment. Individual soldiers and civilians swam across the Warthe and in this way were saved by the troops in the Altstadt. Even if a military operation had been impossible, one could at least have maintained contact with the German troops that had been cut off.

Following the fall of the Neustadt, in which, according to my reckoning, some 5–600 civilians still remained, the situation in the Altstadt was as follows. The Russian front in the north-east stood on the Warthe, in the south-east on the boundary of the Altstadt, in the south-west – except for a small bridgehead – on the Oder-Vorflut Canal. The fortress area was now reduced to only the Altstadt and was barely 2 kilometres long. The fortress was divided into two parts by the Oder. The Russians increased their rate of fire from all sides in the days that followed. The suburb of Kietz had already been razed to the ground by shelling and fires. All the buildings had been destroyed by the shelling and especially by fire. The defence possibilities were made even more difficult by the constrictions within the fortress. Heavy weapons had difficulty engaging any more. Many buildings had to be demolished in the Altstadt in order to provide fields of fire. The psychological pressure on the troops also increased under these circumstances. The Altstadt was known to be completely built up, the old buildings having been constructed with a lot of timber. Fire extinguishing equipment was largely lacking. Water could only be obtained from the fire-extinguishing wells, but extraction was limited. Everyone knew that should the Russians set fire to the Altstadt with their Stalin-Organs, nothing would be saved.

Conditions in the cellars became increasingly unbearable. The Altstadt cellars at this time of year were always flooded from 10 to 20 centimetres. As the water continued to rise, so did the danger. Nevertheless, the troops beat back all the Russian attacks repeated daily.

Once the civilian population had been removed from Küstrin, the district administration's main task was at an end. I then handed over the majority of the staff to the Volkssturm. The remainder were dressed and armed as well as the Wehrmacht could provide. On the orders of the fortress commandant, these 32 men then formed a unit under the title 'Combat Team Körner' which was then employed exactly the same as the troops. This team had a specific section to occupy and, in an alert, had to occupy that section with everyone. Nevertheless, the men of the district administration had to work until late at night loading textiles and foodstuffs to be conveyed by the nightly ammunition convoys to Seelow, where they were taken over by the Landeswirtschaftsamt (regional economic office). The textile stocks were almost entirely removed this way, but the foodstuffs were mainly retained in the fortress as, with the closing of the ring, the possibility of transporting them came to an end, and it can be taken for certain that they were destroyed in the subsequent fighting. Apart from this, I had all the cattle, horses, etc. gathered together and sent off from the fortress in treks in order to maintain the people's food supplies. The men of the district administration thus not only served as brave and courageous soldiers, but also carried out some hard work worthy of recognition.

The fire brigade demonstrated quite exemplary conduct. I agree with the fortress commandant that their commitment to duty was quite unique. Many of the firemen were old men who, for example, on one occasion were on duty day and night for four days without enjoying an hour's rest. They were in constant danger from enemy artillery, bombers and air attacks.

The police in Küstrin also set an outstanding example. They were always on duty and more prepared to help than the Wehrmacht. In both the last two weeks, when buildings and cellars were being destroyed almost every day, their work saved the lives of several people.

Unfortunately, I saw that the troops were not prepared to assist in this kind of work in their free time. Naturally there were individual exceptions. The whole Küstrin garrison had only a limited fighting capacity. As far as I could determine, the fortress garrison consisted of about one-third policemen gathered in from the Warthegau, one-third of Waffen-SS men, and the final third of soldiers of all branches of the Wehrmacht. They were all mixed up together and did not know each other, lacking unity. There were individual good officers and NCOs to reinforce them, men who gathered others around them and achieved extraordinary things in battle. Unfortunately there were too few of these good soldiers. I believe that the fortress was able to hold out as long as it did mainly due to the Probationary Battalion, which consisted of soldiers with a zest for attack. Apart from this there were companies of potential officers, who also had a fighting spirit that successfully fought several defensive battles. One such potential officer company sustained 90 per cent casualties in an attack on the bucket elevator. Another potential officer company started off with 150 men and ended with only 15. It should be considered whether it is right to commit soldiers selected for leadership qualities en masse, for this way we lose all this officer potential. Nevertheless, there was a need for taking action in Küstrin. There was a feeling among the troops that did not hold back in its criticism of the local military leadership. In my opinion, not everything was in order in the military camp. The SS-Gruppenführer and Lieutenant General of the Waffen SS held the Oak Leaves and was highly regarded and respected. I got on well with him in the best possible way. He is a National Socialist and values cooperation with the Party. Those around him were not so inspired. His chief of staff, Major Michalski, was a reservist and by career a theologian from a university. He was a very nervous man with no comradely contact with other officers, thoroughly distant, and I had the impression that he opposed the Party. I cannot assess his military capability, but believe that he was not all that good, as some of his actions revealed. The first liaison officer was Captain Lotz, who simultaneously held a pass as a special emissary of the Reichsführer-SS. In official circles he was known as boastful and pompous. I too had the same impression of him. These men were permanently around the general. I was often told that there was a shortage of officers in the fortress. On the other hand, there were many officers with absolutely nothing to do or who had only trifling jobs.

From the start the Volkssturm in Küstrin were engaged militarily. Later the men were withdrawn and used almost exclusively in the construction of defences. For the most part the Volkssturm showed their worth. It was a shame that the men of the Volkssturm were treated as second-class in everything. They often had to change quarters or positions that they had prepared with love and care to make way for the Wehrmacht. Apart from this, their provision of clothing, boots, etc., was very miserly. Most Volkssturm men had only what they stood up in and had no possibility of changing their clothing. The men were used partly to man the defences and partly to build them. This overstress was accepted but was hardly reasonable. As the Volkssturm came completely under the Wehrmacht in action, the question arises whether the district administration is necessary in such a case. The battalion commander received his orders directly from his Wehrmacht superior and also dealt with him directly. The district staff thus sat between two stools. Their work was simply in the notification of dependants and the execution of other formalities for the Volkssturm men. In this direction, it seems to me necessary to have clear relationships.

I therefore think it realistic that either the district staff should be disbanded in emergencies, or that the Wehrmacht superiors should issue their orders via the district staff. Then the battalion commander would have to deal with the Wehrmacht superiors via the district staff.

On the whole it is worth considering whether the Volkssturm should have remained in Küstrin. The defence of a fortress is a completely military task, for which the best and well-trained soldiers are already good enough. After the Volkssturm had been committed to action in the first military thrust and held the enemy until the Wehrmacht could organise proper defensive positions, in my opinion they could have worked on the most important defensive works in the fortress. Their further employment in the rear of the front would have been more appropriate. I have left unmentioned that during the first five weeks of the siege the Volkssturm men were only poorly armed. It could be anticipated that a breakout attempt by the remains of the garrison would be organised at the end of the battle for Küstrin. It was certain that this action would be allied with physical stress and much fighting and could only be achieved by well-trained soldiers. The predominantly old men of the Volkssturm were thus a hindrance and would also largely not survive the fall of Küstrin.

I remained with my district staff in Küstrin to the last hour and was militarily engaged with all my men in accordance with the commandant's orders. At least the intention was correct, but it was of no significance. It remains to be considered whether the political leadership should be withdrawn in the future once their actual task has been accomplished. One likes to put one's men at the disposal of the Wehrmacht, but even the Wehrmacht had already withdrawn their own administrative offices from Küstrin to Seelow or Müncheberg weeks before. This was annoying to the unwilling ones among the soldiers, but was necessary and useful. The bakery, abattoir, etc. could not continue operating under constant bombardment and lack of working space. They continued their duties in Seelow and Müncheberg and administered the supply of the Küstrin garrison from there. These supplies ceased at the point when the ring around Küstrin became completely closed. The district staff remained an inexplicable presence in Küstrin during the fighting. We were well established with the Wehrmacht and carried out some important work in saving textiles and foodstuffs for the Reich but, as a result of many requests, our role was gradually taken over entirely by the Wehrmacht. Until the men of the district staff were accepted by the Wehrmacht for rationing purposes, it was not easy for them. This was because we were not accepted as members of the Wehrmacht. After the district staff lost their bunker yet again in the last days from a direct hit, and had to find themselves new accommodation, it became impossible. In battle the Wehrmacht is always more important. Quite often we were asked: 'What are you doing here? You have already done your job.' I always replied that the person posing the question would very probably have been the one to shout loudest and shake his head over cowardly political leadership if we had not been there.

After most of my men had lost even the poorest items of their clothing, despite my protests to the fortress commandant it was still impossible to get them new clothing. This was partly because the uniforms were at an end, but the main reason was because, on the orders of the commandant, the officers and Wehrmacht officials regarded the district staff as unimportant in the combat area and made no effort to supply them with the necessary items.

When officials and their associates or even those of other important roles (Reichs Post, town administration, etc.) are requested or expected to remain in the combat area to the last shot, then the Wehrmacht should be given an explicit order to treat these men exactly as their own soldiers.

In general, however, I can say that the presence of a political leader until the last minute within the Küstrin fortress worked positively with regard to the Wehrmacht, Volkssturm, etc. One noticed that the soldiers when visited suddenly in their positions expressed surprise and pleasure at seeing a brown uniform. It was especially so when firing broke out during a visit. If one took the first good rifle in one's hands and joined in without suddenly curtailing the visit, one had the soldiers feeding out of one's hand and could do with them as one liked. On such visits the soldiers did not know how they should respond to 'all the best'. Mostly I came away with a rich donation for the WHW [Winter Relief Fund]. In one visit to Second-Lieutenant Hollmann's platoon, I came away with a donation of RM 4,000, which meant that every soldier in this little unit had contributed RM 120. Almost always one had to promise to return. My relationship with many of the officers was much the same. I was, and remained until the end, a free person to whom the officers could speak freely and openly whatever had to be said. While the officers had to follow their paths of duty and not waver from setting a good example, they often came to me with their thoughts and concerns. This did not involve personal matters but only concerned the basic faults in the military leadership that they could see. SS-Gruppenführer Reinefarth was always grateful for advice on such matters, although he never or seldom expressed his thoughts to me. An uncomfortable trouble-maker remained, if the reports were accurate, among those officers around the Gruppenführer.

So the battle for Küstrin continued. The enemy artillery fire, air attacks, etc., became ever stronger. Our own situation regarding ammunition, foodstuffs, etc., was frequently affected. More and more vehicles and weapons were knocked out and supplies became scarcer. Every day the fortress suffered a large loss of men. Care for the wounded, despite the superhuman efforts of the doctors, was always very scanty. Again and again new cellars had to be found for the wounded, until they too were knocked out and hardly any accommodation could be found for them. For those men remaining in combat, the whole ten weeks of the battle for Küstrin were an undesirable test of the nerves. It was not only enemy action, but the fact that no help was coming from outside, and at the end we could do absolutely nothing about the enemy aircraft, which depressed everyone. There were also many cases of death among the soldiers, policemen, firemen, etc., due to heart attacks and other natural causes.

So the day came for Küstrin when the 'corridor' was closed. This 'corridor' involved not just a drivable route, but included a narrow strip of land that German troops had held free until then and through which the convoys brought ammunition every night. Because of the state of the ground, this route could only be used by tracked vehicles. This meagre last connection with the outside world also fell, despite the anticipated help from outside, and the constant hope it gave to the Küstrin troops that one day the main road from Küstrin to Seelow would be fought free again. The men were simply shattered by this misfortune, and the feeling spread that Küstrin had long since been written off, and that all their efforts and courage had been for nothing. One should also particularly recall that no field post had been arriving in Küstrin. The Volkssturm men for the most part knew nothing about the fate of their families. The field post traffic had slowly died out, and was soon at an end with this closure. The confidence of the soldiers sank even lower when they were told that it was no longer possible to retain this small connection for supplies, and that it was no longer possible for the Wehrmacht to undertake the relief of Küstrin. But at the same time the Küstrin troops came to terms with the idea that their fate was as good as sealed. No one doubted that he would have to fight to the death in the fortress. As soon as a Wehrmacht vehicle appeared on the streets, Russian aircraft shot it up. One result from all the casualties was that more effort was demanded from those remaining. They were all overstressed and overfatigued. A new unrest set in when the Russians shelled the Oder Bridge connecting the two parts of the Altstadt fortress and rendered it unusable. The fate of the fortress appeared to be sealed from day to day. One had no doubt that, if the Russians made a determined attack with their vast superiority, they would take the Altstadt without too much difficulty. On the other hand, the core elements of the fortress troops were tough enough to fight to the last bullet and use their assault knives if necessary.

On the 22nd March the day began with an unusually strong artillery barrage. This was followed by several attacks by the Russians coming from all sides, but they were beaten back. This was repeated in the days to come. If the enemy artillery was not firing, their aircraft were over Küstrin.

On the 25th March there was a concentrated artillery bombardment on the north-eastern part of the Altstadt from all points of the compass. It was immediately clear that this part of the town had been targeted. The uninterrupted bombardment by weapons of all calibres lasted five hours. Then came the enemy aircraft in several waves dropping German bombs of the heaviest kind. Duds lying around confirmed the German origin of these ten-hundredweight bombs. The Wehrmacht observation posts reported 165 enemy aircraft. After these heavy bombs had been dropped, more aircraft arrived and dropped phosphor canisters, setting light to everything.

On the 26th March and during the preceding night, the concentrated bombardment was repeated on the north-eastern part of the Altstadt as far as the Marktplatz, including the town hall. During the night of the 26th/27th March the artillery continued to fire on the burning part of the Altstadt. Whenever it stopped, the enemy aircraft prevented the fire brigade from putting out the flames with their machine guns. This part of the town was reduced to the ground and most of the cellars were destroyed.

The attack was resumed on the 27th March with artillery fire and bombers on the south-west part of the Altstadt, reducing the whole of this part of the town to dust and ashes. Even the Schloss, until then apparently exempt, was set on fire. The last ammunition dump went up in the air. In my estimation there were several hundred wounded lying in the Schloss and the Oelkeller that surely must have all died. With the destruction of this part of the Altstadt, the fortress commandant also lost his command post, and there was no other suitable bunker available that he could transfer to. At noon the Russians launched a major attack on the Altstadt from Sonnenburg. Despite fierce resistance, they were able to reach as far as the Marktplatz. I spoke to the fortress commandant twice on this day and recommended that as the ammunition was running out and as resistance could only be sustained for a little while longer, he should consider how at least some of the combatant troops could be saved. Through my liaison officer, SS-Captain Siedke, the news was brought to me that evening that the Gruppenführer was moving his command post to the Artillery Barracks on the other side of the Oder. I was asked to join the Gruppenführer with my men. The Gruppenführer with his staff of ten men and I with about fourteen men set off, led by one of the district staff who was familiar with the area. We crossed the railway bridge to the Artillery Barracks. In the subsequent discussion, the Gruppenführer asked me and my men to move into the front line, as there was no room for us. That same night I set off with my staff for Kuhbrücken-Vorstadt. The sector commander likewise informed me that there were no cellars or bunkers available even for his soldiers, so we moved into the front line.

The general feeling among the officers and men was that they fully understood that the fortress had to be held until the last minute, but they did not see why the order should not be given to break through to the German lines when the ammunition ran out and so save at least some of the troops. It was known that the ammunition would run out within a few hours and, if there were no further orders, about 1,500 men would have to wait until the Bolsheviks came and slaughtered them. I believe there were also officers who were determined to risk a breakout with their men should no order come from the local command for a combined one. All, however, were determined only to leave the fortress at the very last moment. It seemed senseless to fire their last round in Küstrin and then await the arrival of the Bolsheviks unarmed. Once it was established that no help could be expected from outside, one often heard that soldiers and even officers were proposing to the local command that they should now act independently. As no such orders came, even more rumours circulated among the troops that the fortress commander was no longer with them and they were leaderless. Encountering such rumours did not help much. When a leader is present he has to deal with this situation himself. The fortress commandant could only deal with it in one way, which was to order a combined breakout by the rest of the men. There was no alternative, for the prerequisite for the defence of the fortress was ammunition, and that was lacking.

At about 0800 hours on the 27th March the Russians started a three-hour bombardment that also covered Kuhbrücken-Vorstadt. Behind it they began an attack from Neu Bleyen and the west. As the Soviet infantry attacked, the German infantry turned and ran. Brandishing a drawn pistol, several officers tried to get their men back into their positions, but it did not work. Some of the foxholes were abandoned by the troops at the main Soviet point of attack. I saw a second lieutenant firing an automatic rifle, and a sergeant with a sub-machine gun, who used it extensively. Then there were about six Volkssturm men, who remained staunch and fired away. A Volkssturm battalion commander set an excellent example by remaining in front with these few men and telling them not to weaken. This Volkssturm officer was from the Warthegau and not known to me. I joined these men with my Party comrades from the district staff at the critical point of attack. We lay down with them and fired away continuously. This small fighting band forced the Bolsheviks to take cover and then, as we began to attack, to withdraw. Meanwhile an SS officer had got some of the men back on their feet and some 10 to 15 of them joined us in our position. More and more soldiers gradually joined us. The Russians attacked several times this day but were always beaten back. The German soldiers avoided fighting with the Russians as they were aware of their superiority in weapons. Soon every second Russian had an automatic rifle or grenade-launcher, the others having quick-firing rifles with 15 to 20 rounds. Behind the Russians were other heavy weapons. In contrast the German soldier had his old-fashioned rifle that had to be reloaded for every shot. As the ammunition in the last weeks had no more than five rounds in a clip, each bullet had to be loaded into the breach individually. During this attack German artillery was called on. They fired from the area of Tucheband, but fired too short into our own lines. After this attack also failed, the Russians used loudspeaker propaganda. They played German marches and the proclamations of German generals in Soviet captivity, always asking the German soldiers to give up the fight. The Russians used this loudspeaker propaganda on the Küstrin fronts every day. The speakers mentioned local events, which had a big effect on the troops. They mentioned the fortress commandant, other officers and also Küstrin officials by name, saying, for example, that I had gone away again or that I felt very comfortable in my home in the Neustadt.

We remained on alert day and night, for a new attack could begin any moment. On the 28th March there was a repeat performance of the day before. The concentration was on that part of the town between the Oder and the Oder-Vorflut Canal. Again we endured hour-long artillery bombardments, aerial bombing and phosphor canisters. As I had to stay in the trenches with my men, I sent my liaison officer to the Gruppenführer with my opinion once more. My question as to how much longer the ammunition would last received a chilling reply: the ammunition for the heavy weapons was all but exhausted and there was only 20 minutes' worth of small-arms ammunition left. The Gruppenführer had assembled his officers for a conference. All the officers were unanimous in their opinion that to fire off the remaining ammunition in 20 minutes and then leave 1,500 men quite helpless was clearly senseless. All agreed that it would be better to try to use these men in the new front near Golzow. The Gruppenführer would send a telegram to the Reichsführer informing him that he had defended the fortress to the last round. My liaison officer, SS-Captain Siedke, returned at about 2200 hours with the information that the Gruppenführer had decided with a heavy heart to break through to Golzow with the remaining men. He had fulfilled his task. Now the last rounds were being kept for the breakthrough fighting. Forty artillery shells were then fired, and other rounds for which there were no longer any weapons were blown up. Everything that might be useful to the Russians was destroyed. Those of the wounded who could walk should join their units, the other wounded having unfortunately died in the flames or the demolitions. The word was passed that only the lightest clothing should be worn for the breakthrough and all pack items, overcoats, etc., should be left behind. The men only had light infantry weapons, i.e. rifles, sub-machine guns, pistols and hand grenades. The Gruppenführer arrived at Kuhbrücken with his men at 2300 hours. I had put a man with local knowledge at the head of the whole platoon of district staff; he knew every tree and bush in the Oderbruch. We set off in a southerly direction from Kuhbrücken under the cover of the Oder dyke towards Kietz. We had to cross the dyke between Kuhbrücken and Kietz individually. Of course, all talking and noise was strictly forbidden.

The local man did not look for a track but for particularly swampy ground and meadows where one could expect the fewest Soviet positions. Thus it was possible for about 1,200 men from Küstrin to move across without firing a shot or the Russians noticing. Once the first Russian lines were behind us, we went in a northerly direction with many diversions to the Schäferei sheep farm. Of course there were many Russian positions and other Soviet bunkers on the way. The rifle-armed Russian sentries thought that only Russian troops could be moving about and let us through unchallenged. The Soviet troops seemed to be sleeping in many of the bunkers but were killed in cold blood without a shot being fired if they drew attention to themselves. Certainly it would have been possible to take a large number of prisoners along with us, but as it remained uncertain what kind of fighting awaited us, this was not done. The troops were in a good fighting mood on this march. On one occasion I saw a solder angrily berating for five minutes a Russian who had surrendered. When the Russians realised that they were confronted by German soldiers, they usually surrendered. We were not fired on once from Russian bunkers or by sentries.

One outstanding advantage for us on this enterprise was the weather: it was a dark night and raining. The stress of the march was nevertheless immense. We stumbled mainly though swampy meadows or ploughed fields. The heavy Oder mud clung thickly to one's boots, making walking difficult and demanding the last of one's strength from everyone. Nearly all the men were completely exhausted, but again and again they gathered up their strength and straightened their backs. Of course we had become all mixed up and there was no longer any cohesion between companies and platoons. The constant firing of flares forced us to keep taking cover, which was physically very demanding. We came to the second Russian lines near Gorgast, where we were accosted by a Russian sentry with a password, and when we failed to reply the Russians opened up on us with two machine guns and five or six rifles. We fired back with the remainder of our ammunition, shouted 'Hurra!' and ran into the fire in an attack. The Russians fled when they saw that we were in earnest. The Russians then started using heavy weapons, firing shells and mortars into our ranks. This developed into a fight lasting one to one and a half hours. However, it did give us time to draw breath. Incidentally, a German soldier fired a Panzerfaust into a bunker at the beginning of the fight that silenced all the weapons in it, after which Russian soldiers immediately surrendered from two other bunkers. As our ammunition was about to run out, we suddenly stopped firing and kept quiet. We marched on. Only then and now did we have to attack with cries of 'Hurra!' and chase the Russians away. The Very lights coming from the German lines were useless. To my knowledge, before we set off the Gruppenführer had radioed that we were trying to break through towards Golzow with 1,200 men and requesting that, should we succeed, to make tactical use of the gap. Opposing light signals were agreed. It was later established that the radio message had not got through, which was why the corresponding light signals were lacking. We had also finally lost our direction during the previous fighting. I believe that we had moved several kilometres between the Soviet and German lines. When the completely exhausted Küstrin team finally found the right direction for Golzow, we came under extraordinarily heavy fire from the German front. We replied to the fire at first, but when we realised that it was coming from the German front line, we stopped firing. With loud shouts and singing the national anthem we eventually made ourselves noticed. I reckon, however, that we had suffered our worst casualties from the German fire. In Golzow we immediately asked that the German casualties lying in no-man's-land should be recovered that same night. I know from SS-Gruppenführer Reinefarth that he too was lying there completely exhausted and that he was finally brought out in an armoured reconnaissance vehicle. As to the extent of our casualties, I have not been able to get any approximate figures so far. We had reckoned from the start that a good half would be left on the wayside in the breakthrough. The wounded could not be brought along, as everyone had been told in advance, for the last of one's strength was needed.

The town of Küstrin is a single heap of rubble. The buildings have been shot through, burnt out and those burnt walls still standing shot through yet again. There is not a single Küstrin family that will find the smallest item of their personal goods again. Certainly Küstrin fortress has shown itself worthy of its great historical past in this war. Only when the town was completely shot up, when the ammunition and food stocks were destroyed and there was no chance of holding on any longer did the troops assemble for a breakthrough battle. When one thinks that during the days and weeks beforehand all the men had become tired and burnt out, the breakthrough battle was a unique performance that deserves recognition. SS-Gruppenführer Reinefarth gave the order to break through at the last minute, making a decision that was fully justified. He did what a responsible and self-confident leader must do in such a situation. Metaphorically speaking, there were only two possibilities. Either the fortress held on for another 20 minutes and then surrendered defenceless to the Bolshevik soldiers, or, taking the last of the ammunition, the men broke out and thus, despite the expected losses, several hundred men were saved for the German front. In the troops' opinion, the garrison should have been taken out through the 'pipeline' as soon as Kietz and the Neustadt were lost, to establish a new Oder front west of Küstrin, which would have saved about 3–4,000 men at no great cost.

It will be understood that one simply cannot accept or believe that any earnest attempt was made to relieve Küstrin. If one had been made, then it is at least astonishing that several divisions with fresh, rested soldiers with tanks and heavy weapons were not able to do what the fought-out and tired fortress garrison of Küstrin achieved in the opposite direction with just a few small arms. There are few fortresses that could hold out for ten weeks against such superior forces.

To finish my report, I would like to make an observation that perhaps would not be unimportant in the continuation of the war. First, the question of why it is that the soldier breaks down so often and runs away. I have only one explanation for it, and that is the lack of good officers who not only lead in a military sense but also establish a close comradely relationship with their men. The men [in Küstrin] were all completely exhausted and weary from week-, month- or year-long fighting. They daily experienced the enemy's superiority in weapons and manpower and were losing confidence in their own resources. They had reached an emotional state in which nothing mattered any more. Although it is not allowed in such a tense situation, one might survive if one were at least allowed to have some leave in limited circumstances. When that is impossible, a solution for the fighting troops should constantly be looked for. A unit after a week's fighting in the forward area should earn a week's rest in a rear area. One still sees full garrisons in the country, so such an exchange of soldiers should be possible. A unit that has been able to sleep comfortably for a week and has had its clothing and weapons repaired and even some training, returns refreshed into battle. Old First World War soldiers often told me that they had never experienced units fighting and fighting until they finally died. For instance, during those ten weeks in Küstrin perhaps a third of the troops could have been stood down. Certainly it was necessary to have a large proportion of the troops familiar with the local terrain remaining in place. It was the same with the Volkssturm in Küstrin. Much of their accommodation was full of lice because they had no change of clothing, which made them dirty and consequently unhappy and discouraged. They could have been brought back once every so often to have a good sleep, sort out their clothing and above all have a good wash and even get half a day's training. These troops would certainly be valuable in the further fighting. Here is an example:

I crawled up to a soldier who was on sentry duty in a foxhole on the Warthe, and so on the front line. I tried to have a chat with him, as in other such cases, but he would hardly say anything. When I asked him what his task was, he still remained silent. I must accept that perhaps my brown uniform put him off. He stared at me stupidly. When I finally offered him a cigarette and then got closer to him and asked how long he had been on sentry duty, he answered since early yesterday. He had been on duty for a day and a half without being relieved. He was completely exhausted, overtired and half asleep. Such a soldier cannot do much if the Russians should really come. This case was reported by me and investigated further.

One always had the impression that those who are really able, if they are unassuming and do not like putting themselves in the lime-light, make little progress in the Wehrmacht. Those holding positions on the staff often have high decorations, but act very pompously and boastfully in their manners and appearance.

Most of the senior officers in Küstrin stemmed from the police. In my opinion, they lacked the tactical knowledge needed for commanding troops that the majority of the Wehrmacht officers had learnt on their way up through the ranks. When they belong with the competent officers, then they should wear Wehrmacht uniform. For the Wehrmacht, especially the officers, it must have been sickening to be commanded by police officers. The battle commander in the Neustadt was Police Colonel Walther, and in the Altstadt, Police Major Kulla. While they knew each other well, they had naturally filled other officer posts in their sectors with police officers. In the current situa-tion it is important, without regard to the body one belongs to, to put the most able men in the right place; in this case, they should have donned Wehrmacht uniform and set aside their police ones.

Often very young SS officers were allotted posts that other officers of the Wehrmacht had to step aside for. An 18-year-old SS second lieutenant had, for example, to lead a combat group that included Wehrmacht and Flak captains and lieutenants. These officers were not only old enough to have been the fathers of this SS second lieu-tenant, but even gave the impression that they possessed ability well above that of the SS officer set over them. Most of these young SS officers were daring types, not weaklings, and certainly engaged bravely in every situation. However, such men should be given special assignments for which they are better suited. Appointments for which knowledge, and not least experience, are required belong, however, to other people. Here is an example:

A fire threatened to spread across from a neighbouring building. This was reported to the SS second lieutenant. He immediately ordered the building to be blown up. When the NCO reported that there was clothing in the cupboards and washing hanging around that someone must have brought there, he ordered the building to be demolished a second time. The NCO came back again and reported that about 70 soldiers who used the cellars were at the moment in action, but all their property, packs, clothing, etc. was lying around in the cellars. The NCO was reprimanded and was told once more to blow up the building. Only a few minutes perhaps would have been necessary for a few men to remove these soldiers' items. Apart from this the fire was in no way so far advanced that the demolition was so urgent. The order had been given without any consideration whatsoever by a young man who had surely never had to buy underclothes with his own money. Thank God the soldiers in this situation were much more sensible and saved their comrades' things before blowing up the building.

The soldiers' lack of fighting spirit was also illustrated in the way that they always quickly let themselves be disarmed. We often went into the cellars when there was a smell of burning with a pistol in the hand to winkle out skivers. It was sufficient with two or three men to round up groups of eight to nine men, who timidly obeyed and willingly dropped their rifles, belts and steel helmets. I collected up many weapons for the Volkssturm in this way with my Party comrades and caught cowardly soldiers. When Gauamtsleiter Party Comrade Dame came to Küstrin and I told him, he did not want to believe it. I suggested that he tried it himself. Party Comrade Dame, who was in civilian clothes, rounded up six soldiers who had fled to the Altstadt from the Neustadt. There was a short interrogation and then Dame forcefully demanded that the soldiers immediately lay down their rifles, belts and steel helmets. All six soldiers obeyed and were apparently pleased to be without their weapons. If a single German civilian can so overwhelm six soldiers, what would happen when these soldiers were confronted by Russians? Whether this failing morale can be restored, I do not know. However, what is possible in my opinion, is that by continually relieving those soldiers who are weary, tired and grown apathetic with the fighting, one can give them back an inner equilibrium before they are sent back into battle, and advise them of the urgency and significance of their fight.

I could say a lot about the looting carried out by German soldiers. One was often ashamed at how senseless and how mean German soldiers were to loot the homes of their countrymen. Often I heard it said: 'The Russians could not be worse!' I presume, however, that the higher commands have been informed of these deeds also from other places.

Heil Hitler!

Körner, Kreisleiter

Notes

Square brackets have been used throughout to denote the sources from which the reference given has been drawn, or to indicate which of several books attributed to an author is applicable.

Chapter 1. The Development of a Fortress

1. Thrams, p. 13.
2. Thrams, pp. 14–15.
3. Thrams, pp. 22–4.
4. Melzheimer, p. 180.
5. Kohlase [BO], p. 161; Thrams, p. 28.
6. Melzheimer, p. 180; Thrams, p. 26.
7. Thrams, p. 31.

Chapter 2. The Vistula–Oder Operation

1. Duffy, pp. 249–51; BMA RH 19/XV/13K3.
2. Chuikov, pp. 148–9.
3. Babadshanian, p. 217.
4. Chuikov, p. 159.
5. MA USSR, Stock 333, List 396, File 396, Sheets 58–9 [Bokov, p. 101]; Chuikov, p. 159.
6. Chuikov, p. 160, Order No. 00172 of 27 January 1945.
7. Babadshanian, pp. 218–20.
8. Kohlase [BO], p. 45.
9. Katukov, pp. 329ff; Spaeter, pp. 321–2.
10. Duffy, pp. 178–9; Tieke, p.12.
11. Kohlase [AKTS], pp. 20–2.

12. Kohlase [AKTS], pp. 33–5.
13. Kohlase [AKTS], pp. 68ff.
14. Kohlase [AKTS], p. 145.

Chapter 3. Defence Preparations

1. Thrams, p. 21
2. Thrams, p. 19.
3. Kohlase [Band 4], p. 72.
4. Kohlase [Band 3], p. 32.
5. Kohlase [Band 4], p. 86.
6. Kohlase [AKTS], p. 89.
7. Kohlase [Band 4], p. 77.
8. Kohlase [AKTS], p. 71.
9. BMA RH XII/23, Sheet 352 and RH 19/XV/3 [Kortenhaus, pp. 105, 107]; Schrode, p. 82.
10. Kroemer and Zobel to the author.

Chapter 4. The Russians are Here!

1. Kohlase [BO], p. 45 [Bokov, p. 88] and [Band 4], p. 99; Thrams, p. 32.
2. Kohlase [Band 4], pp. 73–4.
3. Kohlase [Band 4], pp. 73–4.
4. Kohlase [Band 4], p. 87.
5. Kohlase [AKTS], pp. 71–2.
6. Thrams, pp. 29–32.
7. Melzheimer, p. 181.
8. Kohlase [AKTS], pp. 61–3.
9. Boehm, pp. 275–7.
10. Kohlase [Band 4], p. 91.
11. Kohlase [Band 4], pp. 29–35. Schmidt's unit was the 8th Bty, IInd Battalion, Flak Regiment 14, 23rd Flak Division. The railway sidings he mentioned were part of the Potato Meal Factory (Norddeutschen Kartoffel-Mehlfabrik), Küstrin's largest employer of labour.
12. Rudolf Dawidowski in Kohlase [AKTS], p. 82.
13. Melzheimer, p. 182.

14. Kohlase [Band 3], pp. 51–2.
15. Thrams, pp. 33–4.
16. Boehm, pp. 277–8; Schrode, p. 82.
17. MA DDR, WF-03/17398, Sheets 461 and 488 [Simon, p. 351]; tanks in Knüppel, p. 104.
18. Kohlase [AKTS], pp. 43–4.
19. Schrode, p. 82. These Ju-87G Stukas were equipped with 37mm cannon underslung from the wings outboard of the fixed under-carriage.
20. Thrams, p. 34.

Chapter 5. The Siege Begins

1. Erickson, pp. 473–4.
2. Zhukov, pp. 327–34.
3. Duffy, p. 188; Zhukov, pp. 330–1.
4. Duffy, pp. 181–2; Guderian, pp. 342–4; Zhukov, p. 337.
5. Duffy, pp. 182–3, as amended from Tessin.
6. Erickson, p. 520.
7. Kohlase [AKTS], pp. 26–7.
8. Kohlase [AKTS], p. 27.
9. Thrams, p. 35
10. Kohlase [AKTS], pp. 21–4.
11. Kohlase [AKTS], p. 27.
12. Kohlase [AKTS], p. 25.
13. Thrams, pp. 35–9.
14. Thrams, pp. 36–8.
15. Kohlase [Band 4], pp. 35–8.
16. Kohlase [AKTS], pp. 72–3.
17. Kohlase [AKTS], p. 44.
18. Kohlase [AKTS], p. 62.
19. Kohlase [Band 3], p. 43.
20. Kohlase [Band 4], pp. 87–9.
21. Kohlase [AKTS], p. 85.
22. Kohlase [Küstrin], pp. 42–3. The main responsibility for this massacre lay with State Secretary Klemm, Oberstaatswalt Hansen, Prison Director Knops, his deputy Rung, Inspector Klitzing, the leader of the special Gestapo commando Krause, and the SS men who had carried out the murders. Rung was later

sentenced to death for his part in this crime, Klitzing died in prison, and Klemm was given a life sentence but released after only a short while.

23. MA DDR, WF-03/5083, Sheet 820 [Simon, p. 20].
24. Bokov, p. 106; MA DDR, WF-03/5083, Sheet 820 [Simon, p. 20]; Schrode, pp. 85–6.
25. Kohlase [Band 4], pp. 38–42. Despite Schmidt's account, one 16-year-old Soviet soldier surrendered [Märkische Oder-Zeitung of 15 November 1996].
26. Kohlase [Band 3], pp. 32–4.
27. MA DDR, WF-03/5083, Sheet 820 [Simon, p. 20].
28. Kohlase [BO], pp. 164–5 [Busse, p. 51.]
29. Thrams, p. 40.
30. Thrams, pp. 40–1.
31. Thrams, p. 41.
32. Kohlase [AKTS], p. 45.
33. Kohlase [Band 4], pp. 77–9.
34. Kohlase [AKTS], pp. 142–3.

Chapter 6. The Russians Close In

1. Chuikov, p. 156.
2. Knüppel, p. 115.
3. Chuikov, pp. 160–1.
4. Erickson, p. 474.
5. Knüppel, pp. 115–16.
6. Thrams, pp. 43–4.
7. Thrams, pp. 41–2.
8. Kohlase [Band 4], p. 42
9. Thrams, pp. 42–3.
10. Thrams, pp. 44–5.
11. Thrams, p. 45.
12. MA DDR, WF-03/5083, Sheets 27, 147 and 950 [Simon, p. 37]: Weber article.
13. Thrams, pp. 45–8.
14. Kohlase [Band 3], p. 56.
15. Kohlase [BO], pp. 164–6. The sources only mention one lunette on the Island but aerial photographs show two side by side protecting the Artillery Barracks from the southern tip, that

nearest the Oder being the remains of an earlier defensive work along the river embankment and balanced by another, since covered by the Altstadt railway station development.

16. Kohlase [BO], p. 166.
17. Thrams, pp. 44–5.
18. Thrams, pp. 48–50.
19. Thrams, pp. 48–9.
20. Thrams, pp. 50–1.
21. Kohlase [AKTS], p. 80.
22. Thrams, pp. 51–4.
23. Thrams, pp. 54–5.
24. Thrams, pp. 56–7.
25. Thrams, pp. 57–8; Kohlase [BO], p. 163.
26. Thrams, p. 58.
27. Thrams, pp. 59–60.
28. Kohlase [Band 4], pp. 42–8.
29. Kohlase [Band 3], pp. 44–6.
30. Thrams, p. 61.
31. Thrams, pp. 61–2.
32. Thrams, p. 62.
33. Thrams, pp 64–5; Kohlase [Band 4], pp. 44–8.
34. Thrams, p. 66.
35. Thrams, pp. 67–8.
36. Kohlase [AKTS], p. 111.
37. Kohlase [Band 3], pp. 44–6.
38. Kohlase [AKTS], p. 90.
39. Kohlase [Band 4], pp. 48–55.

Chapter 7. Evacuation

1. Thrams, pp. 69–72.
2. Kohlase [AKTS], p. 143.
3. Kohlase [BO], p. 169; Thrams, pp. 44–5.
4. Kohlase [Band 4], pp. 55–9.
5. Thrams, pp. 72–4.
6. Kohlase [Band 4], pp. 91–2. The reactive mortars referred to were large rockets packed in wooden cases that also served as their launching racks.
7. Thrams, pp. 74–5.

8. Thrams, pp. 76–8.
9. Thrams, pp. 78–9.
10. Thrams, pp. 79–80.
11. Kohlase [Band 4], pp. 79–80.
12. Thrams, pp. 80–1
13. Thrams, pp. 81–2.
14. Kohlase [Band 3], pp. 34–5.
15. Thrams, pp. 83–4.
16. Thrams, pp. 84–6.
17. Thrams, pp. 69–79.
18. Kohlase [AKTS], pp. 111–12.
19. Thrams, pp. 86–7.
20. Thrams, pp. 87–9.
21. Kohlase [AKTS], p. 112; Thrams, p. 89.
22. Thrams, pp. 90–1.

Chapter 8. Assault on the Neustadt

1. Kohlase [K], p. 58; Thrams, pp. 92–3.
2. Kohlase [K], p. 58; Thrams, p. 94.
3. Bokov, p. 119; Hahn, p. 8; Thrams, pp. 94–6; article in *War Literature*. The Seydlitz-Troops were mentioned in a telephoned report to HQ 9th Army (exhibit in Seelow Museum).
   Seydlitz-Troops was the name given to the turncoat German units raised by the National Committee for a Free Germany within the Soviet Union from prisoners of war. The members were initially used for disseminating written and oral propaganda encouraging German soldiers to desert, but later went into actual combat against them; they also spread false orders among retreating troops in order to trap them. General Walter von Seydlitz-Kurzbach, captured at Stalingrad, was the vice-president of the committee, but had disassociated himself from all but the propaganda purposes of these troops and was later officially exonerated.
4. Kohlase [AKTS], pp. 47–8.
5. Kohlase [Band 4], p. 80.
6. Kohlase [AKTS], p. 85.
7. Kohlase [AKTS], p. 36.
8. Kohlase [AKTS], pp. 46–7.

9. Thrams, pp. 96–100.
10. Kohlase [Band 3], p. 46.
11. Kohlase [Band 3], pp. 52–3.
12. Kohlase [AKTS], pp. 75–6.
13. Kohlase [AKTS], p. 37.
14. Kohlase [Band 4], pp. 80–1.
15. Thrams, pp. 100–3.
16. Kohlase [Band 3], p. 35.
17. Kohlase [Band 3], pp. 46–7. Peters was given his marching orders on 13 April, being sent to Engineer Replacement and Training Battalion 3 in Brandenburg. He eventually got across the Elbe to the Americans, who handed him over to the Russians in a group of 50,000, but he managed to escape before they crossed back over the Elbe and found his way home safely to Ringelheim, near Salzgitter.
18. Kohlase [Band 3], p. 53. The Goliath was a small, tank-like tracked vehicle used for demolition purposes. It could be steered by cable or wireless to a range of 650–1,000 metres and was only 67cm high.
19. Thrams, p. 103.
20. Kohlase [AKTS], p. 48.
21. Kohlase [Band 4], pp. 74–5.
22. Kohlase [AKTS], pp. 112–13.
23. Thrams, pp. 104–5.
24. Kohlase [Band 4], pp. 74–5.
25. Kohlase [Band 3], pp. 37–40.

Chapter 9. Assault on the Altstadt

1. Brückl, p. 15 [Simon, p. 44]. The only elevation of 16.3 metres in the area is a hillock within the Kalenziger Wiesen, giving an actual elevation of about 7.3 metres above the surrounding area. This was already occupied by the 60th Guards Rifle Division.
2. Thrams, pp. 105–11.
3. Kohlase [AKTS], pp. 47-8.
4. Kohlase [AKTS], pp. 76–7.
5. Kohlase [303], pp. 35–6.
6. Kohlase [303], p. 36; Schöneck, pp. 31–42.
7. Kohlase [AKTS], pp. 48–50.

8. Thrams, pp. 111–12.
9. Boehm, p. 289; Hahn, p. 9; Thrams, pp. 112–14; Zobel to author.
10. Kohlase [303], pp. 36–9.
11. Kohlase [AKTS], pp. 50–1.
12. Kohlase [AKTS], pp. 63–4.
13. Thrams, pp. 114–15.
14. Kohlase [303], p. 39.
15. Chuikov, p. 169; Thrams, p. 115.
16. Kohlase [303], p. 41.
17. Kohlase [303], p. 41.
18. Kohlase [AKTS], pp. 90–2.
19. Kohlase [AKTS], pp. 85–6.
20. Busse, p. 154; Guderian, pp. 353–4; MA DDR WF-03/086, Sheets 262ff [Simon, pp. 48–9].
21. Duffy, pp. 243–5.
22. Boehm, p. 280; Hahn, p. 9; MA DDR W-03/5086, Sheets 170, 223 [Simon, pp. 48–9].
23. MA DDR W-03/5086, Sheet 261 [Simon, p. 50]; Thrams, p. 115.
24. Kohlase [303], p. 41.
25. Thrams, p. 117.
26. Kohlase [303], pp. 41, 43.
27. Kohlase [AKTS], p. 64.
28. MA DDR W-03/5086, Sheet 505f [Simon, pp. 50–1].
29. Boehm, p. 281; MA DDR W-03/5086, Sheets 505ff [Simon, pp. 50–1].
30. Hahn, p. 9; MA DDR W-03/5086, Sheets 292, 313 [Simon, p. 51]; Zobel to author.
31. Thrams, pp. 117–18.
32. Kohlase [AKTS], p. 83

Chapter 10. Breakout

1. Thrams, pp. 118–20.
2. Kohlase [AKTS], pp. 38–40.
3. Kohlase [303], pp. 48–9, 52.
4. Kohlase [Band 3], pp. 53–4. There were no Königstigers in Küstrin.
5. Kohlase [AKTS], p. 92.
6. Kohlase [Band 4], p. 91.

7. Kohlase [Band 4], p. 86.
8. Kohlase [AKTS], p. 64.
9. Thrams, pp. 120–1.
10. Kohlase [AKTS], p. 65.
11. Kohlase [AKTS], pp. 51–3.
12. Kohlase [AKTS], pp. 39–40.
13. Thrams, p. 121.
14. Report dated 1993 in the author's possession.
15. Kohlase [Band 4], p. 93.
16. Kohlase [AKTS], pp. 53–4.
17. Kohlase [AKTS], pp. 39–41.
18. Kohlase [AKTS], pp. 65–6.
19. Kohlase [AKTS], p. 86.
20. Kohlase [303], pp. 48–9, 52–5, 57–60.
21. Kohlase [Band 3], p. 54.

Chapter 11. Consequences

1. Kohlase [Band 4], p. 56; Thrams, p. 122.
2. Melzheimer, p. 185.
3. Thrams, p. 136.
4. Thrams, p. 121.
5. Kohlase [AKTS], pp. 54–5.
6. Kohlase [Band 4], pp. 93–5.
7. Report by Second-Lieutenant Karl-Hermann Tamms, in the author's possession.
8. Davies, p. 545.
9. Davies, p. 252.
10. Davies, p. 279.
11. Kohlase [AKTS], p. 161.
12. Kohlase [AKTS], p. 188.
13. Kohlase [AKTS], p. 14.
14. Article in *Alte Kameraden* taken from Oberstleutnant Ulrich Saft's *Das bittere Ende der Luftwaffe* (Verlag-Saft, Langenhagen).
15. Antipenko, p. 279.
16. Zhukov, pp. 609, 612.
17. Thrams, pp. 136–7.
18. *Twierdza Kostrzyn 2015.*

Bibliography

Antipenko, Lt-Gen. N.A., *In der Hauptrichtung* (Militärverlag der DDR, East Berlin, no date)

Babadshanian, Col. A.H., *Hauptstosskraft* (Militärverlag der DDR, East Berlin, 1981)

Boehm, Oberst a.D. Prof. Erwin, *Geschichte der 25. Division* (Stuttgart, undated)

Bokov, Lt-Gen. F.I., *Frühjahr des Sieges und der Befreiung* (Militärverlag der DDR, East Berlin, 1979)

Chuikov, Vassili I., *The End of the Third Reich*, revised edition (Progress Publishers, Moscow; Panther edition, London, 1969)

Davies, Norman, *Rising '44 – The Battle for Warsaw* (Macmillan, London, 2003)

Duffy, Christopher, *Red Storm on the Reich* (Routledge, London, 1991)

Eichholz, Diedrich, *Brandenburg in der NS-Zeit* (Verlag Volk und Welt GmbH, Berlin, 1993)

Erickson, Prof. John, *The Road to Berlin* (Weidenfeld & Nicolson, London, 1983)

Guderian, Col.-Gen. Heinz, *Panzer Leader* (Ballantyne Books, New York, 1965)

Hahn, Gerhard, report dated 21 January 1978

Katukov, Marshal Michail Jefremovitch, *An der Spitze des Hauptstosses* (Militärverlag der DDR, East Berlin, 1985)

Kazakov, V.I., *Always with the Tanks, Always with the Infantry* (Moscow, date unknown). Title translated from the Russian.

Knüppel, Fritz, *Kreis Lebus: Ein leidgeprüftes Land* (Heimatkreis Lebus, 1990)

Kohlase, Fritz, *Mit dem Fusilier-Bataillon 303 in Küstrin* (Brandenburgisches Verlaghaus, Berlin, 1993) [303]

Kohlase, Fritz, *Küstrin-Aus der Geschichte der ehemaligen preußischen Festungsstadt* (Author, 1993)

Kohlase, Fritz, *Als Küstrin in Trümmer sank* (self publication, 1996)

Kohlase, Fritz, *Brennendes Oderland* (Author, 1998) [BO, Band 2, Band 3, Band 4]

Kortenhaus, Werner, *Lothringen, Elsass, Ostfront: Der Einsatz der 21. Panzer-Division* (unpublished ms.)

Lammers, Frank, *Küstrin – Stadtgeschichte und Stadtverkehr* (Verlag GVE, 2005)

Melzheimer, Werner, *Die Festung und Garnison Küstrin* (Landmannschaft Berlin-Mark Brandenburg, Berlin, 1989)

Scheel, Klaus, *Hauptstossrichtung Berlin* (VEB Deutscher Verlag der Wissenschaften, East Berlin, 1983)

Schöneck, Friedhelm, 'Die Zunge: Tagebuch & Erlebuisberichte aus dem Jahr 1945' (unpublished ms.)

Schrode, Wilhelm, *Die Geschichte der 25. Division: Die Wiederaufstellung der 25. Panzergrenadier-Division, Herbst 1944 bis Kriegsende* (Ludwigsburg, 1980)

Simon, Hauptmann Manfred, *Die Bildung und Erweiterung des Küstriner Brückenkopfes* (Friedrich Engels Academy, Dresden, 1987)

Spaeter, Helmuth, *Die Geschichte des Panzerkorps 'Grossdeutschland'*, part III (Podzun-Pallas-Verlag, Friedeberg, 1968)

Thrams, Hermann, *Küstrin 1945: Tagebuch einer Festung* (Landesmannschaft Berlin-Mark Brandenburg, Berlin, 1992)

Tieke, Wilhelm, *Das Ende zwischen Oder und Elbe: Der Kampf um Berlin 1945* (Motorbuch Verlag, Stuttgart, 1981)

Twierdza Kostrzyn 2015 (Burmistrz Miasta, Kostrzyn nad Odra)

Wewetzer, Horst, 'Erinnerungen zum Ausbruch aus Küstrin' (unpublished article)

Zhukov, Marshal Georgi K., *Reminiscences and Reflections* (Progress Publishers, Moscow, 1974, English translation 1985)

Index

303

ARMED FORCES INDEX
German Armed Forces